THE EVENT OF LITERATURE

THE EVENT OF
LITERATURE
TERRY EAGLETON

YALE UNIVERSITY PRESS
NEW HAVEN AND LONDON

For information about this and other Yale University Press publications, please contact:
U.S. Office: sales.press@yale.edu   www.yalebooks.com
Europe Office: sales @yaleup.co.uk   www.yalebooks.co.uk

Set in Arno Pro IDSUK (DataConnection) Ltd
Printed in Great Britain by TJ International Ltd, Padstow, Cornwall

Library of Congress Cataloging-in-Publication Data

Eagleton, Terry, 1943-
    The event of literature/Terry Eagleton.
    pages cm
    Includes bibliographical references.
    ISBN 978-0-300-17881-4
    1. Literature—Philosophy.   2. Criticism.   3. Literature—History and
    criticism—Theory, etc.   I. Title.
    PN45.E24 2012
    801′.9–dc23

                                                              2012000109

A catalogue record for this book is available from the British Library.

10 9 8 7 6 5 4 3 2 1
For permission to reprint lines from Alan Brownjohn's poem 'Common Sense' from
The Saner Places: Selected Poems (2011) the author and publishers gratefully
acknowledge the Enitharmon Press.

For David Bennett

Contents

Preface

Literary theory has been rather out of fashion for the last couple of decades, so that books like this one are becoming rare. There are some who will be eternally grateful for this fact, most of whom will not be reading this Preface. It would have been hard to foresee in the 1970s or '80s that semiotics, post-structuralism, Marxism, psychoanalysis and the like would become for the most part foreign languages to students thirty years later. By and large, they have been nudged aside by a quartet of preoccupations: post-colonialism, ethnicity, sexuality and cultural studies. This is not exactly heart-warming news for the conservative opponents of theory, who were no doubt hoping that its decline might herald a return to the *status quo ante*.

Post-colonialism, ethnicity, sexuality and cultural studies are not, of course, innocent of theory. Nor do they simply date from its decline. It is rather that they have emerged in full force in the wake of 'pure' or 'high' theory, which for the most part they have put behind them. Not only put behind them, indeed, but served to displace. In some ways, this is an evolution to be welcomed. Various forms of theoreticism (though not of obscurantism) have been cast aside. What has taken place by and large is a shift from discourse to culture – from ideas in a somewhat abstract or virginal state, to an investigation of what in the 1970s and '80s one would have been rash to call the real world. As usual, however, there are losses as well as gains. Analysing vampires or *Family Guy* is probably not as intellectually rewarding as the study of Freud and Foucault. Besides, 'high' theory's steady loss of popularity, as I have argued in *After Theory*, is closely bound up with the declining fortunes of the political left.[1] The years when such thought was at its zenith were those in which the left, too, was buoyant and robust. As theory gradually ebbed, what slipped noiselessly away with it was radical critique. At its height, cultural theory posed some arrestingly ambitious questions to the social order it confronted. Today, when that regime is even more global and powerful than it was then, the very word 'capitalism' scarcely soils the lips of those busy celebrating difference, opening themselves to Otherness or dissecting the Undead. That this is so is testimony to the power of that system, not to its irrelevance.

Yet there is a sense in which this book is an implicit rebuke to literary theory as well. Much of my argument, apart from the final chapter, draws not on literary theory but on that very different animal, the philosophy of literature. Literary theorists have too often cold-shouldered this sort of discourse, and in doing so have played their stereotypical role in the age-old contention between the Continentals and the Anglo-Saxons. If literary theory springs largely from the former sector of the globe, the philosophy of literature hails for the most part from the latter. Yet the rigour and technical expertise of the best philosophy of literature contrasts favourably with the intellectual looseness of some literary theory, and has addressed questions (the nature of fiction, for example) left mostly unexamined by those in the other camp.

Conversely, literary theory contrasts favourably with the intellectual conservatism and timidity of so much philosophy of literature, as well as with its sometimes fatal lack of critical flair and imaginative audacity. If the theorists are open-neck-shirted, the philosophers of literature (who are in any case almost all male) rarely appear without a tie. One camp behaves as though it has never heard of Frege, while the other acts as though it has never heard of Freud. Literary theorists tend to give short shrift to questions of truth, reference, the logical status of fiction and the like, while philosophers of literature often display a marked insensitivity to the texture of literary language. There seems these days to be a curious (and quite unnecessary) relation between analytic philosophy and cultural and political conservatism, which was certainly not the case with some of the major practitioners of this style of thought in the past.

Radicals, for their part, tend to suspect questions such as 'Can there be a definition of literature?' as aridly academicist and unhistorical. But not all attempts at definition need be this, as many in the radical camp might agree when it comes to defining the capitalist mode of production or the nature of neo-imperialism. As Wittgenstein suggests, sometimes we need a definition and sometimes we don't. There is an irony at stake here, too. Many of those on the cultural left for whom definitions are fusty affairs to be left to the conservative academics are probably innocent of the fact that when it comes to art and literature, most of those academics argue *against* the possibility of such definitions. It is just that the most perceptive among them give more cogent, suggestive reasons for doing so than those for whom definitions are by definition futile.

Readers will be surprised, perhaps dismayed, to find themselves plunged at the outset into a discussion of medieval scholasticism. Perhaps it is the stink of the scholastic in me, to adopt a Joycean phrase, which helps to account for my interest in the issues which this book raises. There is certainly a connection between the fact that I was raised as a Catholic, and therefore taught among other things not to distrust the powers of analytic reason, and my later career as a literary theorist. Some might also attribute my interest in the philosophy of literature to the fact that I have frittered away too much of my time on this earth in the egregiously Anglo-Saxon citadels of Oxford and Cambridge.

Yet you do not have to be a former papist or ex-Oxbridge don to appreciate the oddness of a situation in which teachers and students of literature habitually use words like literature, fiction, poetry, narrative and so on without being at all well equipped to embark on a discussion of what they mean. Literary theorists are those who find this as strange, if not quite as alarming, as encountering medics who can recognise a pancreas when they see one but would be incapable of explaining its functioning. Besides, there are many important questions which the shift away from literary theory has left in suspension, and this book tries to address some of them. I begin by considering the issue of whether things have general natures, which has an obvious bearing on the question of whether one can speak of 'literature' at all. I then go on to look at how the term 'literature' is generally used today, examining each of the features which I take to be central to that meaning of the word. One of these features, fictionality, is complex enough to require a special chapter to itself. Finally, I turn to the question of literary theory, asking whether the various forms of it can be shown to have central features in common. If I were to be immodest, I would say that the book offers a reasonable account of what literature (at least for the present) actually means, as well as drawing attention for the first time to what almost all literary theories have in common. But I am not immodest, so I will not say so.

I am grateful to Jonathan Culler, Rachael Lonsdale and Paul O'Grady, who all came up with intelligent criticisms and suggestions. I am also indebted to my son Oliver Eagleton, who talked over the idea of pretending with me and put me right on a number of vital points.

T.E.

CHAPTER 1

Realists and Nominalists

1

Let us begin with what might seem like a pointless diversion. Like many of our theoretical wrangles, the dispute between realists and nominalists is of ancient provenance.[2] It flourishes most vigorously, however, in the later Middle Ages, when a number of eminent schoolmen of opposite persuasions line up to do battle. Are general or universal categories in some sense real, as the realists claim in the wake of Plato, Aristotle and Augustine, or are they, as the nominalists insist, concepts which we ourselves foist upon a world in which whatever is real is irreducibly particular? Is there a sense in which literature or giraffeness exists in the actual world, or are these notions entirely mind-dependent? Is giraffeness simply a mental abstraction from a multitude of uniquely individual creatures, or are such species as real as those individuals, if not necessarily in the same way?

For the nominalist camp, such abstractions are posterior to individual things, being ideas derived from them; for the realists they are in some sense anterior to them, as the power which makes an individual thing what it is. Nobody has ever clapped eyes on crocodilicity, as opposed to spotting this or that scaly beast basking in the mud; yet nobody, as the methodological individualists are eager to remind us, has ever clapped eyes on a social institution either, which is not to suggest that Fox TV or the Bank of England does not exist.

Halfway houses are possible here. The great Franciscan theologian Duns Scotus proposed a moderate or qualified form of realism for which natures have a real existence outside the mind, but become completely universal only through the intellect.[3] Thomas Aquinas would have agreed. Universals were not substances, as an extreme realist like Roger Bacon considered, but neither were they mere fictions. If they had no real existence as such outside the mind, they nonetheless allowed us to grasp the common natures of things, and these common natures were in some sense 'in' the things themselves. A more radical position than that of Scotus' is adopted by William of Ockham, for whom universals have a merely logical status.[4] Nothing universal exists outside the mind, and common natures are nothing more than names. Scotus does not press his own case to this limit, but he has a marked penchant for the particular, best known to the world of letters through his disciple Gerard Manley Hopkins's adoption of his notion of 'thisness' or *haecceitas*. Whereas Thomas Aquinas was content to regard matter as the individuating principle of a thing, in contrast to the form it shared with other entities, the Subtle Doctor discerned in each piece of creation a dynamic principle which made it uniquely, intrinsically itself. If he was much taken with particularity, it was partly on account of his peculiarly Franciscan devotion to the person of Jesus Christ.

Haecceitas sets off a thing from another thing of the same nature (no two snowflakes or eyebrows are identical), and as such represents the ultimate reality of a being, one known fully to God alone. It is, so to speak, the excess of a thing over its concept or common nature – an irreducible specificity which can be grasped not by intellectual reflection on what an object is, but only by a direct apprehension of its luminous presence. In a veritable revolution of thought, the singular now becomes intelligible per se to the human mind. Scotus, remarks one of his commentators, is a 'philosopher of individuality'.[5] The American philosopher Charles Sanders Peirce, who thought the medieval Franciscan one of the greatest of all metaphysicians, praised him as the thinker who 'first elucidated individual existence'.[6] We have set our foot on the long road leading to liberalism, Romanticism, Theodor Adorno's doctrine of the non-identity of an object with its concept, the postmodern suspicion of universals as snares to trap the politically unwary and a good deal more. As Charles Taylor remarks, we can recognise with hindsight the nominalist passion for the particular as 'a major turning point in the history of Western civilisation'.[7]

Realists, by contrast, tend to the view that the intellect is incapable of grasping individual particulars. There can be no science of an individual cabbage, as opposed to a science of the genus as such. In Aquinas's view, the mind cannot seize hold of matter, the individuating principle of things. This is not to say, however, that we cannot have an understanding of individual things at all. For Aquinas, this is the function of *phronesis*, which involves a non-intellectual knowledge of concrete particulars, and which is the lynchpin of all the virtues.[8] It is a kind of sensory or somatic interpretation of reality, a point relevant to what I shall have to say later of Aquinas's reflections on the body. Much later, at the heart of the European Enlightenment, a science of the sensory particular will be born to counter an abstract universalism, and its name is aesthetics.[9] Aesthetics begins life as that oxymoronic animal, a science of the concrete, investigating the logical inner structure of our corporeal life. Almost two centuries later, phenomenology will launch a similar project.

For a realist philosopher like Thomas Aquinas, a thing's nature is the principle of its existence, and through its existence it participates in the life of God. For a realist theology, God's signature can be found at the core of beings. By sharing in the infinite in this way, a thing, paradoxically, is able to be itself. Hegel will later give this doctrine a secular twist: *Geist* is what enables beings to be fully themselves, so that infinity is constitutive of the finite. There is also a Romantic belief that if a thing is to be absolutely autonomous and self-identical, then what it most closely resembles, paradoxically, is the infinite, which acknowledges nothing beyond itself for the obvious reason that there can be nothing.

There are many different phenomena in the world, and thus many different ways of talking; so that one needs to know the nature of a thing in order, as Wittgenstein would put it later, to know what language-game to play in a given situation. Pluralism and essentialism go together. If things have given natures, however, it is easy to see how this can set a limit to the power of the deity who fashioned them. God could always have chosen in his wisdom not to manufacture turtles or triangles, since if he is free there can be no necessity to what he creates. Everything that exists is purely gratuitous, in the sense that it might just as easily have never sprung into being, and is continually overshadowed by this mind-warping possibility. This is true not least of human beings, whose sense of their own possible non-existence is generally known as the fear of death. But it is also true of the modernist work of art, plagued as it is by a sickening or delightful sense of its own contingency. That a thing came into existence was, for Aquinas and others, a matter of gift and gratuity on God's part, not of logical inference or iron necessity. It is a question of love, not need. It is this that the doctrine of Creation is trying to capture. It has nothing to do with how the world got off the ground, which is a question for scientists rather than theologians. Indeed, Aquinas thought it possible that the world might have had no origin at all, as did his mentor Aristotle.

Given that turtles and triangles do happen to exist, however, they exist in a determinate manner, and God is obliged to acknowledge this fact just as we ourselves must. He cannot whimsically decide that $2 + 2 = 5$, as Descartes thought he could. Having made his cosmos, he is forced to lie in it. When it comes to the way things are, he cannot behave like a capricious monarch or a pampered rock star. God is a realist, not a nominalist. He is constrained by the very essences he has created.

An empiricist age is likely to be sceptical of such common natures for a number of reasons. For one thing, since they are intelligible rather than sensible, they offend the empiricist prejudice that only what is perceptible is truly real. If there are no such essences, however, God's sovereignty is assured. He can make a turtle sing 'Pennies from Heaven' if the fancy takes him. The only reason for a thing is *quia voluit* (because he willed it). As Carl Schmitt describes this view, paraphrasing the thought of the philosopher Malebranche, 'God is the final, absolute authority, and the entire world and everything in it is nothing more than the occasion for his sole agency'.[10] The problem, however, is that this arbitrary power renders the deity darkly enigmatic and impenetrable. He becomes a hidden God whose ways are not ours, inscrutable to reason, existing at some infinite remove from his creatures, as remote from them as a celebrity from the common herd. He is the God of radical Protestantism, not the God of the New Testament who in the Johannine phrase pitches his tent amongst us.[11]

By purging essences or common natures from reality, you can soften the stuff up, hence making it more pliable to the touch of power. There are, to be sure, more progressive forms of anti-essentialism than this, but their champions are usually unaware that the doctrine has also served in its time to legitimate human dominion. If God, or the Humanity who in the fullness of time will come to assassinate him and usurp his throne, is to be omnipotent, essences will have to go. Only by draining the world of its inherent meanings can you seek to erode its resistance to one's designs upon it. True mastery over things, as Francis Bacon knew, involves a knowledge of their inherent properties; but it can also come to be at odds with a respect for their specificity, or for what Marx calls their use-value.

If we can cuff Nature into whatever baroque shapes we fancy, a perilous hubris is likely to follow, as Man comes to fantasise that his powers are divinely inexhaustible. In a later phase of modernity, humanity will be ousted in its turn by the codes, structures, forces and conventions that put it in place, and these, not Man, will now act as the supreme donors of meaning. For all the anti-foundationalist fervour of their apologists, they come to act as a new species of foundationalism, signifying as they do a ground (call it Culture, Structure, Language and so on) beneath which our spades cannot sink. Having wrested sovereignty from God, Humanity will in turn be toppled from its throne by Discourse.

Let us return, for now, to the moment of modernity. Only by paring its sensory textures and specific densities down to a mathematical thinness, defining its various features by our own strategies of measurement and calculation, reducing the thickness of the world to our own mental representations of it, can Creation be stripped of its recalcitrant Otherness and delivered wholly into our hands. Things are now to be defined in terms of how they respond to our procedures and techniques, while how they are in themselves slips over the horizon of our cognition. We may not know things as God knows them, but at least we can know the objects that we ourselves produce, which lends the act of labour a fresh importance. It belongs to a Protestant optimism that we can wield such transformative powers, just as it belongs to Protestant angst that we exercise them in a world which, like the ocean in Lem's *Solaris*, has become featureless, elusive and finally unintelligible. Is the price of freedom the loss of reality? In any case, if the self has no essence either – if it is merely a function of power, a congeries of sense-impressions, a purely phenomenal entity, a discontinuous process, an outcrop of the unconscious – then who is the agent of this worldly transformation, and whom does it serve?

In this bleak scenario, an absolute subject confronts a purely contingent world. The other face of anti-essentialism is voluntarism – the flexing of a power which, like the subject who wields it, is ultimately its own end and reason, bearing its grounds and motives within itself. Yet if the world must be indeterminate for such power to flourish, how can it provide determinate grounds for the appropriate uses of it? If reality is fluid and arbitrary, how can it stay still long enough for us to accomplish our projects, and hence be free in the positive sense of the term? In any case, what joy is there in exercising sovereignty over an intrinsically meaningless surge of matter? The more we gain dominion and authority, the more hollow a ring they would seem to have. Because reality is no longer significantly structured, no longer thickly sedimented with meaningful features and functions, it no longer thwarts our freedom of action as much as it once did; yet by the same token, the more vacuous that freedom now appears. Is there not something absurdly tautological about an animal that bestows upon the world with one hand the very sense it extracts from it with the other?

Nominalists like William of Ockham thought that the realists confused words with things, rather as literary theorists like Paul de Man think they do. Because we can say 'boulevard' or 'beech tree' we tend to suppose that there is some identifiable substance which corresponds to these terms. Realism on this view is a form of reification. Besides, since we can never really know things in their uniquely individual being, realism can also be seen as a form of scepticism. Ockham, by contrast, believes that we know specific entities by direct intellectual intuition, thus abolishing all conceptual mediation between subject and object. Among the entities that we can know in this way – indeed, the one we can apprehend most surely and instantaneously – is the self. Universals, as for a later empiricism, are simply generalisations from discrete particulars. They no longer represent the inner truth of an object, which means that how such objects behave can no longer be deduced from their divinely bestowed natures. Instead, we need a discourse which investigates the behaviour of things without recourse to such improbable metaphysical conceptions. This discourse would come to be known as science.

Aquinas, like Abelard and Karl Marx, is more insistent on the fact that all thinking presupposes universals. The Angelic Doctor is anti-empiricist at least in this sense, if not perhaps in one or two others. Marx speaks in the *Grundrisse* of the need to employ abstract or general concepts in order to 'rise' to the concrete. In his view, the concrete is not an empirical, self-evident affair; it is rather the meeting-point of a host of determinants, some of them general and some specific. It is the concrete for Marx which is richly complex; but in order to construct it in thought, general concepts, which he regards as more simple than concrete ones, must inevitably be deployed. There is no question here of simply deducing the particular from the general in the manner of the rationalists, or deriving the general from the particular in the style of the empiricists.

Moreover, Marx believes that universals are actually part of the furniture of the world, not simply convenient ways of viewing it. The later Marx, for example, regards what he calls 'abstract labour' as a real component of capitalist production, without which it could not function. There is no question of it being simply a way of looking. The early Marx of the *Economic and Philosophical Manuscripts* holds that humans are the distinctive individuals they are by virtue of their participation in a specific form of 'species-being', and that the process of individuation is itself a power or capacity of this common nature. In this materialist version of human nature, individual and universal are not treated as antithetical.

The running battle between realists and nominalists is among other things a question of how seriously one takes the sensuously specific. This is a political matter as well as an ontological and epistemological one. It is also a question of the status of abstract reasoning in a progressively empiricist world. What is the yardstick of the real? Is reality only what is proved upon our pulses? Abelard claims that realism, in its emphasis on general natures, destroys all distinctions between things. In the night of realism, all cows are grey. Anselm, by contrast, rebukes nominalism for being 'so wrapped up in material imaginings that it cannot extricate itself from them'.[12] On this Platonic view, the nominalists are too sunk in the trough of their senses, too enraptured by sensory immediacy, unable to see the wood for the trees. Their thought clings myopically to the textures of phenomena, rather than rising above them to gain a more synoptic view. It was on these grounds among others that the full-bloodedly essentialist Plato expelled the poets from his republic. Caught in that sensual music, they were unable to rise to the dignity of an abstract idea. The same goes for a great many literary types in modern times. It accounts for a large part of their hostility to literary theory.

For their part, the nominalists riposte that thought must stay close to the bone rather than read the world off from rationalist first principles or metaphysical essences. For them, it is as though the rationalists and essentialists can know what reality looks like even before they have come to inspect it. One must buckle the mind to the actual in Baconian style, drawing general scientific laws from individual facts rather than (in high-rationalist style) the other way round. General or universal categories thin and dilute the vivid *haecceitas* of things. There is a crooked path here from Duns Scotus and William of Ockham to Gilles Deleuze, a Scotist whose libertarian distaste for general categories goes hand in glove with a species of political anarchism. In Nietzschean fashion, such categorical thought can only be seen as oppressive and constricting, riding roughshod over the unique identities of objects. Postmodernism inherits this prejudice. It is, among other things, displaced theology. It has its obscure origins in the late medieval cult of the arbitrary will.

For Hegel and Lukács, by contrast, a knowledge of essences can liberate the individual object into its true nature, revealing what it covertly is. In aesthetic terms, this involves a curious double operation, in which one first extracts the type or essence from a host of empirical particulars, then coats it once more with a sheen of specificity. In a similar way, the role of the Romantic imagination is to transform phenomena into the image of their essences, but to do so while preserving the fullness of their sensuous presence. This double operation is in some ways a troubling one. For if empirical reality is organised in the literary text according to a ghostly paradigm of things, secretly informed by the typical or essential, that reality is clearly imbued with a certain necessity. Perhaps this was what Paul Valéry had in mind when he observed that art is 'the passage from the arbitrary to the necessary'. In suppressing contingency, the work seems to claim that under the compulsion of their inner natures, things just had to take this particular shape and no other. And this tacit denial of other possibilities is a characteristically ideological gesture. In a similar way, the idea that poetry embodies a certain ineluctable verbal design – a question of 'the right words in the right order', not one letter of which can be altered without transfiguring the whole – would seem in danger of suppressing the contingency of the sign, another typically ideological gesture. Language is 'essentialised' or 'phenomenalised', rendered not semiotic but iconic, linked by an unbreakable bond to a reality which, so it appears, can only ever be signified in this particular way.

Nominalism, as Frank Farrell has argued, represents a kind of disenchantment with the world, one which dimly prefigures the travails of modernity.[13] Creation is no longer as sacred as it once was. It is not difficult to see how a secular, empiricist, individualist, scientific-rationalist modern age, with its belief in the sovereign will as the agent of human history, has some of its sources in the late medieval world. Let us glance briefly at one sense in which this is so. God for Aquinas is not a being on the same scale as humans and toadstools, only incomparably higher. If he is a being at all, which many a theologian would take leave to doubt, it is in a way wholly incommensurate with created things. The Creator on this view is the unfathomable depth in which all things have their being, the ground of their possibility, the love that sustains them in existence. He cannot be reckoned up as one particular entity among them. There are many grounds on which the religious believer may be mistaken, but the charge that he or she has trouble in counting, holding that there is one more object in the world than there actually is, is not one of them.

Duns Scotus, by contrast with Aquinas, sees God as a being in the same sense that snails and oboes are, but infinitely different and superior. This then has the paradoxical effect of shoving the Creator away from the world in the act of claiming a certain kinship between the two. God is on the same ontological scale as ourselves, but inconceivably further up. A split accordingly opens between this sublimely remote deity and his actual Creation. Aquinas's God is immanent as well as transcendent, which means that he can be approached to some extent through human reason. It also means, as we have seen, that things in the world bear his imprint in their inmost being. The world, in short, is sacramental. It is the eminently *lisible* text of its Author. As this sublime Author soars beyond reach of his handiwork, however, he will become gradually inaccessible to human reason, knowable only by faith; and finite things, which are purely contingent, do not speak of him as they do for Aquinas. As far as intimations of the deity go, the text of reality has become illegible.

There is a paradox here. If God exerts absolute sovereignty over his Creation, he crushes the independent life out of it and leaves it unable to bear witness to his glory. So the world is emptied of his presence precisely to the extent that it falls entirely under his sway.[14] There is now nothing in reason or human nature that would suggest the divine origin and end of humanity and the world, a truth that we can derive only from revelation. Since things now exist in their own right, however, rather than as obscure allegories of the Almighty, they can become the object of ordinary human knowledge. If God is removed to the remote realm of faith, dissociating value from fact, a thoroughly secular world can be born. The sacramental yields to the scientific.

In one sense, this is an exhilarating emancipation. Rational investigation is no longer constrained by a reverence for divinely bestowed essences. Philosophy is able to cut the cord that tethers it to theology. And since Man himself is equally unconstrained by such an immutable nature, he can evolve into the historical, self-fashioning, self-determining agent of modernity. Things are stripped of their mystifying auras and yoked instead to the use and welfare of humankind. The idea of progress is no longer impious. We can intervene in the laws of Nature, which are no longer to be treated as sacrosanct, and can do so for the benefit of our species. Nothing is now in principle off-limits to human investigation. The material world can be affirmed in its full autonomy, not as a shadowy symbol of a domain elsewhere. It is no longer to be seen as a sacred text, a set of hieroglyphs or cryptic signifiers whose sense lies outside itself.

At the same time, this movement towards modernity represents one long catastrophe. The arbitrarily absolute God of some late medieval thought becomes a model for the self-determining will of the modern epoch. Like the Almighty, this will behaves as a law unto itself; unlike the Almighty, it threatens to crush the life out of things in the act of exerting dominion over them. The idea of a will which carries its grounds and ends within itself, a power prior to reason though (since it has a built-in inclination to do what ought to be done) in no sense arbitrary or irrationalist, is already present in Scotus. For Ockham, too, the will reigns sovereign. It is not to be slavishly subjected to reason, since some act of will must already be exercised in our choice of reasons for what we do. Once the will becomes all-powerful, however, reason ceases to be a moral faculty and finds itself reduced to purely instrumental status. It is now no more than the humble handmaiden of passion, interest, appetite and desire. The route thrown open by Scotus and Ockham will reach its modernist terminus in the Nietzschean will-to-power, after which time, in the era of postmodern culture, the subject is really too depleted and decentred to will very much at all.[15] Even so, it is interests, power and desire which remain foundational for postmodernist thought, and reason's capacity to engage in critical reflection upon them is notably curtailed. For the postmodernists as for some of the schoolmen, reasoning takes place within the framework of such interests and desires, and so cannot pass fundamental judgements upon them. We shall be seeing some of the implications of this case for literary theory later, in the work of Stanley Fish.

Thomas Aquinas takes a quite different view of the will. In his eyes, it is not a power to be exercised arbitrarily or autonomously, but a joyful acquiescence in the good, a susceptibility to being drawn towards the inherent value of a thing. It thus contains a vital element of openness, a readiness to be acted upon, which is hardly how the will has been portrayed in later Western thought. 'The exercise of the will [for Aquinas],' writes Fergus Kerr, 'is more like consenting to the good that one most deeply desires, rather than imposing oneself on something indifferent or recalcitrant . . . [it] is aligned conceptually with desire, consent, delighted acquiescence, in short, with love.'[16]

The nominalists' bracing concern for the individual also plays its ruinous role in a history of possessive individualism. In this view of things, individuals are autonomous, and the relations between them are external, contractual and non-constitutive. Since relations are not perceptible in the way that radishes are, they cannot be said to exist in the strongest sense of the word. As John Milbank writes, 'It is within voluntarist theology that the key philosophy of "possessive individualism" has its origins'.[17] To transform this condition would require a sense of the social totality; but since nominalism is averse to universals and abstractions, this, too, must come under censure. As that unwitting Ockhamite Margaret Thatcher observed, there is no such thing as society.

The liberation of things from the restrictive categories of scholasticism proved to some degree self-defeating. Science may trade in empirical particulars, but it usually has scant concern for their sensory bodies. In emancipating things from the sway of metaphysical essences, it subsumes them to an equally abstract set of general laws. What is retrieved with the one hand is removed with the other. One modern phenomenon above all is thought to hold out against this abstraction, and its name is art.[18] For a precious Romantic legacy, it exists to remind us of the sensuous specificity of which we have been plundered.

This is one reason why literary types tend to be militant champions of the particular. Most of them find abstractions instinctively unappealing. The only general category for which some of them can muster a morsel of enthusiasm is that of literature itself. Only when this is felt to be under assault do the apologists for the uniquely individual have instant recourse to abstract thought.[19] One reason why literary theory has proved such a scandal is that the phrase itself is almost an oxymoron. How can something as irreducibly concrete as literature be the subject of abstract investigation? Is not art the last refuge of the chance particular, the delectably offbeat detail, the wayward impulse, the idiosyncratic gesture, of everything that defeats a straitjacketing dogma and a unitary vision? Is not its whole point to give the slip to the tyranny of the doctrinaire, the schematised view of reality, the programme of political action, the sour stink of orthodoxies, the soul-destroying agendas of bureaucrats and social workers?

Most literary types are in this sense natural-born nominalists, whether of the old-style liberal or newfangled postmodernist kind. 'The movement away from theory and generality,' remarks Annandine in Iris Murdoch's novel *Under the Net*, 'is the movement towards truth. All theorising is flight. We must be ruled by the situation itself and this is unutterably particular.' It is a case that one can find reproduced a thousand times in the annals of modern literary commentary. Even Lenin came up with a version of it. Theory is one thing, while art or life is another. One scarcely needs to point out that Annandine's statement is a theoretical claim in itself. In fact, Murdoch's fiction contains an uncommon amount of abstract reflection, put into the mouths of various spoilt saints, Oxford bohemians, ruined visionaries and upper-middle-class metaphysicians. It would also be interesting to know how any human situation could be unutterably particular and still prove intelligible. How could we speak of an absolute identity, one entirely without relations to what lies outside itself? By what conceptual means (and all concepts are unavoidably general, including 'this', 'unique', 'inimitable', 'unutterably distinctive' and so on) could we come to identify such a state of affairs?

It is, one should note, a remarkably recent view of art. Samuel Johnson, who was enthused by the general and bored by the individual, would certainly have found it strange, as would a great many pre-Romantic artists. It is an ideology of art only a little over two centuries old, and even then one which fails to make much sense of many a precious artefact of that period. It is hard to see how it sheds much light on, say, Samuel Beckett, whose work seems deliberately cast in the teeth of such liberal-humanist pieties. It is also unclear how far it can illuminate the great lineage of literary realism, in which by a kind of sleight of hand or *trompe l'oeil* what looks free-floating and particularised is covertly ordered into a more 'typical' or generic set of fables, characters and situations. One author who has been known to indulge in such strategies is Iris Murdoch. The two texts set cheek by jowl in Joyce's *Ulysses* – an apparently random day in Dublin and the surreptitious, rigorously schematising Homeric subtext – constitute a parody of this classical realism, one in which stray contingency and conceptual scheme are now pulling apart and becoming caricatures of themselves, achieving only an ironic, self-consciously synthetic kind of unity with each other. This formal property of the novel is itself a moral statement. Realism may appear in love with the stray particular, but this is to overlook some rather vital aspects of the form.

Once the wave of existentialism had receded, the latest chapter in the history of nominalism was written by post-structuralism and postmodernism. Thinkers like Foucault, Derrida and Deleuze, in their aversion to the general concept, the universal principle, the informing essence, the totalising political programme, are among other things the improbable heirs of certain late medieval schoolmen. When Tony Bennett writes that what is needed is not

'a theory of *Literature*, but a theory of *literatures*: concrete, historically specific and materialist', he speaks as a left-nominalist.[20] Are
we to suppose that there are no significant relations between these
different bodies of work? Are they to be treated as rigorously
discrete and autonomous? If so, why do we call them all literature?
Anyway, can there not be a concrete, historically specific, materialist investigation of universals such as death, sorrow and suffering?
(Some might consider that there is indeed such an inquiry, widespread and persistent, if not exactly universal, known as tragedy.)[21]

Bennett wants to ditch the discourse of aesthetics altogether,
suspecting it of being idealist and unhistorical. He does not seem
aware that there are a number of philosophers of art who would
cheerfully endorse his view of literature, and who would do so
precisely as aestheticians. He also passes over the fact that while
the category of literature may be historically mutable, some of its
components – fiction, for example, or poetry – would seem to be
universal to human cultures. What, after all, is more striking: the
fact that what the Nuer and the Dinka know as storytelling is not
what Peacock or Saul Bellow know as storytelling, or the fact that
both camps share a recognisably common form across such vast
tracts of cultural difference? Continuities and shared features may
have just as much historical force as difference and discontinuity.
Even the most turbulent historical eras reveal permanence and
persistence alongside rupture and revolution. Nor does 'universal'
necessarily mean 'timeless', as nominalists like Bennett tend to
suspect. Universals have a specific material history quite as much
as individuals.

There is an extraordinary irony at stake here. Postmodernist
theory casts a jaundiced eye on the science, rationalism, empiricism and individualism of the modern age. But it remains deeply
indebted to that epoch in its rampant nominalism, however
ignorant it may be of the history of that doctrine. In this sense, it
signifies only a partial break with what it imagines it has left
behind. Nor does it grasp the secret affinities between nominalism

and the insolence of power. It does not see how essentialism has served among other, darker purposes to protect the integrity of things from the insistence of the sovereign will that they be cravenly pliable to its demands. Instead, it maintains in universalist spirit that the doctrine of essences is always and everywhere reprehensible. Jeremy Bentham, not exactly one of postmodernism's cultural icons, would have emphatically agreed.

It is worth recalling that schemes of classification vary from culture to culture. In *The Savage Mind*, Claude Lévi-Strauss claims that objects in tribal societies may be assigned to a certain category not simply because they possess properties definitive of that class, but also on the basis of symbolic associations with existing members of the species. As Simon Clarke puts it, 'A classification [in such societies] does not have an overall logic, but a series of "local logics", since items can be associated with one another according to very different criteria. The rules in question are many and varied, and can differ from society to society.'[22] We are not compelled to choose between one universally binding scheme of classification and pure difference, whatever that might look like. The point has a bearing on the account of literature I am about to offer.

Not all universals or general categories need be oppressive, any more than all difference and specificity are on the side of the angels. One would expect those with a distaste for universals to be a little less grandly universalising in these matters. For an archnominalist like Michel Foucault, all classification would seem an insidious form of violence. For more reasonable souls such as socialists and feminists, grouping individuals together in certain respects for certain purposes may contribute to their emancipation. It is not to be taken as implying that they are alike in every other respect as well.

One further point may be made. Essentialism has almost always been treated by philosophers in ontological terms – as a question about the nature of a thing's being. But what if one were to approach it ethically instead? What if the 'essence' of a human being were whatever it is one loves about them? One might add, since we are now about to turn to the problem of difference and identity, that love has also been seen as resolving this apparent opposition, at least when it crops up at the human level. Since the word 'love' is not normally admissible in literary-theoretical discussion, however, and is plainly indecorous in such a context, I shall pass over these suggestions as abruptly as I broached them. In any case, the point is not much use when it comes to considering the essence of unlovable phenomena like slugs or screwdrivers.

CHAPTER 2

What is Literature? (1)

1

We may now descend from the Supreme Being to the more profane question of whether something called literature actually exists. The point of this brief excursus has been to demonstrate just how much is at stake, intellectually and politically, in the apparently arcane question of whether there really are such things as common natures in the world.

Almost thirty years ago, in *Literary Theory: An Introduction*, I argued a strongly anti-essentialist case about the nature of literature.[1] Literature, I insisted, has no essence whatsoever. Those pieces of writing dubbed 'literary' have no single property or even set of properties in common. Though I would still defend this view, I am clearer now than I was then that nominalism is not the only alternative to essentialism. It does not follow from the fact that literature has no essence that the category has no legitimacy at all.

Stanley Fish writes that 'the category "work of fiction" finally has no content ... there is no trait or set of traits which all works of fiction have in common and which could constitute the necessary and sufficient conditions for being a work of fiction.'[2] The choice is clear: either a work of fiction has an essence, or the concept is vacuous. Fish, in short, is an inverted essentialist. He believes with Thomas Aquinas that things without essences have no real existence; it is just that Aquinas holds that things do in fact have essences while Fish thinks they do not. Otherwise they are in perfect agreement. In similar vein, E.D. Hirsch argues that 'literature has no independent essence, aesthetic or otherwise. It is an arbitrary classification of linguistic works which do not exhibit common distinctive traits, and which cannot be defined as an Aristotelian species.'[3] Once again, we are offered a Hobson's choice between the essentialist and the arbitrary.

The most persuasive alternative to this false dilemma remains Ludwig Wittgenstein's theory of so-called family resemblances, first advanced in his *Philosophical Investigations*. It is one of the most suggestive solutions to the problem of difference and identity that philosophy has yet come up with; and if such a formidable gap did not yawn between Anglo-Saxon and Continental philosophy, it may well have saved the post-structuralist cult of difference from some of its more extravagant excesses. In a celebrated move, Wittgenstein invites us to consider what all games have in common, and concludes that there is no single element they share. What we have instead is 'a complicated network of similarities overlapping and criss-crossing'.[4] He then famously compares this tangled web of affinities to the resemblances between the members of a family. These men, women and children may seem alike, but not because they all have hairy ears, a bulbous nose, a slobbering mouth or a streak of petulance. Some will have one or two of these features but not the others; some will combine several of them, along perhaps with yet another physical or temperamental trait, and so on. It follows that two members of the same family may share no features at all in common, but may still be linked to each other through intervening items in the series.

Literary theorists were not slow to spot the bearing of this model on their own concerns. Only four years after the appearance of the *Investigations*, Charles L. Stevenson can be found using it to illuminate the nature of poetry.[5] Morris Weitz also draws on the idea in the process of rejecting the view that art can be defined.[6] Robert L. Brown and Martin Steinmann appeal to the notion of family resemblances to enforce the anti-essentialist point that 'there are no necessary and sufficient conditions for counting a piece of discourse as a work of art'.[7] Colin Lyas argues that there is a set of properties definitive of literature, such that any work defined as literary must exemplify at least some of them. But not all so-called literary works will display all of them, and no two such works need share any of them in common.[8] Why we call one work literature may not be why we award the accolade to another. John R. Searle remarks in *Expression and Meaning* that literature is a 'family-resemblance notion'.[9] More recently, Christopher New has rehearsed the case once more: in his view, 'all literary discourses would resemble some other literary discourse in one way, but they would not all resemble each other in a single way'.[10] For his part, Peter Lamarque points out that there is no set of properties that all works must manifest to win themselves the honorific title of literature.[11]

It is hard to deny the resourcefulness of this model, and not just when it comes to literature. What is it that inspires us to group such strikingly diverse works as Plato's *Republic*, Nietzsche's *Beyond Good and Evil*, Heidegger's *Being and Time*, Ayer's *Language, Truth and Logic* and Habermas's *Theory of Communicative Action* under the same heading? What if anything do Kierkegaard and Frege have in common? The family-resemblance response to this query appeals neither to an abiding essence nor to some arbitrary effect of power. The likenesses between things are taken to involve real features in the world. The hairy ears and bulbous noses are not just 'constructs', mere functions of power, desire, interests, discourse, interpretation, the unconscious, deep structures and so on. Yet it is still possible for both Frege and Kierkegaard to be called philosophers without sharing any inherent features in common. This is not because calling them both philosophers is a decision independent of such features, but because, as we have just seen, one member of a class may be linked to another through a range of intermediary cases.

Even so, Stanley Cavell has argued that Wittgenstein is not in fact out to discredit the notion of essence but to retrieve it.[12] Essence is explained in grammar, Wittgenstein remarks in the *Philosophical Investigations*, meaning that it is the rules that govern the way we apply words which tell us what a thing is. This, to be sure, is a very different conception of essence from Aquinas's divinely manufactured natures. Hard-nosed forms of essentialism claim that what makes a thing a member of a particular class is a certain property or set of properties it possesses which is both necessary and sufficient for it to belong to that class. For a strong form of essentialism, these qualities determine and can explain all the other qualities and behaviours of a thing.[13] But there are in fact no kinds or species all of whose members are identical in respect of all their properties. It is possible to defend a softer version of essentialism, as I did in *The Illusions of Postmodernism*,[14] but this hard-headed version of the creed is egregiously hard to swallow.

Definitions of the literary or fictional have also depended to some degree on what one takes to be their opposites, rather in the way that notions of leisure are parasitic on conceptions of labour. But this, too, has been notably unstable over the centuries. The opposite of literature may be factual, technical or scientific writing, or writing which is thought to be second-rate, or works which do not inspire us imaginatively, or texts which do not issue from a certain 'polite' or genteel milieu, or those that do not yield us intimations of the godhead and so on.

Not all philosophers of literature are eager to endorse the family-resemblance theory. Peter Lamarque rightly points out that resemblances can hold between any two objects, and that what must therefore be at stake here are 'significant' similarities. Yet this, he suspects, involves a certain circularity, since what counts as a significant similarity 'seems to presuppose rather than illuminate the idea of literature'.[15] It is not clear that this is the case. Stein Haugom Olsen, in a work whose title might be said to reflect a certain wishful thinking, rejects the family-resemblance model on the conservative grounds that it would let in too much – that the lattice of overlapping elements that constitutes literature extends into what he considers the non-literary (popular fiction, for example), thus jeopardising the notion of literature as writing which is especially valuable.[16] We shall be looking into this dubious conception later on. In the meanwhile, it is worth noting that family-resemblance-type definitions are indeed leaky at the edges, in ways that the literary purist may not consider desirable.

Lamarque is right to insist that the affinities in question must be significant ones, and right, too, to be alert to the danger of begging the question here. There are countless features shared by so-called literary works (assonance, for example, or narrative reversals, or dramatic suspense) that scarcely seem constitutive of the category of literature itself. There is, moreover, one notorious objection to the family-resemblance model. This is the claim that if one does not spell out the affinities in question the concept is simply vacuous, since any object can be said to resemble any other in any number of respects.[17] A tortoise resembles orthopaedic surgery in that neither can ride a bicycle. If, however, one does give a name to the resemblances at stake, one seems to be back to the business of sufficient and necessary conditions for a thing being what it is, which the family-resemblance notion might be thought to have disposed of. All we have done instead is to relocate this kind of talk at the level of the general category rather than the individual entity. Individual things, for example, do not all need to have the same specific feature in common in order to belong to a particular species of things; but there are features that are constitutive of the species itself, and the individual entity must display at least one of them if it is to count as a member of that species. Not every member of the Smith family need be afflicted with a bulbous nose, but a bulbous nose is one way we recognise the Smiths as a family.

When it comes to some phenomena, the family-resemblance idea is less than illuminating. Take, for example, the category of art.

We have seen that from a family-resemblance viewpoint there is no need for every object we call a work of art to display the same property or set of properties. There will be a criss-crossing and overlapping of such features. Yet to arrive at a definition of art as such, it must be possible to specify which of these common features are taken to be constitutive of the class itself; and the fact is that art is made up of too amorphous a set of objects for this to be done with any great plausibility. Not many philosophers of art nowadays would contend that art can be defined by certain intrinsic properties, or that any such property is both necessary and sufficient for something to be ranked as an artwork. As Stephen Davies puts it, 'Artworks do not form a natural kind.'[18] This is one reason why most of those who think a definition of art is nonetheless possible tend to look instead to art's functional or institutional nature.

Any functional definition of art will naturally take account of the daunting diversity of its uses and effects. Some things, like spoons and corkscrews, can be fairly easily defined by their functions, which historically speaking have remained fairly stable. But literature has had a much more chequered history of functions, all the way from consolidating political power to glorifying the Almighty, providing moral instruction to exemplifying the transcendent imagination, serving as a form of ersatz religion to augmenting the profits of large commercial corporations. One of the most vital functions of the work of art since Romanticism has been to exemplify that which is gloriously, almost uniquely free of a function, and thus, by virtue of what it shows rather than what it says, act as an implicit rebuke to a civilisation in thrall to utility, exchange-value and calculative reason. The function of art on this viewpoint is not to have a function.

It is conceivable that a haiku, a warrior's decorated mask, a pirouette and the twelve-bar blues have certain so-called aesthetic effects in common, but it is hard to see that they share any very distinctive intrinsic qualities. Perhaps they all reveal what is occasionally called 'significant form' or integral design. Even if they do, however, there are a good many avant-garde and postmodern phenomena that do not, yet to which we give the name of art all the same. There are also plenty of objects like spades and tractors which display significant form but are not generally regarded as works of art, except perhaps by socialist realists.

Literature, however, is a less amorphous phenomenon than art in general. A crime thriller and a Petrarchan sonnet are scarcely lookalikes, but they would seem to have more in common than do impasto, a bassoon solo and a glissade in ballet. So perhaps family resemblances can be more easily picked out in the case of works that people call literary. My own sense is that when people at the moment call a piece of writing literary, they generally have one of five things in mind, or some combination of them. They mean by 'literary' a work which is fictional, or which yields significant insight into human experience as opposed to reporting empirical truths, or which uses language in a peculiarly heightened, figurative or self-conscious way, or which is not practical in the sense that shopping lists are, or which is highly valued as a piece of writing.

These are empirical categories, not theoretical ones. They derive from everyday judgements, not from an investigation of the logic of the concept itself. We may call these factors the fictional, moral, linguistic, non-pragmatic and normative. The more of these features that are combined in a specific piece of writing, the more likely it is in our kind of culture that someone will dub it literary. We may note that not all of the aspects I have listed are on the same footing. To talk of the value of a literary work is just to talk in a certain way about its language, moral vision, fictional credibility and so on. It is not dissociable from these features. We shall see later that the other aspects of literariness also interact in important ways and present some significant parallels with one other.

Texts that combine all of these factors – *Othello*, for example, or *Light in August* – are generally taken as paradigmatically literary. But no work classified as literary needs to meet all of these criteria, and the absence of any one of these features need not be enough to disqualify it from the category. In this sense, none of these attributes is a necessary condition of literary status. Sometimes, but not always, the presence simply of one of them may be enough for us to regard a piece of writing as literature. But no single one of these qualities will be enough to secure literary status for a work, which is to say that none of them is a sufficient condition of it.

People may call a work literary because it is fictional and verbally inventive even though it is morally shallow, or because it yields significant moral insights and is 'finely' written but non-fictional, or because it is non-fictional and morally trivial but superbly written and serves no immediate practical purpose, and so on. Some people might count as literature a pragmatic but verbally opulent text (a verbal charm ritually chanted to banish evil spirits, for example), whereas others might regard the fact that the chant has a practical function as outweighing its rhetorical allures. A private diary kept by a survivor of Nazi Germany may be ranked as literature because of its historical value, along with the depth and poignancy of its moral vision, despite being non-fictional, pragmatic (it was kept, let us say, to inform the public of this history) and appallingly written. And so on. Many permutations are possible. But not just anything goes, even though Shelley wished to include parliamentary statutes under the heading of poetry because they created harmony out of disorder. This would seem a more cogent reason to include them under the heading of ideology.

There are, then, many different ways in which the word 'literature' is used, which is not to say that it can be used in just any old way. A ham sandwich is not literature even for the most generously pluralistic of postmodernists. But the fact that the word has several overlapping uses, in a family-resemblance kind of way, accounts for why works such as John Le Carré's *Smiley's People*, Newman's *Apologia pro Vita Sua*, Thomas Browne's *Pseudodoxia*, Seneca's moral essays, Donne's sermons, Clarendon's *History of the Rebellion*, the Superman comics, Herder's reflections on national cultures, Hooker's *Laws of Ecclesiastical Polity*, Bossuet's funeral speeches,

Boileau's treatise on poetry, the *Beano* annual, Pascal's *Pensées*, Madame de Sévigné's letters to her daughter and Mill's *On Liberty* have all been included in the category of literature from time to time, along with Pushkin and Novalis. When the police speak of having removed some literature from the premises, they are sometimes including pornography or leaflets inciting racial hatred in that category. As with any class of things, moreover, there will always be hybrids, anomalies, liminal cases, twilight zones, undecidable instances. Since concepts emerge from the rough ground of our social practices, it is not surprising that they are ragged at the edges. They would be far less use to us if they were not. Aquinas himself allows for hybrid, indeterminate cases. He is not a hard-line essentialist.

The notion of family resemblances is a dynamic one, in the sense that it contains a built-in capacity for expansion and transformation. This is one reason why some conservative critics are so wary of it. Let us imagine that in a particular culture the literary means primarily the fictional. Because of certain mythological beliefs, however, a good many literary works tend to combine this fictional status with images of elephants falling from immense heights. After a while, such images might become one of the constituents of literature itself. There might be heated controversies over whether texts which did not present the sky as raining elephants counted as literature at all. Then, after a while, the expectation that literary works should be fictional might gradually fade away, and the elephant image might come to team up with some other feature, so that this combination in turn would become typical of the literary.

Here, then, is another reason for the roughness of the family-resemblance model. There is a sense in which it is self-deconstructing. Both temporally and spatially, it points beyond itself. And this capacity to proliferate is part of what puts the conservative on guard. Relations, as Henry James remarks, stop nowhere. A work may be thrown up by the existing criteria of literariness which ends up questioning that whole prevailing orthodoxy, inaugurating in avant-garde fashion not simply a new artefact but a new version of art itself.

A good deal of critical controversy and interpretive labour are involved in establishing what is to count in any given context as fictional, valuable, richly figurative, non-pragmatic and morally significant. All of these categories are culturally and historically variable. In the eighteenth century, for example, only one of these criteria – that a piece of writing should be highly esteemed – was essential for a work to be ranked as literary, and even then the esteem in question was as much social (a question of 'polite letters') as aesthetic. At the same time, however, there is an impressive degree of continuity on this subject across histories and cultures. The *Odyssey, The Changeling* and *The Adventures of Augie March* are called literature for much the same kinds of reason, whatever they may have been dubbed in their own time. All of them are fictional, non-pragmatic, verbally inventive moral inquiries, and all of them are highly rated. Such continuities need alarm only those postmodernists who for some astonishing reason regard all change and discontinuity as radical and all continuity as reactionary. Nor is it simply a question of our own literary institution picking out those features of older works which best suit its own sense of literature. On any estimate, the literary features in question are central to these texts as such. This does not alter the fact that what counts as fictional, non-pragmatic, verbally inventive and so on may change from place to place and time to time.

All of these facets of literature, as I hope to demonstrate, are porous, unstable, fuzzy at the edges and tend to merge into their opposites or into each other. There is no need to maintain that what fiction or the non-pragmatic means to Philip Roth is exactly what it meant to the authors of the Icelandic sagas. Indeed, having identified these five dimensions of literature, I shall spend a good deal of time showing how easily they can come apart in one's hands – a fact which, I trust, will give pause to those commentators eager to conclude that I have now abandoned my earlier radical view of the nature of literature for a more middle-aged approach. Most of the rest of this study will be devoted to illustrating how these factors *fail* to yield us a definition of literature, in the hope that in this process of self-deconstruction, some light will be shed on the workings of what people call literary texts. When I use terms like 'literary texts' and 'literature' in this book, incidentally, I mean what people nowadays generally regard as such things.

The mistake of some modern theorists is to imagine that because categories like these are leaky and labile, as is the case with the great majority of human concepts, they have no force at all. Having pitched your idea of a class or concept at an unworkably idealised level, you then regard whatever falls short of it as useless. Because we have no precise definition of fascism or patriarchy, the notion crumbles to dust. The belief that definitions must of their nature be exact is one of several senses in which the wilder sort of deconstructionist is the prodigal son of the metaphysical father. The metaphysical father fears that without watertight definitions we are plunged into chaos; the wild-deconstructionist son shares the illusion that definitions must be watertight if we are not to have pure indeterminacy, but unlike his austere father revels in the indeterminacy. For Derrida, indeterminacy is where things come unstuck; for Wittgenstein, it is what makes things work. As he inquires in the *Investigations*, is an indistinct photograph of someone not a photograph of them at all? Do we need to measure our distance from the sun to the nearest millimetre? Does it not make sense to say 'Stand roughly there'? Is a field without an exact boundary not a field at all? And isn't conceptual fuzziness sometimes exactly what we require?

It so happens that several of the literary features I have listed have a central place in the evolution of a human life. Small children learn to speak by first rehearsing the whole range of human sounds in their babbling. Poets are simply those emotionally arrested creatures who continue to invest their libidinal energies in words rather than objects, and who thus regress to the infantile state of oral eroticism which Seamus Heaney has called 'mouth music'. In this sense, the 'deviant' (childish babbling) is the condition of the non-deviant (adult language), just as play is the condition of non-play, and the non-pragmatic of the pragmatic. Children's fiction, fantasy, speech, mimesis and make-believe are not cognitive aberrations but the very seedbed of adult knowledge and behaviour. To learn how to speak is also to learn how to imagine. Since language could not operate without the possibility of negation and innovation, the imagination, which cancels the indicative in the name of the subjunctive, is built into its very nature.

As for mimesis, children learn how to think, feel and act by being born into a form of social life and miming its characteristic modes until these things come to seem natural to them. This is one reason why Bertolt Brecht saw theatrical performance as our natural condition.[19] There can be no human reality without mimesis. Among other things, then, the literary returns us to the ludic roots of our everyday knowledge and activity. It allows us a glimpse of how our distinctive ways of feeling and acting are a semi-arbitrary selection from a whole gamut of possibilities built into our language and infantile fantasises. (I say 'semi-arbitrary' because some of these ways of feeling and behaving are also species-based. It is natural to weep at the death of a loved one, not just a 'social construct'. Sodden handkerchiefs are cultural, but grief is natural.) This is one reason why creative writers and literary critics are more commonly liberals rather than conservatives. There is something about the imagination that baulks at the status quo.

Have we, then, arrived at a point where we can now say what is literature and what is not? Unfortunately not. One reason why we have not is that none of the features I have listed above is peculiar to what people call literature. There are, for example, plenty of non-literary forms of fiction: jokes, lies, advertisements, statements by spokespersons for the Israel Defense Force and so on.

Sometimes the only distinction between a literary work and a superbly recounted tall tale is the fact that the former is written down. A joke may be rich in wordplay and moral insight, work non-pragmatically, deliver a fictional narrative stuffed with fascinating characters and be highly esteemed as a piece of invention. In which case there is nothing, formally speaking, to distinguish it from a literary text as I have just described it. Someone might breathe admiringly 'That's pure literature!' on hearing such a comic story.

This is not, of course, to suggest that poems and jokes are the same thing. Socially speaking, they are clearly different practices. Differences and resemblances depend on a lot more than formal qualities. Quite often it is the material context or social situation which enforces a distinction between what is literature and what is not. The whole point of a joke is to be funny, which is not true of a lot of what we call literature. It is certainly not true of *The Malcontent, John Gabriel Borkman* or *Mourning Becomes Electra*, except for those with a peculiarly perverse sense of humour. Even comic literary works are rarely *just* funny, and some renowned works of comedy, like some jokes, are not funny at all. We are not usually carried out of Shakespeare's comedies by our companions convulsed with helpless laughter.

The difference between a joke and a literary work may simply be functional, which is to say situational or institutional. A joke is not commonly bound in an expensive leather volume and placed on a library shelf, even if a really conceited comedian might always get round to doing so. There may be times when we find it hard to distinguish a joke from a poem, but this does not mean that we cannot tell *Le Bateau ivre* from a cheap crack about one's mother-in-law. Apart from the odd anomaly, jokes are obviously not poems. The social context suggests as much. People are not awarded the Nobel Prize for mother-in-law jokes. They do not read their jokes out to enraptured audiences breathless with fine feelings. They do not write 'Joker' in their passports, find themselves compared with Stevens or Neruda or publish volumes entitled

Collected Jokes 1978–2008. Jokes and poems are different social institutions, whatever formal properties they may share in common. We may call a poem a bad joke, but this is rather like calling an inept lawyer a comedian. All the same, there are times when context will not be enough to determine the difference. There may be cases (Sterne's *Tristram Shandy* is perhaps one of them) where there is no clear distinction between a jest and a literary work.

How are we to distinguish novels from dreams, given that a dream may be awash with imagery, rife with wordplay, replete with grippingly dramatic events, rich in moral insight, furnished with fascinating characters and powered by a compelling storyline? In one sense, this is rather like wondering whether machines that dispense chocolate bars can think. Do they know that you are in frantic search of a Mars Bar? It is obvious that they do not, just as dreams are obviously not novels, even if both happen to share the same formal qualities. People do not wake up from their novels in panic, or dog-ear their dreams so as to remind themselves how far they have got in them. Even so, a written account of such a dream may display all the qualities we associate with literature, while actually being part of a psychoanalyst's clinical records.

So these five features fail to deliver a hard-and-fast definition of literature, in the sense of securing the frontiers between it and other phenomena. Sometimes we can do so by appealing to the institutional context, but such appeals are not invariably decisive.[20] There are many cases where we simply cannot decide, and where the fact that we cannot decide does not really matter. There is no such thing as an exact definition of literature. All such attempts at exclusive definition are vulnerable to a triumphant 'But what about ...?' The features I have set out are simply guidelines or criteria to help cast light on the nature of literature-talk, and like all such criteria have a certain rough-and-ready quality about them. But rough definitions may be preferable both to Platonically precise ones and to anything-goes-ism.

Anything-goes-ism in this context is objectionable among other reasons on democratic grounds. It seems to suggest that when people use the word 'literature' they have no idea what they are talking about. They imagine they are discussing a relatively determinate phenomenon, but in fact they are not. My own inclination is to invest more faith in common-or-garden discourse than this. People do indeed have a sense of what they mean by literature, and of how it differs from other social forms, and much of what I am doing here is simply trying to focus that sense more sharply. As with all efforts at more exact (and so, perhaps, more fruitful) formulation, however, problems then emerge which were not obvious beforehand. What you gain on the swings you lose on the roundabouts.

2

Since fictionality is probably the thorniest of the factors I have touched on, I shall devote a separate chapter to the subject later on. Meanwhile, let us take a glance at a couple of the other criteria, beginning with the linguistic. René Wellek and Austin Warren insist in their *Theory of Literature* that there is a special literary use of language, a claim that has turned out to have embarrassingly few adherents.[21] Literary theorists these days are well-nigh unanimous in their conviction that there are no semantic, syntactical or other linguistic phenomena peculiar to literature, and that if this is what the Russian Formalists, Prague structuralists and American New Critics believed, then they were grievously mistaken.

Whether it is indeed what they believed is another matter. The Formalist case that all literary devices work by a form of estrangement or 'deautomatisation', in which the reader becomes newly conscious of the stuff of language, sounds essentialist enough, as though the whole of world literature could be scooped up into a single strategy. Indeed, it has a claim to rank as the most astonishingly ambitious critical programme of the modern era, one which sees itself as having stumbled upon the key to all literary mythologies and laid bare the long-preserved secret of poetry, narrative, folklore and prose fiction in a single, enormously versatile, device.

The Formalists, however, are out to define 'literariness', not literature, and regard such literariness as a relational, differential, context-dependent phenomenon.[22] One person's 'self-focusing' sign or flamboyantly self-conscious trope may be another's routine idiom. In any case, making-strange does not exhaust the repertoire of literary tactics. The Formalists characterise the process mainly in terms of poetry. Their treatment of non-poetic genres usually involves finding versions of such devices there, too, though generally of a structural rather than semantic kind. They thus make the mistake of so many schools of literary theory, granting privilege to one particular literary genre and then defining others in its terms. We shall see later that the speech-act theorists assign a similar unwarrantable privilege to realist narrative. The Prague structuralists likewise see poetry as involving what Jan Mukařovský calls 'the maximum of foregrounding of the utterance',[23] though for them as for the Formalists, verbal deformations and deviations are perceptible only against a normative linguistic background, and so alter from context to context.

It is worth adding that though formalist theories of literature are notably shy of history, they themselves tend to arise under distinctive historical conditions. One such condition is when literary works no longer appear to serve any very definite social function, in which case it is always possible to pluck a virtue from necessity and claim that they represent their own function, ground and purpose. Hence the formalist view of the literary work as autonomous. Another condition is when the basic stuff of literature – language – is felt to have become tarnished and degenerate, so that literary works have to wreak a certain systematic violence on this unpropitious material, alienating and transforming it in order to wrench some value from it. The poetic is thus a kind of alienation to the second power, defamiliarising an already distorted medium.

The Russian Formalists, Prague structuralists, American New Critics and English Leavisites all write in civilisations which are living through the early impact of so-called mass culture, along with accelerating scientific and technological advances, on the everyday language that forms the literary artist's raw materials. At the same time, that language is buckling under the strain of new urban, commercial, technical and bureaucratic pressures, as well as being thrown increasingly open to cosmopolitan cross-currents. In this situation, only by being brought to a certain crisis can it be restored to health.

In *The Phenomenon of Literature*, Bennison Gray believes that he has grasped the essence of his subject. A literary fiction must constitute a coherent statement (a claim which seems deliberately designed to exclude most modernist and experimental writing from the category of literature), and involves a particular use of language in the sense that it must present an event in moment-by-moment style rather than simply reporting it. Thus 'Pussy cat, pussy cat, where have you been?' is literature, but 'Thirty days hath September ...' is not (these are Gray's own examples, not my sardonic travesties).[24] Thomas C. Pollock argued with portentous vagueness some decades ago that literature consists in a certain use of language that evokes the author's experience. Whatever this is supposed to mean, he would find himself nowadays pretty much in a minority of one.[25] For it is generally agreed that there is no kind of language, no verbal or structural devices, that literary works do not share with other bits of writing, and there is an abundance of so-called literary writing (naturalistic fiction, for example) in which language is not used in especially deviant, ambiguous, figurative, deautomatising, self-referential or self-focusing ways. Emile Zola's *Nana* or George Gissing's *The Nether World* are not remarkable for the way they flaunt the materiality of the signifier. It is also true that there is as much metaphor in the Bronx as there is in Balzac. Jan Mukařovský speaks of an 'unstructured aesthetic', meaning the proverbs, metaphors, invectives, archaisms, neologisms, imported expressions and the like which are to be found as vivifying devices in ordinary speech.[26] Jacques Rancière sees the concept of litera- ture, as it emerges in the late eighteenth century, as signifying a certain self-referential or non-representational use of language, but this is to make a particular type of literary work exemplary of the phenomenon as a whole.[27] Rather similarly, Philippe Lacoue- Labarthe and Jean-Luc Nancy claim that the concept of literature as we know it, in the sense of a kind of writing creative in its very essence, was invented by the Jena Romantics in the late eighteenth century, along with the notion of literary theory. For all its sugges- tiveness, this is once more to confine the concept of literature to a specific version of it.[28]

As far as self-referentiality goes, the British Banking Act of 1979, not generally acclaimed as a poetic masterpiece, contains the following sentence: 'Any reference in these regulations to a regula- tion is a reference to a regulation in these regulations.' Since this sentence draws attention to itself as a tongue-twister or piece of wordplay, one might see it as an instance of the self-referentiality it speaks of, hence qualifying it for literary status on a formalist view of the matter. One or two more traditionally minded critics, however, regard heightened verbal effects as inimical to literary merit. 'Since Flaubert,' the American critic Grant Overton comments with a barely concealed frisson of distaste, 'it has dawned on us slowly that literary style – prose which in any way obtrudes itself as prose – is something less than the most enviable condition in a novel.'[29] Authors should say what they mean in plain, honest- to-goodness, American-as-apple-pie prose rather than indulging in fancy French flourishes.

There is a difference, not much noted in literary-theoretical circles, between writing which is rhetorically heightened or self- focusing in the manner of *Paradise Lost* or *The Wreck of the Deutschland*, and works which are simply well written according to some institutionally defined criteria of fine writing. You can write in literary vein without sounding too cloyingly like the opening pages of Lawrence's *The Rainbow* or the more purple stretches of *Moby-Dick*. People sometimes grant the title of literature to works which are finely but not self-consciously written, rather than simply to those which are verbally self-regarding. They may see an economy and lucidity of language, or a certain sinewy plainness, as more admirable than a bristling thicket of exotic tropes. Fine writing, like good manners, may be thought to involve a certain self-effacing unobtrusiveness – though if it becomes understated enough, as with Roland Barthes's 'degree zero' writing, it becomes obtrusive once more. Hemingway is the standard example. Stylelessness can be a style in itself. Even so, literature cannot be usefully defined as good writing, since, as Dorothy Walsh points out, all writing should be well-written.[30] Neither 'good' writing nor rhetorically burnished writing, then, will serve to define the category.

Monroe Beardsley claims that there is indeed one property of literature which is both necessary and sufficient, namely the fact that 'a literary work is a discourse in which an important part of the meaning is implicit'.[31] But some works pigeonholed as non-literary are richer in implication than some poems and novels. And without some measure of implicit meaning, no piece of writing could function at all. The sign 'Exit' tacitly requests us to take it as a descriptive rather than an imperative, otherwise theatres and department stores would be permanently empty. There is, to be sure, a question of degree here; but Swift, whose hard, muscular, artfully depthless style the critic Denis Donoghue once finely described as lacking all tentacular roots, presumably qualifies as literature in Beardsley's eyes, as one suspects do Hemingway and Robbe-Grillet. In any case, a discourse may be freighted with implication in one cultural setting and not in another. Implications are a function of the relations between a work and its contexts, not fixed properties of it.

There is a paradox in the idea of the self-flaunting sign. In one sense, this kind of language keeps the world at arm's length, drawing our attention to the fact that the text is writing and not the real thing; yet it seeks to put flesh on real things by unleashing the full range of its resources. The paradox of the poetic sign is that the more densely textured it becomes, the more it expands its referential power; but this density also turns it into a phenomenon in its own right, throwing its autonomy into relief and thus loosening up its bond with the real world. Moreover, because the sign's sound, texture, rhythmic and tonal value are so palpable, it can enter more easily into connotative relations with the signs around it, rather than seeming to denote an object directly. To 'bring up' the sign is thus to 'fade down' its referent, as well as, paradoxically, to bring it into sharper focus.

The busier the sign, then, the more referential work it accomplishes; but by the same token the more it draws our eye to itself, displacing it from what it denotes. F.R. Leavis is keen on signs which smack of material reality (Shakespeare, Keats, Hopkins), but takes a stern view of autonomous ones which seem to cut adrift from the real (Milton). There is, however, a fine line between words which are redolent of the taste and texture of things, and words which appear to have become things themselves. Fredric Jameson sees modernism as involving a reification of the sign, though one that emancipates it from its referent into its own free space. There is thus loss and gain together. In one sense, the world is well lost, but the price some modernist works are forced to pay for this freedom from the importunity of the real is alarmingly steep.[32] By contrast, the poet who rejects the autonomous sign choosing instead a language full of the feel of (let us say) tangerines and pineapples might be better off as a greengrocer. Words which really merged with their referents would cease to be words at all.

Theorists may have largely abandoned the case that literary works are verbally peculiar, but they have been more reluctant to jettison the view that they insist on a peculiar degree of vigilance from the reader. F.E. Sparshott tells us that a literary discourse is one we attend to for its inherent qualities rather than for its referent.[33] But there are also critics for whom the literary cannot be distinguished by such inherent qualities because these qualities do not exist. Stanley Fish, who correctly sees that there is no general intrinsic difference between 'literary' and 'ordinary' language, insists that what we call literature is simply language around which we draw a frame, indicating a decision to treat it with a peculiarly focused attentiveness.[34] It is this act of focusing that will produce the so-called inherent qualities of the language, which for Fish have no existence independent of it.

This skates with suspicious speed over the question of why we should want to do this in the first place, if there is nothing in the work itself to warrant it. On what grounds are such a decision taken? Why encircle this text rather than that? It cannot be because of a work's innate properties, since, as I have just pointed out, Fish does not believe that it has any. 'Formal units,' he writes in boldly counter-intuitive style, 'are always a function of the interpretive model one brings to bear; they are not "in" the text.'[35] His epistemology thus disqualifies him from accepting that in a specific cultural context, some texts display properties that are judged to reward a sensitive reading more than others, and that this is one reason why the literary institution 'decides' that they are to be handled with an answerable delicacy and responsiveness. It is hard otherwise to see what the grounds of such a decision are; and decisions taken without rational criteria, like so-called existentialist ones, are only in a loose sense of the word decisions at all. Why are so many frames drawn around texts in metre, for example, or ones that are fictional? Is this choice simply arbitrary? Might the literary institution just as easily have selected *Nuts* magazine and the racing results as Kleist and Hofmannsthal?

Of course, given enough futile ingenuity, you can coax *Nuts* magazine and the racing results to yield up a few lavishly poetic meanings. The question is rather why the literary institution does not generally invite us to do so. The obvious answer – that it considers Kleist and Hofmannsthal to be more rewarding in this respect – will not do for Fish, since if texts have no inherent properties none of them can be said to be preferable in itself to any other. By the same token, however, there can be nothing for Fish inherent in *Nuts* magazine (its illustration of certain popular-cultural forms, for example) which would make it worth drawing a frame around any more than around Kleist, since it has no inherent properties either. Or, at least, it has no perceptible verbal qualities that would seem to make it either worth reading or not worth reading before the frame is sketched around it. The case thus yields no more comfort to the critics of the canon than it does to the champions of it. It also begs the question of what is meant by something being 'in' a text in the first place, as though believers in 'inherent' meanings are bound to assume that meaning resides in a work rather as brandy resides in a keg.

Fish's theory could be seen as the critical equivalent of decisionism in ethics, though in this case it is institutions rather than individuals that do the deciding. He cannot ground the decision to treat a text as literary in facts about the work, since in his view there are no such unimpeachable facts. Facts are simply well-entrenched interpretations. Why they become so well embedded in specific circumstances he fails to inform us. It cannot be because they are part of the way the world is, since for Fish 'the way the world is' is itself a product of interpretation. Interpretations generate facts, not vice versa. The so-called facts of the text are generated by a reading of it. So all you would be doing, in appealing to textual evidence to support your critical hypothesis, is grounding one interpretation in another. Not only that, but the so-called textual evidence is actually a product of the hypothesis in question, so that the case becomes circular. The concept of evidence is thus seriously weakened. It is turtles all the way down.

On this thesis, it is hard to account for situations in which texts appear to resist our interpretations of them, forcing us to revise or abandon our critical hypotheses in the light of new evidence. How we can ever be surprised by a poem or novel, or conclude that our reading of it has in some sense gone awry, becomes unclear. Textual properties in Fish's world are simply not real enough to offer such resistance to our designs on them. We get out of a literary text only what we surreptitiously put into it, since everything we 'discover' in the work is in fact a product of our institutionally determined reading of it. Fish would seem to be a literary equivalent of the man in Wittgenstein's *Philosophical Investigations* who passes money from one of his hands to the other and thinks he has made a financial transaction.

'The properties of the text (whether they be literary or "ordinary" properties),' Fish observes, 'are the product of certain ways of paying attention.'[36] Robert C. Holub suggests that Fish must at least 'admit the existence of words or marks on pages . . . as "something that exists prior to interpretation",'[37] but he is being far too charitable. For Fish, the phrase 'marks on a page' is positively bristling with interpretations. Even semicolons are a social construct, in the sense that they are as much a product of interpretation as some outlandish hypothesis about *Eugene Onegin*. What it is we are interpreting, then, must remain as mysteriously inaccessible as Kant's noumenal realm, since the answer to that question could only be another interpretation. The case, one should note, runs different senses of the word 'interpretation' illicitly together. Because all empirical observations are theory-laden, as Fish rightly insists, they become interpretations in the same sense that seeing Malvolio as a merchant banker is one. They are thus unable to validate or invalidate such claims.

Strangely for a neo-pragmatist, Fish does not take Wittgenstein's point that we use the word 'interpretation' only in certain practical contexts. We generally use the term when there is some possibility of doubt or obscurity, or of alternative possibilities, which is true of semicolons only for the short-sighted. I do not 'interpret' that I have two knees. To imagine that I always have to 'interpret' the words 'Stanley Fish' every time I see them is like supposing that I have to 'infer' or 'deduce' that someone is grief-stricken from his torrent of tears. We can speak of an interpretation of Mozart's clarinet concerto because there are different ways of performing it, but when I look out of a window I do not generally interpret that I am looking out of a window.

Fish believes that we have to construe meanings from black marks on a page, which is as wrong-headed as believing that we have to construe a black and white patch on our eyeballs as a zebra.[38] When we look at a word we see a word, not a set of black marks that we interpret to be a word. This is not to deny that we can be unsure whether certain black marks actually are a word, or that we can be uncertain of what a word means, or bemused by how it is being used in a particular context. (Though one cannot be bemused about how a word is being used unless one knows what it means. I am never in the least puzzled about how the word 'ziglig' is being used in a certain context, since I have no idea what it means.) The point is simply that we should reserve the term 'interpretation' for cases of doubt or diverse possibilities, for fear of it losing all force. Otherwise I could preface all my observations with the words 'I interpret that . . .', a phrase that would then behave like a cog in the machine of language which was failing to mesh with anything. Instead of saying 'There's my old pal Silas Rumpole', I could say 'I interpret that there's my old pal Silas Rumpole', and so on. It is possible that this could become a little tedious after a while.

That Fish does not see how the concepts of doubt and interpretation go together is evident from the fact that he sees reading as a process of interpretation, but denies that it involves any possibility of doubt. A reader will generally be sure of the meaning of the text, just as she will be sure that she is in the presence of a pain-maddened rhinoceros. The fact that we supposedly need to 'interpret' a cluster of black marks to denote a penguin does not mean that we could ever do otherwise. This is because the individual reader is merely a function of the so-called interpretive community to which she belongs, and for this community, meaning is always determinate. It is, so to speak, the community which does the interpreting for the reader, to the point where she will spontaneously see a meaning just as it determines her to see it. Readers are just the obedient agents of their interpretive communities, as the CIA are the obedient agents of the US government. From the standpoint of the interpretive community, everything in the world is an interpretation; from the standpoint of the individual, nothing appears to be. In a striking irony, Fish sees the need for interpretation where there is none, and fails to see the need for it where there is.[39]

Reading for Fish, then, is largely an unproblematic affair. The whole process is well-nigh automatic, as the interpretive community takes the strain and the reader is able to lie back. For the case at its most self-parodic, there is no untidy overlapping of such communities, no ambiguity about their conventions or how to apply them, no indeterminacy about their boundaries, no conflicts and inconsistencies within them, and no possibility of collisions between the sense the interpretive community makes of a text and the meaning that the reader tries to pluck from it. Fish tends to see interpretive communities in implausibly homogeneous terms. Readers, and human beings more generally, are the product of a single set of ways of doing things, which means that you cannot fundamentally challenge these conventions as long as you belong to them. According to what conventions would you do so? Indeed, since the human subject is actually constituted by these institutions, it could not submit them to fundamental critique without leaping out of its own skin. Any such radical critique, as we shall see later, could be launched only from the vantage point of some other interpretive community (which would then make it irrelevant to your own), or from some metaphysical outer space.

Fish's epistemological radicalism thus has some interestingly conservative political implications. It implies among other things that nobody can disagree with him. If he can understand your criticisms, then you and he are natives of the same interpretive community and there can be no fundamental dissension between you. If he cannot understand you, this is probably because you inhabit an interpretive community incommensurable with his own, and your criticisms may thus be safely ignored.

Epistemological constructivism in general sees the world as the product of one's interpretations, and can thus slip easily into scepticism. It becomes possible to believe with Fish that 'what we know is not the world but stories about the world'. In which case, if the stories are 'about' the world (though how do we know that, and how is it not just another story?), it is hard to see how we are not knowing the world when we are knowing them. For the Kantians, it is phenomenal appearances which intrude their ungainly bulk between us and the world as it is in itself; for the postmodernists it is discourse or interpretation. The idea that in pronouncing the word 'biscuit' we know only the word itself, or the concept it signifies, rather than the actual piece of confectionery, rests on a naive misconception of what a word is, and a reificatory one to boot. It imagines that words or concepts are objects which intervene between ourselves and reality, which is rather like supposing that my body is what prevents me from making contact with the world.

This mistake was especially rife in the 1970s and '80s among Saussureans, Althusserians, discourse theorists, some radical feminists and others, and is still to be found in postmodern thought today. For an alternative viewpoint we can have recourse once again to Thomas Aquinas, not the most fashionable of thinkers among postmodernists, who points out in the fifth book of his *De unitate intellectus contra Averroistas* that there is no problem with how concepts relate to whatever they are concepts of, since a concept is not what we understand of a thing but just *is* our understanding of a thing. It may be a false understanding, to be sure; but this is not because the concept is getting in the way of the object, or because it is merely a derivative version of it. Behind this misconception lies the treacherous metaphor of concepts as pictures in one's head. Nor do you elude this snare by maintaining that the concept actively constructs the object rather than passively reflecting it. Behind a good deal of epistemological constructivism lurks the reified view of a concept as a quasi-thing, rather than as a way of doing things; so that, for example, the disciples of Louis Althusser (among whom I myself could at one time be somewhat ambiguously counted) used solemnly to contrast the real object in the world with one's conceptual construction of it, the latter being the only thing we could know of that object. This involves an error about the grammar of the word 'concept' from which cultural theory has yet wholly to recover.

This swashbuckling brand of anti-realism, common in the cultural climate of the late 1970s, is strongly counter-intuitive. Does Fish really mean that blank verse, heroic couplets or the character of Miranda are not properties internal to a text but features bestowed on it by the reader? One might defend the case by claiming in Nietzschean fashion that there are no such things as inherent qualities in any case – that a nasty dent in the skull is as much a verbal construct as Apollo. But this then makes Fish's point about literary works trivial and self-evident. If it is true of the whole of reality, it cancels all the way through and leaves everything exactly as it was. It has meaning but no force. The claim that literary works lack inherent qualities is informative only if one believes that such things exist in the first place. Fish either has to come clean and declare that he does not think they do, or explain why rhubarb has inherent properties but the drama of Georg Büchner does not. (The fact that the latter is a piece of discourse is no answer, since in Fish's view so in a sense is rhubarb.) In fact, Fish appreciates the point that his case cancels all the way through, and is actually rather pleased about it. He is that odd kind of pragmatist who has no wish for his theories to make a practical difference to the world. They simply redescribe what we do in any case. The point is to interpret the world, not to change it.

For the Formalist Roman Jakobson, the poetic represents a 'set towards the message' – meaning that it is a question of orienting ourselves to a piece of language as valuable and significant in itself. It is hard to see how this clearly distinguishes poetry or fiction from, say, history or philosophy. The language of such works is not always a purely instrumental affair, inviting us to pass straight from the sign to the referent in brisk disregard of the former as a value in itself. Think of Tacitus, Hume, Lecky or E.P. Thompson. Fish, however, does not insist that we should pay close attention to texts marked as literary in an 'aesthetic' way, savouring their verbal strategies and relishing their intricate designs. He thinks rather that what we should attend to is the moral content of the work, which a sensitivity to the language of the text will persuade us to bring into unusually sharp focus. In a dichotomy of form and content worthy of Sir Arthur Quiller-Couch, the work's language is simply instrumental to an exploration of its content. It is merely a clue to the fact that we are in the presence of some weighty moral issues.

This overlooks what we can call after Louis Hjelmslev the form of the content, as well as the content of the form.[40] It fails to see, as almost all philosophers of literature do as well, that a work's moral outlook, if it has anything so cohesive, may be secreted as much in its form as its content – that the language and structure of a literary text may be the bearers and progenitors of so-called moral content. A neoclassical poem which exploits the order, symmetry and equipoise of the heroic couplet; a naturalistic drama which is forced to gesture off-stage to realities it cannot credibly bring into view; a novel which garbles its time sequence or shifts dizzyingly from one character's viewpoint to another: all these are instances of artistic form as itself the bearer of moral or ideological meaning. Even a piece of poetic nonsense, a snatch of wordplay or non-cognitive verbal *jeu*, can have an implicit moral point, delighting in a bout of creative energy for its own sake, refreshing our perception of the world, releasing unconscious associations and the like. It is remarkable how often the philosophy of literature ignores the morality of form in its high-minded pursuit of ethical content.

Peter Lamarque also divorces form and content, severing questions of verbal quality from the ethical and cognitive. Why should truth and falsity, he inquires rhetorically of his readers, 'have anything to do with whether something is well or badly written?'[41] One needs only to unpack that anodyne phrase 'well or badly written' to grasp the bond between the ethical insights of a work and such stylistic features as metaphor, irony, texture, tonal shifts, heightened rhetoric, understatement, hyperbole and the like. 'In literary art,' writes Victor Erlich, 'ideological battles are often acted out on the plane of the opposition between metaphor and metonymy, or metre and free verse.'[42] The same can be true of a work's structural aspects.

The later Henry James's cobwebby prose, so Lamarque considers, 'is only admired, if at all, because it serves the literary purpose of exhibiting the complexities, ambivalence, and fragility of human relations'.[43] It is a curiously puritanical view of literature. Formal devices are there to serve some moral purpose beyond themselves, as children's television in the United States seems to assume that toddlers' play is acceptable only if some edifying moral message can be grimly tied to its tail. But the exhausting, exhilarating process of tracking the microscopic twists and turns of meaning in *The Ambassadors* or *The Golden Bowl* is itself a moral experience, rather as the inordinate length of the Proustian sentence, its capacity to propel itself through any number of intricate sub-clauses and around any number of hairpin syntactical bends without losing its steady semantic thrust, is a stylistic performance with intimate relevance to questions of moral value.

In any case, 'exhibiting the complexities, ambivalence, and fragility of human relations' is by no means just a 'literary' purpose, if by this is meant one confined to that realm. And does not a prose style belong to a literary purpose as well? Part of what has traditionally been meant by literature is a species of writing in which the formal and moral are notably hard to separate – which is not to suggest that a good many 'literary' effects do not arise from playing the one off against the other.[44] The two are analytically distinct, if not existentially so. There need be no suggestion of an 'organicist' unity of the two here. But to respond to the 'moral content' of a work (a misleading phrase in itself) is to respond to that content as it is constituted by tone, syntax, figure, narrative, viewpoint, design and the like. One of the instructions silently encoded in a work of literature is 'Take what is said in terms of how it is said'. Belletrism on the one hand, and moralism on the other, are the upshot of ignoring this interdependence of method and moral substance.

Lamarque and his colleague Stein Haugom Olsen do not share Fish's idealist doctrine that texts lack inherent properties. Like him, they see literature as a species of writing that invites and rewards a certain kind of attention, and one that is intended to do so; but in their view this is on account of the features it manifests. More exactly, it is on account of those really existent features of the work that the social institution of literature selects as aesthetically relevant. Such qualities include design, formal complexity, unifying themes, moral depth, imaginative creativity and so on. Because the literary institution has classified a piece of writing as literary, we know from the outset what procedures to put in hand, what questions to ask of a text, what operations count as valid, what to be alert to and what to set aside. As Charles Altieri inelegantly puts it, 'we know what a literary work is when we know what we characteristically learn to do when we are told that a text is a literary one'.[45] This curiously circular sentence reflects in its very syntax a certain canonical self-confirming.

As with Fish, Lamarque and Olsen, this is a suggestively pragmatic approach. Literature is a question of what we do, a set of enabling strategies, a certain way of conducting or orienting ourselves in the presence of a piece of writing. Rather as the hermeneuticists see reality as that which returns a coherent answer to our questioning of it, so for this theory a literary work, like an affectionate pet, is one which responds positively to a certain way of being handled. Yet we can always argue the toss over what exactly it is we should be doing, a point that these theorists, champions as they are of the orthodox literary institution, seem rather less eager to grant. Altieri, for example, assumes that what we should get up to with texts includes imposing coherence on them when they seem not to display it, a view we shall be querying later. Lamarque and Olsen assume just the same.

There are other problems as well. For one thing, it is doubtful that a work must be intended to be read as literature, either by the author or the literary institution, for it to qualify as such. Take, for example, that torrid tale of lust, murder, adultery and sexual vengeance known as 'Goosey Goosey Gander':

Goosey, goosey, gander
Where shall I wander?
Upstairs and downstairs
And in my lady's chamber.

There I met an old man
Who wouldn't say his prayers
So I took him by the left leg
And threw him down the stairs.

It is not hard to see what is afoot here. Returning home unexpectedly, the speaker of the poem is alerted by his faithful pet goose to the fact that his wife's lover is lurking somewhere in the house. But where? he asks the animal – in code, naturally ('Where shall I wander?'), so as not to put the lover on his guard if he happens to be listening. Upstairs or downstairs? Is he in the wife's bedroom? Perhaps the goose confirms the latter suggestion with a fractional upward jerk of his beak. Bursting in on the adulterous scene in his lady's chamber, and maybe all the more outraged because the lover turns out to be disgustingly decrepit ('old man'), the speaker forces the wretch to his knees with a snarl of 'Say your prayers, you bastard!' But the lover proudly refuses; so seizing him by the offending organ (one takes 'leg' here to be a metaphorical substitution) the speaker hurls him down the stairs to his death. In a darkly ironic twist, a goose turns out to be more loyal than a wife.

If such a reading were to gain credence, as I am quietly confident that it will, one might have succeeded in turning a fairly trite snatch of verse into a more complex, suggestive one – in short, into literature as it is currently understood.[46] One would also have augmented its value in the process, as the piece has proved capable of evoking significant moral resonances in the reader's mind. Part of its literary effect, once recast in this way, is the chilling contrast between its pat rhymes and jaunty rhythms and the ugly realities glimpsed between the lines. The poem is a kind of *trompe l'oeil*: the leanness and economy of its language, its lines which travel no more than a couple of inches or so, its trim uniformity on the page, its air of artless explicitness, its innocence of figurative effects, its regular rhythm which curtails any elaborate improvisation on the part of the speaking voice – all this seems curiously at odds with the modernist elusiveness of its meaning, the failure of its narrative to cohere and its lack of definitive closure, along with the sense that it is really a set of fragments or terse notations masquerading as an achieved whole.

In any case, is 'Goosey Goosey Gander' really much more banal than some of the more simple-minded of Wordsworth's contributions to *Lyrical Ballads*, or William Blake's 'Little Lamb, who made thee?' We treat the Blake poem as literature largely on account of the value and significance it accrues in the wider context of *Songs of Innocence and of Experience*, which in the eyes of the literary institution is a major work; but taken in itself, and read non-ironically (which as often with Blake may well be a mistake), it is embarrassingly feeble.

One might note that for a conventionally worthless piece of art to become a precious one, such a reinterpretation would be necessary. This is because, though someone might experience a state of mystical ecstasy in the presence of a kitschy statue of the Sacred

Heart, the statue could not be said to be the cause of it. It is part of what we mean by 'kitschy', 'threadbare', 'brittle', 'meretricious' and so on that things of this kind cannot by their nature provoke profound responses. Responses are (in the phenomenological sense of the word) intentional, bound up with the nature of their object. But you can always try to make such objects more interesting, and hence more valuable. Walter Benjamin had a magnificent knack of plucking the most fertile meanings from the most humble, inauspicious of texts, a practice that in his case was political as well as critical. One should not assume, however, that complexity is *ipso facto* aesthetically desirable, as Lamarque and Olsen, along with a good many other critics, seem to do. A work may be complex but emotionally bankrupt, just as it may be coherent but monotonous. And what of the stark, poignant simplicity of a tragic ballad?

The question of what constitutes an 'aesthetic' effect is rather more fraught than Lamarque and Olsen seem to suspect. What may function as such in one context may not do so in another, as the Formalists were keenly aware. The 'aesthetic' is a more culturally and historically variable matter than these theorists seem to imagine. Lamarque and Olsen regard the literary institution as the ultimate court of appeal in questions of meaning, value and the nature of literature; but there is no single such institution, and we may expect any such complex of social practices to be shot through with anomalies and contradictions, which does not appear to be the case for these particular scholars. Like Fish, they seem to assume in their conservative way that everything runs smoothly all of the time – that the conventions that govern literary reception always hold and are always well defined, that the distinction between the literary and non-literary is fairly waterproof, that a skilled professional will just *know* how to proceed and so on.

There is an unpleasant smack of self-satisfaction about this case, as when Olsen draws a remarkably patronising comparison between the professor's view of a literary text and the judgement of the hapless undergraduate ingénue. The superiority of the former's approach, he writes, can be recognised only by those who know what critical practice involves – who know not merely what texts are labelled literary, but who can appreciate them as such.[47] So the professor's way of proceeding is correct because it is confirmed by . . . the professor. The circularity of the argument reflects the closedness of the club. Only those judgements are valid which conform to the view of the experts. Would these be the professors who howled in fury at *The Waste Land*, dismissed John Clare as a crackpot and were sickened to their stomachs by *Ulysses*? If Olsen has not occasionally read undergraduate essays which outshone the work of some academics, perhaps because of rather than despite their authors' untutored state, then his professional life is the poorer. Traditionally minded literary scholars have a number of virtues, but imaginative flair and critical audacity are not usually among them. In fact, there is something in the very conception of traditional scholarship which militates against these qualities. This is one reason why the scholars may sometimes need to be educated at the hands of their students.

Like some other philosophers of art, Lamarque and Olsen generally assume that 'aesthetic' means aesthetically successful, that 'appreciation' signifies positive appreciation and that 'literature' is always and everywhere a term of approbation. 'Appreciation,' Olsen comments, 'starts from an expectation of value.'[48] But what if that expectation is dashed, or partly frustrated? Do, say, *The Plumed Serpent* or the drama of Sheridan Knowles then cease to be literature?[49] And how are they to be described instead? Not, one imagines, as bad literature, which would surely be an oxymoron in Lamarque and Olsen's eyes. These are not questions they overlook altogether, but they grant them too little weight. Negative judgements of esteemed works would seem if not impermissible, then mildly distasteful. Nothing in such artefacts would ever appear to falter or backfire. We hear almost nothing of works generally deemed to be literary, perhaps pre-eminently so, which contain wretched prose, soul-numbing rhyme schemes, stale perceptions, histrionic emotion or improbable narrative turns. Yet all of this and more is to be found in the so-called literary canon, not least because what E. D. Hirsch has called literature by association – meaning the principle by which if, say, Wordsworth's *Prelude* enters the canon, his third-rate sonnets scramble in as well by clinging to its shirt-tails.[50] What would Lamarque and Olsen call a piece of writing that veered from the sublime to the abysmal? Are the good bits literature and the bad bits not?

One cannot define literary works as those which demand especially scrupulous attention, since the same might also be said of reading an order for one's execution. It is unlikely one would grant such a document no more than a bored, perfunctory glance while continuing to shovel down one's supper. No doubt it is also true that one would be unlikely to peruse it as one would a piece of Elizabeth Bishop, perhaps lingering over the way 'guilty before God' rhymes with 'firing squad'. But not all literary works demand this kind of attention either. Bertolt Brecht liked his audiences to watch his plays with a certain mild distractedness or studied nonchalance, which is why he encouraged them to smoke. In this way they might resist being drawn into a hypnotic empathy with the events on stage that might blunt their critical assessment of them. Can't one read a work too closely, as one can stand too myopically close to a painting?

René Wellek and Austin Warren argue in their greatly influential *Theory of Literature* that literary texts are those in which the 'aesthetic function' is dominant. But aesthetic features, as we have seen, are not restricted to works we dub literary. Assonance, chiasmus and synecdoche may be more common in an advertisement than in a piece of naturalistic fiction. In any case, as William Ray points out, 'if ambiguity and self-focusing derive from the violation of norms, *any* text can be made code-inventive simply by reading it according to conventions it seems to violate'.[51] Lamarque and Olsen would doubtless acknowledge that there may be as much synecdoche in soap ads as in Heinrich Heine. The literary in their eyes consists in assuming a certain attitude to these features – treating them as central, savouring them in themselves, knowing what we can legitimately expect of a work that deploys them for their own sake. Yet they continue to maintain a fairly rigorous distinction between the literary and the non-literary.

Design, formal complexity, unifying themes, moral depth and imaginative creativity, however, are fortunately not the monopoly of literature. They can be just as characteristic of a treatise on human psychology or a history of modern Burma. Singling out poems and novels as 'imaginative' writing, with the implication that one can only write about netball or brain tumours unimaginatively, is a fairly recent historical development. Nor can the difference be that we attend to the 'literary' as an end in itself, but make use of other kinds of writing. Political theory, to be sure, is supposed to guide our action in the world; but then so in a sense is literature. What would it mean to read Anselm, Husserl or Burckhardt 'instrumentally' rather than for their inherent qualities? To gather useful ideas and insights from them, perhaps. But this is not easily separable from the quality of their prose or the design of their arguments. In any case, we do much the same with what we call literature.

Besides, you can treat a piece of writing 'aesthetically', in the sense of 'disinterestedly' or non-instrumentally, without it containing a single image, symbol, deft piece of design or shapely bit of narrative. Its language may be drably utilitarian, but this does not mean that you have to treat it in a utilitarian way. How texts are verbally constituted or institutionally classified, *pace* Lamarque and Olsen, need be no absolute guide to how we resolve to treat them. Conversely, a text could be richly freighted with aesthetic devices but nevertheless invite a purely practical response. A car repair manual written by a frustrated poet might serve as an example. There could be reports on rodent control in Montana couched in gorgeous prose, or road signs full of surreal wordplay. The *dulce* and the *utile* are not always on separate planets. Advertisements sometimes exploit poetic devices for the distinctly non-poetic goal of making profit. Conversely, it is possible to speak of finding a use for Calderón's tragedies or Cavafy's poetry, absorbing them into one's experience in ways that make a moral difference. There is no hard-and-fast distinction between focusing on the text as an end in itself and finding some function for it.

The literary procedures described by Lamarque and Olsen are of fairly recent vintage. These ways of treating a text as 'literary' were not for the most part shared by, say, the bardic caste of early medieval Ireland. Nor were they all that popular in the political theatre of the Weimar Republic. 'Literary discourse and informative discourse,' Olsen observes, 'are two mutually exclusive categories.' Is this true of Virgil's *Georgics*, Castiglione's *The Courtier*, a Tudor dietary manual, Richard Burton's *Anatomy of Melancholy* or Goethe's *Italian Journey*? The critic William Hazlitt quotes a colleague who describes John Locke and Isaac Newton as 'the two greatest names in English literature'.[52] Nowadays they would scarcely be considered literature at all, let alone eminent examples of it. The literary has not always turned on such an emphatic distinction between fact and fiction, art and historiography, imagination and information, fantasy and practical function, dreaming and didacticism. In eighteenth-century England, Shaftesbury's philosophical reflections would have counted as literature, but it is doubtful that *Moll Flanders* would have made the grade.

Lamarque and Olsen see valuable literary works (a phrase which in their eyes is surely a tautology) as those which prove responsive to the normative reading strategies of the established literary institution. The interpretation of a work is thus tilted from the outset towards a positive evaluation of it. It is as though the literary institution informs you that a certain text is worthwhile by presenting it to the critic to be inspected, and the critic then obediently proceeds to unearth the evidence that will confirm the correctness of this view by rehearsing the very critical procedures by which the institution has already reached its judgement. The point of this operation is not entirely clear. In any case, it begs one or two questions. Works worth reading are those which respond to specific critical strategies; but any work will respond positively to some kind of critical strategy, which leaves unanswered the question of why Lamarque and Olsen choose the particular ones they do. It must surely be because these techniques reveal what has already been judged to be most rewarding about pieces of writing. There is no suggestion that they might reveal something that might alter our opinion about such matters, or that other techniques might have equal or greater validity.

Richard Ohmann argues a similar case, claiming that 'our readiness to discover and dwell on the implicit meaning of literary works – and to judge them important – is a consequence of our knowing them to *be* literary works, rather than that which tells us that they are such'.[53] Literature, in short, is a quality of attention. It is the way we find ourselves already biased and attuned when we pick up a book. We submit some texts to especially close scrutiny because we take the word of others that they will turn out to deserve it. There is no suggestion that these judges might be disastrously mistaken, as were those who appointed John Masefield and a whole series of equally dreary hacks to the Poet Laureateship, or that we might discover that works conventionally dismissed as worthless might merit this kind of attention more than Swinburne. What about a courageous critical pioneer who first proclaims the value of such writing in the teeth of the literary institution, like F.R. Leavis on the early T.S. Eliot?

Berys Gaut includes the fact of 'belonging to an established literary form' among the conditions for a work being regarded as art.[54] But what of the work that sets out to demolish or transform that set-up, to dismantle the prevailing definitions of literature and revolutionise the rules of the game? Does the literary institution really instruct us so assuredly in what to do with, say, *Finnegans Wake*, and is that work at risk of being denied the honorific title of literature if it does not? Richard Gale tells us that 'words and sentences occurring in a fictional narrative do not acquire a new meaning, nor do our ordinary syntactical rules cease to apply to such sentences'.[55] To this extent, we always know in principle how to handle them. But there are many experimental works that bend words and syntax well out of their customary shape. Why do philosophers of literature always seem to take Jane Austen and Conan Doyle as their paradigm, rather than the poetry of Paul Celan or Jeremy Prynne? Charles Altieri is in no doubt that we should withhold the name of literature from a work which proves unresponsive to canonical procedures.[56] In a similar way, Soviet psychiatrists used to withhold the name of sanity from those who proved resistant to their treatment. Good works of literature are those that resemble other good works of literature, allowing us to do with them what we are accustomed to doing. The literary canon submits itself to no other court of judgement. It is self-confirming.

Yet why should such canonical procedures go unchallenged? There is an assumption among many champions of the canon, for example, that an authentic work of art must always and everywhere forge unity out of complexity – a prejudice that survived with astonishing tenacity from the age of Aristotle to the early twentieth century, when modernists and avant-gardists dared to query what political ends were served by this fetishistic obsession with integrity. Why should artworks never have a hair out of place? Why should every one of their features be slotted precisely into place, organically related to every other? Can nothing ever simply freewheel? Is there no virtue in dispersion, dislocation, contradiction, open-endedness?[57] This compulsion to coherence is by no means beyond the reach of criticism. On the contrary, it has ideological and even psychoanalytic implications of which the custodians of the canon appear innocently unaware. Yet it continues to crop up in the work of philosophers of literature as more or less axiomatic. And this spontaneous conformity to a deeply questionable dogma is sufficient grounds for scepticism when we are informed by the aestheticians that they have the key to the nature of literature in their possession.

CHAPTER 3

What is Literature? (2)

1

We can turn now to the moral dimension of literary works. I use the word 'moral' to signify the realm of human meanings, values and qualities, rather than in the deontological, anaemically post-Kantian sense of duty, law, obligation and responsibility.[1] It was literary figures in nineteenth-century England, from Arnold and Ruskin to Pater, Wilde and – supremely – Henry James, who helped to shift the meaning of the term 'morality' from a matter of codes and norms to a question of values and qualities. It was a project consummated in the twentieth century by some of the age's most eminent critics: Bakhtin, Trilling, Leavis, Empson and Raymond Williams among them.

Indeed, the literary had become the very paradigm of morality for a post-religious world. In its fine-grained sensitivity to nuances of human conduct, its strenuous discriminations of value, its reflections on the question of how to live richly and self-reflectively, the literary work was a supreme example of moral practice. Literature was a danger not to morality, as Plato had suspected, but to moralism. Whereas moralism abstracted moral judgements from the rest of human existence, literary works returned them to their complex living contexts. At its most overweening, as with Leavis and his disciples, this became a new kind of evangelical campaign. Religion had failed, but art or culture would replace it.

On this viewpoint, moral value lies in the form of literary works as much as their content. There are several senses in which this is so. For some Romantic thinkers, the fruitful coexistence of the work of art's various components could be seen as the prototype of a peaceable community, and thus as politically utopian. Within its bounds, the artwork is innocent of oppression or domination. Moreover, the poem or painting offers in its very form a new model of the relation between individuals and totalities. It is governed by a general law or design, but this is a law entirely at one with its sensory particulars, and cannot be abstracted from them. In organising its elements into a whole, it brings each of them to a supreme degree of self-realisation; and this, too, foreshadows a utopian order in which individual and community can be reconciled.

Besides, if the work of art is morally exemplary, this is not least because of its mysterious autonomy – of the way it seems freely to determine itself without external coercion.[2] Rather than stoop to some external sovereignty, it is faithful to the law of its own being. In this sense, it is a working model of human freedom. There is an ethics and politics of form at stake here, of which the philosophy of literature has been for the most part quite oblivious.

There is a lineage from Shelley and George Eliot to Henry James and Iris Murdoch for which morality itself is a question of imagination, and thus an inherently aesthetic faculty. It is by this divinatory power that we can feel our way empathetically into the inner lives of others, decentring the ego in order to grasp the world selflessly from their standpoint. The classical realist novel is thus a moral practice in its very structure, shifting as it does from one centre of consciousness to another to constitute a complex whole. Literature can therefore be seen as a moral project even before it has come to utter a moral sentiment. It was this that led the critic I.A. Richards to remark, with a brio that might seem in retrospect a touch premature, that poetry was 'capable of saving us'. He did not seem to recognise that if our salvation depends on something as rare and fragile as poetry, our condition must be dire indeed.

The imagination, however, has its limits, which not many literary types seem keen to acknowledge. Few ideas have been more unequivocally commended. To criticise the imagination would seem as impious as to scoff at Nelson Mandela. Yet the imagination is by no means simply a creative power. It is capable of dreaming up noxious scenarios as well as positive ones. Serial-killing requires a fair amount of imagination. The faculty is often seen as among the most noble of human capabilities, but it is also unnervingly close to fantasy, which is one of the most infantile and regressive. Nor is the imagination a special or privileged power. If it is what inspired Mahler's 'Resurrection' symphony, it is also an essential component of everyday cognition. Since the imagination makes absent things present, it is through it that we have a sense of futurity, without which we would be unable to act at all. There is no point in putting the beer can to your lips unless you have a dim premonition that the contents will thereby course down your throat.

Only on a Cartesian view of the world do I need through an act of imagination to occupy your body or mind from the inside in order to know what you are feeling. There is generally an assumption here that the body is a brute lump of matter thwarting our access to each other's inner lives, so that we are in need of some special faculty (empathy, moral sense, imagination) to break into each other's emotional innards. We shall be looking at this assumption later on. In any case, knowing what you are feeling will not necessarily inspire me to treat you benevolently. A sadist needs to know what his victim is feeling, but not so that he can cease to torture him. Conversely, I can treat you benignly without having to recreate your interior world in my head. I can also empathise with a neo-fascist while still feeling the need to lambaste his politics. Morality is not a question of feeling, and is thus not a question of the imagination either.

To love others is not in the first place to feel in a certain way about them, but to behave in a certain way towards them. This is why the paradigm of charity is the love of strangers, not of friends.

In trying to love strangers, we are less likely to confuse love with a warm glow in the pit of one's stomach. Genocide is not the result of a breakdown of the imagination, as some have suggested. It was not that the Nazis could not imagine how those they slaughtered were feeling. It is that they did not care. There is a good deal of critical cant about the imagination, just as there is about the idea of vision. Pol Pot was one of the great visionaries, along with William Blake and Thomas Jefferson. When Shelley writes in his *Defence of Poetry* that 'the great instrument of moral good is the imagination', he valuably enriches a certain rather arthritic sense of morality while making a number of deeply dubious assumptions.[3] Few documents have urged the value of poetry as magnificently as the *Defence*, and few have so absurdly exaggerated its importance.

When it comes to reading literary works, what we might call the empathetic fallacy holds that the point of the activity is to get inside someone else's life. Catherine Wilson argues that literature is neither a question of knowing *how* nor of knowing *that*, but of knowing *what* something feels like.[4] But getting on the inside of someone else – becoming imaginatively at one with them – will not yield us knowledge of them unless we retain our own reflective powers in the process. Pure empathy is at odds with the critical intelligence required for understanding. Living through a situation, as Monroe Beardsley points out, does not necessarily constitute knowledge.[5] 'Becoming' Lear will only yield you the truth of Lear if he grasps the truth about himself, which would seem to be far from the case. We do not watch *Timon of Athens* in order to feel misanthropic. We watch it to grasp something of the meaning of misanthropy, which is an emotional as well as intellectual affair. We do not read a lyric poem to know how the poet was feeling when she wrote it (perhaps she was feeling nothing much beyond her tussle with tone and image), but to know something new about the world by viewing it in the light of the poem's fictionalised feelings.

Why should literature so often be seen as a kind of emotional prosthesis or vicarious form of experience? One reason has to do with the drastic impoverishment of experience in modern civilisations. Literary ideologues in Victorian England considered it prudent to encourage working-class men and women to stretch their sympathies beyond their own situation through reading, partly because this might foster tolerance, understanding and hence political stability, and partly because allowing men and women to enrich their experience in this way might compensate them to a degree for their dispiriting conditions of life. It might also distract them from inquiring too querulously into the causes of this deprivation. It would scarcely be too much to claim that for these cultural commissars, reading was an alternative to revolution.[6] The empathetic imagination is not as politically innocent as it may appear.

Moral values and literary meanings have in common the fact that they are not objective in the sense that hydroelectric dams are; but they are not purely subjective either. For a moral realist, moral judgements pick out real features of the world rather than simply expressing attitudes to them. To call anti-Semitism offensive is not just to register how I happen to feel about it. Not to call it offensive would be to fail to give an accurate description of, say, what was taking place in a pogrom. Moral values are real in the same sense that meanings are, or indeed works of art. Lamarque and Olsen speak in *Truth, Fiction, and Literature* of 'subjective knowledge' in literature, to be contrasted with scientific knowledge of the 'external' world. But literary meanings, like works of art or moral values, are not the expression of subjective states of mind. They are part of the furniture of the actual world, and can be discussed and debated without reference to some putative subject. It is true that literary works often produce the effect of lived experience, but all they actually consist of is written signs. Everything that happens in a literary work happens in terms of writing. Characters, events and emotions are simply configurations of marks on a page.

The 'literary' conception of morality we have been examining has more in common with so-called virtue ethics than it has with

Kantian deontology.[7] Like virtue ethics, the object of moral judgement in a poem or novel is not an isolated act or set of propositions but the quality of a form of life. The most effective kind of moral inquiry, from Aristotle to Marx, asks how human beings are to flourish and find fulfilment, and under what practical conditions this would be possible. It is within this framework that judgements of individual actions or propositions play their part. Literary works represent a kind of praxis or knowledge-in-action, and are similar in this way to the ancient conception of virtue. They are forms of moral knowledge, but in a practical rather than theoretical sense. They are not to be reduced to their 'messages', in John Searle's revealingly reductive term.[8] Like virtue, they have their ends in themselves, in the sense that they can achieve those ends only in and through the performances they signify. Virtue has its effects in the world – for Aristotle it is the only way for a human life to thrive – but only by being true to its inner principles. Something similar is true of literary works of art.

When it comes to what we call literature, then, there can be no simple translation of lived experience into laws and norms. Instead, in a of unity of theory and practice, such works yield us a type of moral cognition which is not readily available in other forms. As Peter Lamarque argues, overstating his case somewhat, 'when we are guided by an artist to see things in a new way, to adopt a new perspective, we cannot formulate a lesson learned, for the particularities resist all effort of generalisation.'[9] The moral import of such works cannot be easily abstracted from their quality and texture, and this is one of the ways in which they are most like behaviour in real life. Even so, one can give *some* kind of account of a work's moral outlook without simply rehearsing the text word for word. Indeed, literary criticism does so all the time, sometimes in highly subtle and sophisticated ways, though this is not best seen, *pace* Lamarque, as 'formulat[ing] a lesson learned'. There are possibilities beyond being struck dumb by the work's ineffable particularity on the one hand, and reducing it to a set of moral tags on the other.

In contrast to Lamarque, David Novitz claims that we can and should draw lessons from literary works. 'Suppose, for instance,' he writes, 'that in the light of Defoe's *Robinson Crusoe*, I come to think of isolation no longer as unproductive and arduous, but as a spur to human resourcefulness . . . I might simply discover that my attitude to isolation has changed,'[10] Defoe's novel, however, is not a Boy Scout manual, or a textbook for entrepreneurs about how to augment their profits. Its moral significance lies as much where Novitz does not look for it as where he does – in its cumulative, relentlessly linear, 'what happens next?' narrative form, its spare, sinewy, non-figurative prose style, its restless refusal of closure, its attention to the primary qualities of objects rather than their secondary ones, its interweaving of story and moral commentary, its formal tension between narrative as pure contingency and narrative as providential design, its rudimentary modes of characterisation, its apparent accumulation of incidents purely for its own sake. Few of these issues tend to catch the eye of philosophers of literature, as opposed to literary critics or theorists.

A work's moral outlook, in short, may be as much a question of form as of content – a parallel between plots, for example, a way of handling a storyline or a two-dimensional mode of depicting character. Richard Gale makes the same mistake as Novitz about the moral force of literary works when he suggests that 'We might give up hunting as a result of seeing or reading *Bambi*'.[11] Some might consider that we would be more likely to take it up. Hilary Putnam, by contrast, has a rather more subtle view of art's moral operations, seeing them as enlarging our conceptual and perceptual repertoire and thus furnishing us with descriptive resources we did not possess before.[12]

Another way of putting the point is that the moral truths of literature are for the most part implied.[13] By and large, they are shown rather than stated. Literary works fit more easily with Heidegger's concept of truth as disclosure or revelation than they do with self-improvement manuals. Like Aristotle's *phronesis*, they embody a mode of tacit moral knowledge that cannot be adequately captured in general or propositional form, which is not to suggest that it cannot be captured there at all. Such forms of cognition cannot be easily abstracted from the process by which they are acquired. This is one thing we mean when we claim that the form and content of a literary text are inseparable. An extreme example of such tacit knowledge is knowing how to whistle *Eine Kleine Nachtmusik*, which is not distinct from the act of doing it and which cannot be taught to someone else. The kind of moral insight at stake in literary works is thus more like personal knowledge than knowledge of facts.[14]

Even so, it is not a matter of the particularity of the artwork 'resist[ing] all effort of generalisation', as Lamarque suggests. For one thing, as we have just noted, we can indeed discuss works of art in general terms, just as we can perfectly well cast our personal knowledge of other people in general, propositional form. For another thing, there is a form of generality at work in the artefact itself. For classical aesthetics, as we have seen already, the work does not dispense with the general. It is rather that its overall law or design is no more than the mutual articulation of its individual parts, and thus not to be alienated or abstracted from them. Art thus represents an alternative mode of cognition to Enlightenment rationality, clinging as it does to the specific without thereby relinquishing the whole. It is not a question of dismissing the general as a violation of the particular, but of grasping a different relation between the two.

Jerome Stolnitz is somewhat more sceptical about the cognitive power of art.[15] The fact that he takes by contrast an extravagantly uncritical view of science, whose truths he seems to regard as beyond dispute, does not greatly assist his case. (One might claim rather that scientific truths are of the kind that can always be wrong.) There are, so he argues, no *sui generis* artistic truths; instead, literary works tend to reveal truths we know already from other sources. He is right to see that literature does not disclose truths that can be found nowhere else, rather as F.R. Leavis denies that there are any moral values which are specifically 'literary'. What Stolnitz fails to grasp is that literary texts tend to present their moral truths phenomenologically; and this means that such insights are largely indissociable from their formal and verbal embodiment. (I say 'largely', since from time to time literary works also come up with more abstract moral propositions, as with Ulysses's speech about cosmic order in Shakespeare's *Troilus and Cressida* or Proust's reflections on jealousy.) Stolnitz fears that we diminish the depth and complexity of a literary work in shifting from what it presents to something called its truth. His mistake is to see this truth as something beyond the depth and complexity in question – as a meaning abstractable from it, rather than as the material form it assumes.

One might put the point slightly differently. If you were trying to present a moral case in written form, you might feel the need to edit, highlight, slant and stylise your materials so as to bring out its salient features. You might also find yourself constructing narratives, or fashioning dramatic cameos of key situations, or creating characters who graphically illustrated the main aspects of your argument. You would, in short, find yourself writing a novel. It would not take much to turn the *Philosophical Investigations* into one. Indeed, its author dreamed wistfully of writing a work consisting of nothing but jokes, rather as Walter Benjamin dreamed of writing one made up of nothing but quotations. Fleshing out your moral case would mean turning it into fiction. Moral content and literary form would gradually converge, until it was hard to tell them apart. There are close links between fictional form and moral cognition, as Plato's dialogues would suggest. One reason why Plato casts much of his thought in dramatic or dialogical form is because the process of arriving at the truth is in some sense part of it, as it is in a different way for Hegel and Kierkegaard.

There are, however, rather more productive ways than Stolnitz's of being sceptical about the link between the literary and the moral. The truth is that literary art has usually been proposed as a paradigm less of morality than of liberal morality. The richly suggestive work of Martha Nussbaum is a case in point.[16] Nussbaum values plurality, diversity, open-endedness, irreducible concreteness, conflict and complexity, the sheer agonising difficulty of moral decision (what the French hyperbolically call its 'impossibility') and so on. These are precious values on any reckoning, but Nussbaum seems largely unaware of just how socially and historically specific they are. They are more typical of a middle-class liberal than a working-class socialist. It is not surprising that she takes her literary cue so often from that doyen of exquisitely agonised liberals, Henry James.

There is no doubt that the mighty lineage of nineteenth-century realism lends itself admirably to this moral approach, though it works a lot better with James and Gaskell than it does with Kingsley, Disraeli or Conrad. But the whole of literary art cannot be tacitly coerced into this highly specific moral ideology. The literary and the liberal are not synonymous, even if they appear so to the metropolitan literati. Are Dante and Spenser notable for their devotion to diversity, their finely ambiguous judgements, their sense of certain irresolvable clashes of value, their preference for the provisional and exploratory over assured and immutable truths? And are they any the worse for not being so? Milton is a militant, doctrinal, politically *engagé* poet who clings to an absolute distinction between the forces of light and the powers of darkness. It is not that he is a great writer despite these things.

The liberal view of morality sets its face firmly against the didactic. Indeed, one of the great clichés of modern criticism is that teaching and preaching are fatal to literary art. 'Works that are too overtly didactic, that too obviously are trying to impart a message,' writes Lamarque, 'are seldom valued highly.'[17] 'Overtly' and 'too obviously' make the point conveniently incontrovertible; but that even a touch of didacticism is distasteful is as received a judgement for the literary establishment as the suggestion that Shakespeare wrote some rather impressive stuff. But it is surely not the case. 'Didactic' simply means a matter of teaching, and there is no reason why all teaching should be hectoring or doctrinaire. Brecht's *Lehrstücke*, Lancelot Andrewes's sermons and William Blake's Proverbs of Hell are didactic works which are also potent pieces of art. *Uncle Tom's Cabin* is not an embarrassingly second-rate novel because it has a specific moral purpose – so does Swift's *A Modest Proposal*, Tolstoy's *Resurrection* and Orwell's *Animal Farm* – but because of the way it executes it. One might contrast it in this respect with *The Grapes of Wrath, The Crucible* or Ibsen's *Pillars of the Community*. Billie Holiday's song 'Strange Fruit' is both superb art and social propaganda.

Nor is there any reason why literary works should always coyly sweeten the pill of their moral purpose, as Lamarque's 'too overtly' would suggest. There is nothing particularly coy about Allen Ginsberg's poem inviting America to go fuck itself with its atom bomb, but it works well enough as a piece of literary rhetoric. Teaching and preaching are ancient functions of literature, and only an age for which the word 'doctrine' has ominous resonances of authoritarianism, rather than more neutrally denoting an established body of beliefs, would feel so chary of its art speaking out from time to time in the cause of specific creeds. Or, indeed, would feel so chary of creeds as such. It is a liberal and postmodern prejudice that conviction as such is potentially dogmatic (with the exception, no doubt, of that particular one). The more passionate the faith, moreover, the more likely it is to breed intolerance. There is no reason to imagine that this is so. History is strewn with the holders of non-dogmatic convictions, from Parmenides to Bertrand Russell. And liberals should hold their views as passionately as their opponents. Anyway, the case generally applies more to other people's convictions than to one's own. One does not commonly find liberal-minded critics denouncing as didactic works which speak up for freedom of opinion, as opposed to those which sing the praises of the Five Year Plan.

Explicit doctrine, to be sure, is not the primary way in which most literature functions. But this does not mean that all committed works of art must be raucous and reductive. One of the most moving passages in the whole of Dickens is his wrathful rounding on everyone from the Queen to his readers after the death of Jo in *Bleak House*, an unabashed piece of social propaganda. There is nothing amiss with propaganda, provided it is done well. Literature is not automatically compromised by being politically partisan, as Milton's defence of regicide, Shelley's 'The Mask of Anarchy' or Edmund Burke's magnificent polemic against Warren Hastings might illustrate. A good many of Vladimir Nabokov's novels are politically partisan, but critics rarely complain of the fact because it is a partisanship most of them share. To their eyes, it appears simply like the unvarnished truth. The word 'doctrinaire' applies only to other people's beliefs. It is the left that is 'committed', not liberals or conservatives. The claim that doctrinal commitment is always and everywhere the ruin of art is a hollow liberal piety.

Of the various components of the 'literary' I have spelt out, the moral seems at first glance the most indispensable. It is clearly not a sufficient condition for literary status, since it is also to be found in historical and philosophical discourse, not to speak of religious pamphlets, birthday cards, love letters, government reports on abortion and a good deal more. But it is easy to see it is a necessary condition. How could there be literature without some inquiry into the value and significance of human life? The opposite of 'moral' in this context would seem to be the practical, technical or informational. It might also, however, be abstract doctrine, which is why one brave academic soul has maintained that Pope's *Essay on Man* is not literature.[18] Yet the *Georgics* is rated as literature, despite being an agricultural manual (sometimes of dubious reliability) which has next to nothing to say about human beliefs, motives, passions and the like. It counts as literature partly because of its form and language, and partly because it is from the same pen as the *Aeneid*.

Lucretius's *De rerum natura* is rated as a literary work, a distinction unlikely to be bestowed on modern scientific treatises even if, like Lucretius's essay, they were written in verse. Lengthy stretches of Dante's *Purgatorio* consist of scientific and theological exposition.

A Tudor dietary manual or seventeenth-century essay on the breeding habits of goldfish may count as literary not because it exhibits any particular interest in human manners and morals, and perhaps not even because it is judged especially well written, but because its archaic language grants it a certain artistic status, and perhaps also because of its value as a historical document. A book on diet or goldfish written today is far less likely to qualify, unless perhaps it is thrown off in an idle moment by Thomas Pynchon. An eighteenth-century treatise on optics might be judged literary on the same grounds. Generally speaking, the more historically remote from us a piece of writing is, the more likely we are to consider it literature. More recent bits of writing have to fight harder for such august status, and need by and large to trade more on their aesthetic qualities to achieve it. Perhaps our bank statements will read as quaintly as 'The Knight's Tale' in a few centuries' time.

We shall see in the next chapter that texts such as essays on fish-breeding, despite being 'non-moral', non-fictional and (let us suppose) indiffferently written might still be deemed literature by being treated 'non-pragmatically', used as an occasion for reflections which range beyond their evident functions. We should also note that non-fictional discourses, such as government reports on the leather industry, as opposed to fictional government reports on public disturbances which once more exonerate the police from all blame, shape and select their materials, occasionally employ narrative form, and are thus not without fictional features.

Christopher New asks whether we 'can confer the status of a candidate for appreciation (as literature) on a plumber's manual'.[19] If it is magnificently written, or dates from 1664, or both, then it is hard to see why not. Its 'non-moral' status might be outweighed by these factors. E.D. Hirsch contends that Darwin and Niels Bohr may pass muster as literature, but surely not a psychological paper on visual disturbances after prolonged perceptual isolation.[20] But does Darwin make the grade because he writes more skilfully than the psychologist, or because historic works of science may be granted the coveted title of literature while less important ones are denied it? What if the paper on visual disturbances were to achieve such celebrity in the fullness of time? We may note here, incidentally, that the view that literary works are especially valuable bits of writing may include their historical as well as their aesthetic value. We may feel inclined to use the word literature of 'non-moral' works such as Leibniz's mathematical studies simply on account of their historical stature.

There can even be forms of fiction that border on the non-moral. A tight-lipped, ultra-Hemingwayesque narrative ('He left the bar and turned past the sleeping border guard and the breeze got up again and there was the same metallic feeling in his stomach and the same soft creaking behind his left eye as though the eyeball was working itself loose') might leave its moral significance so implicit as to be well-nigh undetectable. Roland Barthes regarded the *nouveau roman* as a precious exercise in purging objects of their moral connotations. The moral point of a work might lie simply in the scrupulous lucidity with which it registers the material world, its refusal of anodyne fantasy and nebulous sentiment. In literary realism, truth-to-life becomes a moral value in itself. The descriptive here is also the normative.

Or consider this extract from Alan Brownjohn's poem 'Common Sense':

An agricultural labourer, who has
A wife and four children, receives 20s a week.
¾ buys food, and the members of the family
Have three meals a day.
How much is that per person per meal?
　　　　　　—*From Pitman's Common Sense Arithmetic, 1917*

A gardener, paid 24s a week, is
Fined 1/3 if he comes to work late.
At the end of 26 weeks, he receives
£30. 5. 3. How
Often was he late?
—*From Pitman's Common Sense Arithmetic, 1917*

. . . The table printed below gives the number
Of paupers in the United Kingdom, and
The total cost of poor relief.
Find the average number
Of paupers per ten thousand people.
—*From Pitman's Common Sense Arithmetic, 1917*

There is surely no doubt that this is a highly moral poem, despite the fact that it makes no moral comment on what it records. It takes up no attitude to its subject-matter. The fact that it is in verse form, however, is sufficient cue for the reader to assume a moral attitude to the piece herself, engaging perhaps in certain Foucauldian reflections on the nature of statistics, social engineering, official attitudes to the poor and so on.

It is a standard postmodern case that different cultures are likely to foster very different moral values. It is true that the moral norms of the *Bacchae* or the *Oresteia* are by no means those of Schiller's *Maria Stuart* or Stendhal's *The Charterhouse of Parma*. Yet it is also striking what a consensus of moral value literary works reveal across the centuries, however grossly unfashionable it may be to point it out. It is hard to think of a major piece of literary art from Propertius to Pamuk that sings the praises of torture and genocide, or which dismisses mercy, courage and loving kindness as so much high-sounding cant. The passion for justice, for example, would seem to be perennial in the human species and its writings, whatever different forms it assumes from one place or time to another. This is one sense in which claims that there are human continuities over long stretches of historical time can be radical, not reactionary. It is one of the several blind spots of postmodernism, with its prejudice that the pliable and mutable are always to be preferred to the persistent and unchanging, that it fails to grasp this simple truth.

2

We come now to the idea of the non-pragmatic as a constitutive feature of what is nowadays called literature. People sometimes use the term of pieces of writing which serve no direct or definite social function, in contrast to parking tickets or recipes for fudge. This sense of the literary tends to be most active in periods like our own, when literature has shed most of its traditional social functions. It is not an account that will do to describe a hymn to the Virgin Mary, a chant designed to drive out evil spirits, a masque staged to celebrate an aristocrat's birthday, a poem celebrating the military exploits of the tribe or a eulogy to a monarch which deftly conceals his exiguous intellectual powers. It is when literature is dislodged from such formal functions that its apologists may seek to compensate for this lapse of status by claiming either that literary works are precious in themselves, or that, having come loose from one particular social purpose, they can now be said to serve a plurality of them.

This, roughly speaking, is the conception of literature championed by John M. Ellis in his *Theory of Literary Criticism*. Ellis agrees with almost everyone else that literary texts are not to be identified by any intrinsic properties. In his view, they are identifiable instead by their uses (though in an irony he fails to point up, these uses may themselves be non-pragmatic, such as enhancing our sense of beauty or deepening our understanding of cruelty). When we treat a stretch of language as literature, Ellis argues, we no longer concern ourselves (as we would with a practical piece of writing) with whether it is true or false, whether it is the kind of information we might act on, and so on. In short, we no longer treat it as part of our immediate social context. Instead, we use it in such a way that 'the text is not taken as specifically relevant to the immediate context of its origin.'[21] One might claim that we seize on the fact that the text is not empirically true or directly functional as an occasion for seeing it as true and useful in some wider or deeper sense. One might also point out, to supplement Ellis's account, that severing a text from its source involves a simultaneous focusing and broadening of readerly attention. On the one hand, we now treat it as of value in itself, rather than in purely instrumental spirit; on the other hand, we release it from one specific context into a diversity of them.

To classify a text as literary on this view is to take a decision not to refer it to its originator or to treat it as a communication from her. (We shall be looking later at the bearing of this contention on so-called speech-act theory.) Such works are not dependent for their meaning on their genetic contexts, and are not to be judged according to their success or otherwise within that situation. They are, so to speak, free-floating, cut adrift from their point of origin, and hence peculiarly portable in a way that a passport is not. A passport, to be sure, is designed to be carried about; but it fulfils a specific, highly limited, set of functions. A concert ticket is even more stationary. Literary texts are those whose functions we cannot predict, in the sense that we cannot predetermine what 'uses' or readings of them may be made in this or that situation. They are inherently open-ended, capable of being transported from one context to another and of accumulating fresh significances in the process.[22] As Wimsatt and Beardsley suggest in their classic essay on the so-called intentional fallacy, a poem is 'detached from the author at birth.'[23]

The claim that literary works are unusually mutable is not some newfangled view of them. It has a venerable history, not least in the ancient Jewish practice of *Midrash* or scriptural interpretation. The Pharisees who gathered after the fall of the Temple to study the Torah were concerned less to extract some innate significance from the text than to assign it fresh meanings, sometimes of an arrestingly improbable kind. This group of men, travestied by the New Testament authors for their own politico-theological ends, were among the first hermeneuticists. The meaning of a biblical text was not seen as self-evident. The term *Midrash* itself, meaning to seek or investigate, suggests this clearly enough. Holy scripture was seen as inexhaustible, and confronted each commentator with a different sense each time it was studied. Unless a piece of scripture could be radically reinterpreted to meet the needs of the day, it was judged to be dead. It had to be revitalised by constant exegesis in the light of the contemporary moment. Revelation was a continuous process, not a once-and-for-all event. The Torah was seen as a radically incomplete text, which each generation of interpreters had to take a hand in bringing to perfection. No one of them had the last word, and the process of deciphering scripture involved an endless collective wrangling.[24] Privileged status was sometimes assigned to the oral Torah, since writing encouraged the reification of meaning.

That a text is cut loose from its origin, however, could be seen as true of all writing, even if it is more obvious in the case of literature. There is a question of degree here. Writing, unlike non-recorded speech, is a mode of meaning that can continue to function in the absence of an author, and this possibility is a permanent structural feature of it. 'Once any account is written down,' remarks Socrates in Plato's *Phaedrus*, 'you find it all over the place, hobnobbing with completely inappropriate people no less than with those who understand it, and completely failing to know who it should and shouldn't talk to.'[25] There is something alarmingly or delightfully promiscuous about writing, which can by its very nature migrate across jealously patrolled borders, is ready like a garrulous old bar-fly to buttonhole any passing stranger, and can convey sacred truths (as the avatars of the Reformation were quick to recognise) into illicit or mutinous hands. When it comes to writing, you don't know where it's been. Even so, there is a danger that the apostles of the transgressive may celebrate this anarchic force a little too naively. Before one waxes too blithely anti-logocentric, it is worth recalling the key role of scripture in the maintenance of oppressive power. It is also true, as I have suggested already, that some pieces of writing are a good deal more mobile than others.

Ellis is a kind of essentialist for whom non-functionality is of the very nature of literary art. In fact, we shall see in a moment that this property is neither necessary nor sufficient for writing to be classified as literature. But there are other problems with this as well. For one thing, Ellis claims that to detach a work from its genetic context is to render it impervious to judgements of truth or falsehood. We shall have occasion to throw doubt on this claim later on. Indifference to truth and falsehood is generally seen as a defining quality of the fictional, but the fictional and the non-pragmatic are not necessarily hand in glove. There can be non-pragmatic texts – spraying an obscenity on a wall just for the hell of it – which are not fictional. Karlheinz Stierle argues that popular fiction falls somewhere between the pragmatic and non-pragmatic, since in his view such works are simply instrumental to illusion-building.[26]

All the same, it is important to see that fiction loosens up the relation between a piece of writing and an actual situation, and in doing so can facilitate the kinds of operation Ellis has in mind. In this sense, if not in every sense, there is indeed a connection between the fictional and non-pragmatic aspects of the literary. Fiction relieves works of their burden of responsibility to the actual, thus making them more easily detachable from it. Richard Ohmann's claim that literary works lack so-called illocutionary force, which we shall be examining later, involves a conception of them as sitting loose to the workaday world of pledges and commitments, and as such is akin to Ellis's view of them as non-pragmatic.

The same effect may be achieved by self-conscious or richly figurative language, which intimates that a text is to be taken as something other than a report on an empirical situation. Because the poetic sign has its own material reality rather than transparently reflecting the world, there is a certain looseness of fit between itself and its referent, one which is akin to the looseness of fit between fiction and real life. There is a relation between such linguistic devices and the non-pragmatic, since they, too, invite us to focus on more than the situation at hand. They act among other things as signals that something more than the practical and immediate is at stake. A similar distancing is involved in our taking a literary work as primarily moral rather than empirical, and thus as not bound to a specific situation in the manner of a laundry list. Here, then, four of the constitutive features of literature I have identified cooperate to the same end.

Another problem with Ellis's case is that even in modern times there are works people call literary which have undeniably practical functions. Burke's political speeches may once more stand as an example. We call these literary because of their figurative fertility, rhetorical brio, emotional bravura, dramatic virtuosity and so on – so that here one constituent of the literary compensates for the absence of another, namely the non-functional. It is too simple to suggest that Burke's speeches on the state of Ireland or the American revolution were practical in his own day but are literary in our own. Many of his contemporaries appreciated them as poetic performances.

Not all literary texts float free of their genetic contexts. Adrian Mitchell's poem 'Tell me lies about Vietnam' is meant to address a highly specific situation, as is Milton's sonnet 'Avenge, O Lord, thy slaughter'd saints'. This is not to suggest that works like these have nothing to say beyond their immediate conjunctures, simply that these conjunctures are mightily important to them. Ellis enforces too sharp a choice here. There are degrees of non-functionality as well, which he fails to acknowledge. The distinction between the pragmatic and the non-pragmatic is by no means impermeable. Everyday communication is not simply practical: think of joking, greeting, cursing and the like. Or think of so-called phatic communication, which focuses on the act of utterance itself ('Great to be talking to you again!'). A sermon may hope to induce some practical effects in its listeners, but probably not on the spot.

There is also pragmatic fiction, such as televised fables illustrating the folly of driving while drunk, as well as non-pragmatic non-fiction like a funny story that happens to be true. A Mallarmé poem is certainly non-pragmatic, but how about Magna Carta, Hölderlin's reflections on tragedy, a scientific treatise on fruit bats or the American Constitution? Is increasing our knowledge of fruit bats any more pragmatic than *The Wind in the Willows* if there is no practical use to which we can put it? Not all writing which floats free of its point of origin is graced with the title of literature. (How far the American Constitution does so is a matter of ferocious contention between so-called legal originalists and their opponents.) In any case, is the literary wholly a question of what we do to writing rather than what writing does to us? Are there not works which in certain contexts invite such dislocation from their sources more than others, perhaps by virtue of their baroque language or self-evidently fictional status? Is there not a sense in which some kinds of text (those cast in heroic couplets, for example) do a fair job of detaching themselves?

Ellis is right to see that 'texts not originally designed for this use may be included [in the category of literature], while texts that were consciously designed for this use may be excluded'.[27] This flexibility is one of the virtues of his case. But he fudges the question of non-functionality by contrasting 'literary' works not, say, with the writings of Newton, Mill or Freud, but with everyday speech. It is clear enough that statements like 'What a magnificent hair do!' 'perish after [their] context has gone', as Ellis puts it, unless it is the only compliment one has ever been paid and the warm glow it occasions lingers on, even on one's deathbed. The appropriate comparison, however, is not between a literary work and everyday language but between, say, Lermontov's *A Hero of Our Times* and Schopenhauer's *The World as Will and Representation*. In what sense is the meaning and value of the latter restricted to its genetic context? What, in any case, if the original context of a work is unknown? And if it is known, do we not sometimes have recourse to it in the case of non-pragmatic works to help decide questions of meaning? Might not part of a work's aesthetic effect involve a tension between what we know it meant originally and what it means to us now? So zealous is Ellis to press his case that he pushes it, unnecessarily and unacceptably, into a full-blooded denial of the importance of a work's genetic conditions. He is not a formalist on this question, but a 'presentist': our contemporary situation is always the overriding one when it comes to assessing the meaning and value of past works.

Yet the idea of context-independence need not entail such an implausible anti-historicism. A work that is recycled, or in Brecht's term 'refunctioned', remains a determinate product of its historical times. And this may exert constraints on how, and how much, it can be refunctioned. Michel Foucault is as averse as Ellis to the genetic investigation of discourse, which would leash it to its moment of conception; but he has no doubt all the same that such discourses are thoroughly historical, emerging at certain times and withering away at others. Besides, the capacity of a work to transcend its genetic conditions, and the nature of those conditions, may be closely related. Certain pieces of writing continue to resonate with us because of the peculiar power with which their original contexts have invested them. In this sense, the work that proves most tenacious over time may be, ironically, the one that belongs most intimately to its own historical moment, or belongs to it in a certain way.

Works that we decide to treat non-functionally, Ellis remarks, are those 'worth treating in the way that literary texts are treated ... When, therefore, we are analysing a literary text, we are always dealing with the features of its structure which are the cause of its being valued highly as literature'.[28] But if critical analysis invariably attends to the features of a text which make it highly regarded, then, as with Lamarque and Olsen, it is hard to see how there can ever be negative criticism of literary art. The very word 'literary' insulates it against such an indignity. That a work is rewarding becomes the precondition rather than conclusion of one's investigation of it, since one would not bother to investigate it if it were not. As with some other commentators we have looked at, there is something inescapably circular about Ellis's whole process of value-judgement.

There are times when Ellis's account of literature runs the descriptive and the normative together, despite his insistence on the need to distinguish them. If, as he sometimes seems to imply, the non-functional is superior to the functional, then value is already built into the definition of literature, though here on account of its non-pragmatic rather than formal, moral or linguistic character. One standard attempt to bridge the gap between descriptive and normative, or fact and value, is to appeal to the concept of function: a good clock is one that fulfils its function of keeping accurate time, so that its value can be factually established. There is a sense in which Ellis stands this strategy on its head. We can move from the non-functional status of a text, which is taken to be a fact about it, to a value judgement on it.

Yet there is no necessary correlation between the precious and the non-pragmatic. There are trivially non-pragmatic bits of writing, such as that excruciatingly mawkish verse I scribbled in a moment of euphoria at the sight of Blackpool pier. Elsewhere in his book, Ellis seems to register this fact. 'Just as a work of literature must be seen primarily as a text that performs a certain task and is treated in a certain kind of way,' he writes, 'so a good work of literature is primarily one that performs that task well and is eminently suitable for its characteristic use as a piece of literature.'[29] So there would indeed seem to be a distinction between the precious and the non-pragmatic, since we can speak of how well a work performs its (non-pragmatic) function.

One thing people sometimes mean by calling a work literary is the fact that its meaning is somehow supposed to be generalised – that what it presents is offered not just for its own sake but as resonant with some broader or deeper significance.[30] And this is clearly bound up with a literary text's fictional status, as well as with its non-pragmatic character. In both of these ways, it can more easily be the bearer of general meanings than an engineer's report or a set of practical instructions. Aristotle thought poetry was to be distinguished from history by its generality. Samuel Johnson speaks in *Rasselas* of the need for an author to avoid the individual and address general propositions, large appearances, questions of the species as a whole. Wordsworth writes in the 1802 Preface to *Lyrical Ballads* of truth 'not individual and local, but general and operative', while Georg Lukács insists in *The Historical Novel* on those features of a text that are 'typical' rather than purely contingent. Claude Lévi-Strauss regards mythological signs as floating in a limbo between the concreteness of images and the generality of concepts, an ambiguity which has a vital bearing on literary works as well.

We expect from so-called literary works more than accounts of specific figures or situations, however compelling they may be. Instead, we expect them in some obscure sense to gesture beyond themselves. As Robert Stecker puts it, 'we look for some general significance in the particulars of a text'.[31] A character in Dermot Healy's novel *A Goat's Song* muses on how 'a feeble story could contain a truth that assembled far beyond the meaning of the words'. Peter Lamarque argues that a literary work not only presents a world but invites thematic interpretation of it, in which its content acquires a broader significance.[32] It is a notable feature of literature that in reading it for what it says, we also take it to be intimating something else. If these two levels are difficult to dissociate, it is because the 'something else' is not another set of significations altogether, but a distinctive way of handling the meanings we are offered, a matter of what the linguisticians call uptake. We are meant to be alerted by the very word 'poem' or 'fiction' to the fact that what follows is to be taken as exemplary – as having an undertow of moral implications beyond the events it depicts or the emotions it registers, which is not generally the case with dishwasher manuals or the financial pages of *The Times*.

Nowhere has this inherent duplicity of literature been more suggestively formulated than by Jacques Derrida:

> The 'power' that language is capable of, the power that there is, as language or as writing, is that a singular mark should also be repeatable, iterable, as mark. It then begins to differ from itself sufficiently to become exemplary and thus involves a certain generality ... But this condensation of history, of language, of the encyclopaedia, remains here indissociable from an absolutely singular event, an absolutely singular signature, and therefore also of a date, of a language, of an autobiographical inscription. In a minimum autobiographical trait can be gathered up the greatest potentiality of historical, theoretical, linguistic, philosophical culture – that's really what interests me.[33]

Language works by a kind of double inscription, both clinging to the singular and departing from it. A lyric poem or realist novel presents what is meant to be an irreducibly specific reality; but because the signs it uses are only signs because they are iterable, capable of being deployed in other contexts, any particular literary statement packs a wealth of general connotations into itself. It is thus that the singular comes to behave as a microcosm, condensing whole possible worlds in its slim compass. The more texts are fashioned or framed to display this duality, the more they conventionally approach the condition of literature. Literary texts typically exploit the doubled nature of discourse by portraying irreducibly specific situations which are at the same time, by the very nature of language, of more general import. In Derrida's term, they are 'exemplary'. This is also true of some of the strategies we associate with fiction.

The phenomenological aesthetics of Maurice Merleau-Ponty finds a similar duality in works of art. There is the 'visible' dimension of such artefacts, meaning their sensuous presence; but sustaining this almost as a sort of scaffolding is a whole 'invisible' context of significant situations and relationships, one which is generally overlooked in everyday life but which it is the function of the artwork to bring into the foreground. A similar thought informs Heidegger's notion of the work of art's 'world'. The artwork for Merleau-Ponty occupies an intermediate space between perception and reflection, in the sense that its sensory immediacy speaks of a more fundamental context of ideas. This context or deeper structure is not as instantly perceptible as the work's characters and events; but because it is related to them as their 'lining', it is not entirely abstract either.[34]

There is a paradox involved in the dual nature of language. This is the fact that the more rigorously one specifies, the more general possibilities one evokes. To depict a thing in all its singularity means laying language on thick; but this then swaddles the thing in a dense web of connotations and allows the imagination to play freely around it. The more language you pile on, the more you hope to net down the *quidditas* of whatever you are describing; yet the more you displace it by evoking a wealth of other possibilities. As with a Giacometti sculpture, the more it is pared down, the more massive the thing seems to loom.

The doubleness we are examining is not true of everything lucky enough to be called literary. We sometimes go to popular literature (an oxymoron in the eyes of many a theorist we have mentioned) simply for a rattling good yarn, with no particular implications beyond itself. Few readers have recourse to Agatha Christie for her moral wisdom. As Richard Gale suggests, 'The literary and social conventions of the time and place of its creation along with the style in which it is written determine whether [a work] is to be taken as suggesting general truths about the world'.[35]

There is, however, no law that commands us to take a text as it seems to want to be taken, any more than we must do so with our friends and colleagues. Even if a piece of writing appears not to invite it, a reader can still engage in such a generalising operation. We can always brood on an Exit sign as an ominous memento mori. We can see that 'Goldilocks and the Three Bears' was probably not intended to be read for anything but the storyline, but this is no reason why we should not allow a few pregnant general meanings to simmer in our mind as we read, such as the danger to domestic order of anarchic young girls on the rampage. In fact, it is hard to see how any narrative, however stubbornly specific, can avoid general implications altogether. When it comes to what we call literature, the question is rather one of editing and treating the specific partly *for the sake* of the general, an operation most obvious in the case of fiction. In fiction, the specific, because it is largely invented, tends to offer less resistance to this aim. Even so, this double-coding is not confined to what is conventionally called literature. Gerald Graff believes that literary works can be distinguished from so-called ordinary-language utterances by the fact that 'the messages conveyed by individual speeches do not exemplify any larger illustrative message, as do the speeches of a literary work'.[36] But a man who boasts to his workmates of his sexual exploits may provoke them not only to a judgement of himself but to certain general speculations on bragging, sexism, masculine arrogance and the like.

In one sense, all our experiences are exemplary ones. Nobody can commit to writing a thought or feeling that is in principle intelligible only to himself, not even the author of *Finnegans Wake*. There are no emotions I can have that nobody else conceivably could, as opposed to emotions I have that they happen not to. To write is already to engage in a shareable kind of sense-making. There is an implicit dimension of generality to even the most apparently private of experiences, which is part of what makes literature possible.

So-called literary works, then, entail a double-reading, as we respond to concrete situations yet inscribe them, if only unconsciously, in some less specific context. Because we are aware that *Emma* is a novel, we do not take the significance of the heroine's behaviour as stopping with herself, as we might with a life of Florence Nightingale. When this dual strategy rises to self-consciousness, it is known as allegory. In the case of literary realism, it involves a precarious balance between individual and general. Because the general attitudes of a realist text are incarnate in its concrete particulars, those particulars need to be realised as compellingly as possible. Indeed, literature is the 'thickest' description of reality that we have. Yet this may then have the effect of undercutting the work's overall way of seeing, drawing the reader's eye from that to the details that instantiate it. The text needs to allude to more than itself, but not at the expense of the very specificity which renders such allusions persuasive. The concrete is the medium of the general, but can always end up by obstructing it.

The novelist Samuel Richardson writes to his friend William Warburton that he does not wish his readers to believe that his novel *Clarissa* is a real-life account, but does not want to confess that it is fiction either. There are various ways of interpreting what he meant by this. He may have meant that while he wanted his story to have the air of reality, he did not want readers to believe the events it depicts actually happened, since its exemplary moral status might thereby be compromised. The book would then become just another real-life report, with no 'typical' dimension to it. We might fail to grasp that the novel is by its very nature a tale about more women than Clarissa, more men than Lovelace and more places than eighteenth-century London. But to declare the book a fiction might risk undermining its realist impact, thus indirectly sabotaging its exemplary status as well. Richardson's comments to Warburton suggest that he wanted to suspend his story somewhere between fiction and reality, hence securing for himself the best of both worlds.

To treat something as fictional is among other things to allow yourself to think and feel around it, imaginatively freewheel, refuse the grim fatality of the factual in the name of the virtual. Because literary works are fictional in the sense of sitting loose to the actual, they can be congenial occasions for such speculative activity. They can deal with the obduracy of the real in cavalier spirit, spinning imaginative hypotheses rather than slavishly conforming to the clamourings of the reality-principle. This is one reason why the imagination and radical politics have so often been linked. If this freewheeling involves holding the work a little at arm's length, it can also mean a more intense experience of it. In fact Coleridge considered that the more engrossed by a literary work we were, the less credence we could give it, since in his view such credence involved an act of will which too wholehearted an immersion in the text would make impossible. Literary works have the power to present things in their tangible presence, and thus to draw the reader in; but like the Husserlian phenomenologist they can also free them up to be viewed from a number of different angles, thus combining the palpable with the provisional. In this interplay of distancing and drawing in, they reproduce in unusually intensive form the doubled or ironic consciousness which is a characteristically human way of belonging to the world.

3

The assumption that works of literature are unusually valuable pieces of writing is widely current among theorists. Stein Haugom Olsen writes that 'a literary work is not understood but appreciated', as though you could appreciate what you do not understand.[37] For him, as we have seen, the act of interpreting a text takes for granted a positive evaluation of it. Why would one bother to interpret a non-canonical work? There is a sense, then, in which interpretation follows on the heels of evaluation and not, as is generally assumed, the other way round. On Olsen's view, a critical account must focus on those features of a work which justify the interest invested in it by the members of one's culture. A valid interpretation is one that identifies the qualities that classify the work as a successful piece of art. So criticism is not actually *criticism*, in the common-or-garden sense of the word. It is no significant part of its task to point out where a work falls short of the distinction we assume from the outset it must manifest. Instead, the word 'criticism' in Olsen's lexicon yields to the belletristic 'appreciation'. 'Appreciation' is less likely to let in the negative than the more rebarbative 'criticism'.

In similar vein, Colin Lyas writes that 'It will be impossible to define literature unless we cite features the possession of which make a piece of writing valuable in a certain way'.[38] Literature for him is an 'approval' word. Charles Stevenson thinks that we should preserve a positive or laudatory sense of the word 'poem', on the grounds that a poem could be so bad as not to be a poem at all.[39] All poems, then, are good poems, just as all sausages are good sausages (since bad ones are not sausages at all). Gregory Currie claims that 'to say of something that it is literature is, except in certain special circumstances, to ascribe to it a certain kind of value'.[40] Christopher New remarks that works whose literary qualities are 'poor and unremarkable ... do not deserve the honorific title of (good) literature'.[41] The brackets are worth noting. It is as though New has suddenly realised that he is just about to rule out the possibility of bad literature, and so hastily insets a 'good'. The effect of the insertion is to turn the claim into a tautology: poor and unremarkable works are not good ones. New also tells us that when 'we contrast serious literary writing with escapist literature, we are using the word "literature" in a neutral, value-free way'.[42] It would appear that what counts as serious and what as escapist can be neutrally established, a case that even the most dedicated positivist might be reluctant to endorse. Paul Crowther writes in an excellent study of aesthetics that 'we would surely not allow that all paintings or poems *ipso facto* are works of art'.[43] So what are we supposed to call them? They may be *bad* works of art, but that does not mean that they are not works of art at all, any more than a diseased liver is not a liver. Descriptive and normative uses of the term 'work of art' are commonly confused in these types of discussion.

What does this theory make of bad literature? You can, to be sure, claim that the notion of bad literature avoids being an oxymoron in this sense, that it refers to a member of a highly esteemed class of works that fails to live up to that promise. A wretched Restoration tragedy or vacuous neoclassical piece of pastoral can thus still be considered as achieving literary status in a generic sense, if not in an individual one. Or one might be speaking of works that aspire to the eminence of the literary but fall miserably short of it. Yet the problem is not to be dismissed so easily. For we have seen already that the so-called literary canon contains a number of items that are fairly shoddy stuff. Equally, there are whole genres like science fiction that some would deem noncanonical yet which have produced some magnificent individual works. Lamarque and Olsen distinguish literature from light entertainment, but there are plenty of fine comedies that fall into both categories. And if literary works are those that prove responsive to a certain kind of treatment, then this is as true of good popular fiction as it is of Cervantes. Is the fiction of P. D. James and Ian Rankin literature, and if not, why not? Because it lacks the requisite fineness of language or depth of vision? But what about Robert Southey or Thomas Beddoes? They are certainly considered literature, but unlike James and Rankin it is doubtful whether they are worth reading.

The view that literature is an inherently valuable kind of writing has a highly specific history. In the sixteenth and seventeenth centuries, so Raymond Williams has argued, the word 'literature' really meant what we mean today by literacy or literary erudition, so that 'a man of much literature' meant an exceptionally well read one.[44] In tracing the evolution of the term 'literature' from the eighteenth century to the present, Williams demonstrates how a 'category which had appeared as objective as "all printed books", and which had been given a social-class foundation as "polite learning" and the domain of "taste" and "sensibility", now became a necessarily selective and self-defining area: not all "fiction" was "imaginative"; not all "literature" was "Literature".'[45] Criticism, as a practice that had performed so many diverse functions in the past, then became the chief way of legitimating this 'specialist and selective category' of literary artefacts. Valid criticism is that which appreciates valid works, and valid works are those that respond positively to valid criticism. The critic becomes the high priest of these literary rites, presiding with a due sense of his own authority over this self-legitimating process.

Indeed, the religious metaphor has a broader significance. Williams argues that the idea of 'creative' or 'imaginative' literature emerges for the first time in the late eighteenth century as a form of resistance to an increasingly prosaic, utilitarian social order. As such, it represents one of the last besieged outposts of transcendent truth in a harshly pragmatic environment. The transcendent imagination and early industrial capitalism are born at a stroke. Literature and the arts become forms of displaced religion, protected enclaves within which values now seen as socially dysfunctional can take shelter. A good many of our own conceptions of literature stretch no further back than this quite recent historical moment.

The truth, however, is that to use the word 'literature' normatively rather than descriptively leads to needless muddle, along with a fair number of self-satisfied prejudgements. It is better to treat the word 'literature' like the word 'intellectual'. 'Intellectual' does not mean 'frightfully clever'. If that were so there would be no dim-witted intellectuals, which is far from the case. The category is a job description, not a personal commendation. The word 'literature' should be similarly confined to descriptive uses. Medbh McGuckian is literature, and so is Maeve Binchy. Which is not to say that readers will not sometimes want to make qualitative distinctions between the two. We should also shake off the intellectual indolence of assuming that a literary work is worthwhile simply because the literary institution tells us that it is.

There is one way of assessing the value of a literary work which is probably unique to the twentieth century, and which crops up in one current of criticism there after another. This is the view that what is precious about literary art is the way it renders our taken-for-granted values freshly visible, thereby opening them to criticism and revision. Derek Attridge writes that 'if the text comforts and reassures by simply confirming prejudices according to some well-known verbal formulae ... it cannot be called ... literature'.[46] This aesthetic has its origins in the Russian Formalist doctrine of 'making strange': by estranging our perceptions, the poem retrieves them from the workaday staleness in which they are commonly sunk and turns them into arresting objects of investigation in their own right. Behind this doctrine in turn lies the dim presence of Husserlian phenomenology, with its shift of focus from the object in the world to the act of consciousness that 'intends' it. In the case of both Formalism and phenomenology, we place reality provisionally in brackets in order to focus more attentively on the mental operations involved in the act of perceiving it.

Reception theory inherits this doctrine, as is clear enough from the early work of Hans Robert Jauss. Jauss speaks of the 'horizon of expectations' against which any work of literature will be apprehended, meaning by this the whole structure of assumptions or system of cultural reference that the reader brings to bear on the text. Aesthetic works vary in value and meaning as they shift in their histories of reception from one horizon to another, or as those horizons themselves change. The most valuable works are those which estrange the background assumptions against which they are read, turning these assumptions into an object perceptible to the reader and hence prising her free of their constraints.[47] A work which simply fulfils readerly expectations – Death on the Nile, for example – is accordingly to be held in low aesthetic esteem. The model presupposes that orthodox beliefs and conventions are aesthetically valuable only in so far as they can be shaken up, a case which might have come as a surprise to Dante or Dryden. In fact, Jauss is forced rather absurdly to lump classical texts with 'culinary' ones, to parcel up Horace's odes with the latest blockbuster, since neither kind of work challenges the conventional horizon of expectations.

Like Formalism, this case takes it as read that common-or-garden norms and perceptions are impoverished, and that dominant conceptual systems (what Jauss calls 'affirmative or institutionalised meaning') are bound to be restrictive. Literary value lies in disrupting or deviating from the prevailing social wisdom. As with the Formalists, it is a negative conception of artistic merit. The same is true in a different sense of Theodor Adorno, the greatest of Marxist aestheticians.[48] The new is valuable in itself, and the normative inherently ossified. The possibility that norms can be defamiliarised in unproductive ways is excluded from the outset. Everyday social discourse is tarnished and debased, so that only by being ruptured, thickened, dislocated, condensed, heightened or pared to vanishing point can it be persuaded to yield up a few rare scraps of value. Behind modernism's fascination with language lurks a profound distrust of its everyday manifestations.

'The relationship between art and society,' Jauss observes in Gadamerian style, 'has to be grasped in the dialectic of question and answer.'[49] He means by this that the authentic artwork puts a question to orthodox social values, and in doing so receives a fresh kind of response. At the same time, the work itself is interrogated in different ways by different generations of readers from within their own shifting horizon of expectations; and this 'fusion of horizons', as Hans-Georg Gadamer names it in *Truth and Method*, in which the historical moment of the text's production encounters a specific moment in the history of its reception, may then transform the conventional meaning of a work, releasing significances which its moment of production could not have anticipated.

One implication of this claim is that all worthwhile literary texts are in some sense radical or subversive – a case that would doubtless have been howled down as the last word in intellectual vulgarity had it emerged from the Marxist camp,[50] but which can pass as a kind of wisdom when it springs from the more politically congenial milieu of hermeneutics, formalist poetics and reception theory. In a naively avant-garde gesture, the familiar is branded as the irretrievably banal. Everyday experience is necessarily bankrupt. Only by alienating the alienation, estranging the commonplace until it becomes well-nigh unrecognisable, can we restore to it its integrity. Yet this is in itself a banal sort of dogma. That many routine norms and conventions may be positive, to be cherished rather than challenged, is scarcely considered. What of the norms that govern the rights of working people to withdraw their labour? Is the view that fraudulent bankers should be punished to be made freshly perceptible so that it may become an object of critique? No doubt the convention requiring all citizens to donate two-thirds of their income to the Emperor is in need of challenging, but not necessarily the laws that grant you the right to gain recompense for being tortured.

The view that conceptual systems are inherently constraining is equally groundless. If Stalinism entails such a system, so does some feminism. And how about reception theory itself? The case reflects a liberal prejudice against doctrinal formulations; but are there no liberal doctrines, agendas or manifestos? Some systems of ideas are oppressive, while others are enabling. One would have expected those wedded to pluralism to be a touch more judicious on this score. Not many liberals denounce the US Constitution, which is a well-formulated enough piece of doctrine, as a charter for slavery. What a particular regime of ideas fails to accommodate – theories of racial purity, for example – may well deserve to be excluded. Not every margin is healthy, nor every system diseased. There are minorities out of line with dominant assumptions who should at all costs be shut out. Neo-Nazis, for example. 'Dominant' does not always mean 'oppressive'.

Jauss was later to abandon much of this case, or at least radically qualify it. In his own way, he came to see it as classically ideological, universalising a specific historical moment (that of Formalism, high modernism and the avant-garde) to the history of culture as a whole. The historical moment which gave birth to the theory is a revolutionary one, all the way from the Bolshevik regime, in which some of the Formalists played their part along with various of their Futurist and Constructivist colleagues, to the dissident modernist coteries of Paris, Berlin and Vienna and the leftist avant-gardes of interwar Europe. It is no surprise that some of the most fertile cultural experiments of the twentieth century, not least Expressionism and Surrealism, sprang from this period of political agitation. Even reception theory, a more moderate, mild-mannered product of this turbulent legacy, can be seen in the context of political upheaval.[51] The pioneering essay by Jauss which heralded the emergence of this current on the critical scene was published in 1969.

Even so, the notions of art thrown up by this history are as limited as they are suggestive. They fail to shed light on literary works which depend on an assured compact with their readers; which regard conventions as enabling rather than stifling; which do not see common experience as vacuous or deluded; and which value the desire to affirm over the impulse to subvert. Such works need not be conservative. They might be feminist texts as much as neoclassical ones. There is a hermeneutic of solidarity as well as suspicion. Radical politics involves affirming common practices as well as demystifying them. It spans the insights of Raymond Williams and E.P. Thompson as well as those of Max Ernst and Georges Bataille.

The claim that the value of literature lies in estranging everyday norms is a central feature of Wolfgang Iser's brand of reception theory. The literary work 'depragmatises' social conventions, prising them loose from their run-of-the-mill contexts and turning them into objects of scrutiny in their own right. It is as though the true referent of the literary work is not so much social reality as the conventions that regulate it.[52] There is a parallel here with the phenomenology by which the early Iser was influenced. What is at stake is less the real object than the modes by which it is appropriated.[53] Literary works of art, by making visible the *doxa* by which we live, raise possibilities banished by the conventional wisdom. Yet since this is hardly the case with, say, whole reaches of medieval art, Iser is forced to regard much of it as 'trivial'.[54] The imprisoning dogma in this case would seem to be his own liberal-modernist outlook.

All our conceptual systems, Iser maintains, must exclude and displace, and the function of literary works is to highlight what has been shouldered aside. Such works deal with 'the inescapable residue that escapes the mastery of the systems concerned', rather as they do for the deconstructionists.[55] In fact, by this point Iser has clearly been to school with Derrida, partly recasting his reception theory in post-structuralist terms. In a simplistic contrast inherited from that style of thought, systems are almost always negative, while what they fail to assimilate is invariably positive. The literary work of art, Iser announces, 'implicitly draws an outline of the prevailing system by explicitly shading in the areas all around that system'.[56]

There is a parallel here with the Marxist critical theory of Pierre Macherey.[57] Macherey's project is to show how the literary work, in drawing upon artistic form to lend a determinate shape to an otherwise amorphous ideology, begins despite its own best intentions to throw the limits of that ideology into relief. Those limits mark the place at which what the work says begins to shade into its 'not-said' – which is to say, into whatever is censored from its speech as ideologically impermissible. Ideology generally refuses to acknowledge its own frontiers, fondly imagining that its scope is universal and eternal; but the effect of formalising or objectifying it in this way is to begin to 'make speak' its gaps, silences and elisions, all of which result from its exclusion of certain social realities. (Iser himself, doubtless under Macherey's influence, writes in his later volume *Prospecting* of the literary work as 'enabl[ing] what is not said to become present'.[58]) The seeds of this suggestive theory lie in Louis Althusser's contention that the authentic work of art opens up an internal distance between itself and its ideological context, one which allows us to perceive that context in an estranging, potentially emancipatory, way.[59] There is a fruitful alliance here between Formalism and Marxism, though one that raises as many problems as it resolves.

Once again – to name simply one of these problems – value would seem to lie solely in the deviant and defamiliarised. It takes root in the cracks and crevices of an ideology which lacks all merit in itself. Literature seems to be on the side of the liberal and radical angels, challenging the status quo purely by virtue of its objectifying form. I toed this questionable line myself in my *Criticism and Ideology*, arguing that literary value arose from the capacity of a work to disrupt the ideology within which it was held.[60] This overlooks the fact that some ideologies are resourceful and productive. 'A fictional text,' Iser writes, 'must by its very nature call into question the validity of familiar norms.'[61] This may be true of Rilke's *Notebooks of Malte Laurids Brigge* or Musil's *The Man without Qualities*, but nobody has ever accused *Mansfield Park, Barchester Towers*, Captain W.E. Johns's *Biggles in the Orient* or the Rupert Annual of acting transgressively, even though they are all works of fiction. It is true that Austen's and Trollope's novels may lend these norms a new kind of visibility, but it does not follow from this that they are brought into question. The effect of turning one's taken-for-granted conventions into objects of scrutiny may be as much to consolidate as to upend them, a point that this theory damagingly overlooks.

Nor is it true, as this theory sometimes seems to imply, that we act on certain assumptions only because we are unaware of them, any more than it is true that ideology is always unconscious of itself.[62] It is perfectly possible to be alert to the cultural relativity of one's values while clinging to them for dear life. The philosopher Richard Rorty spun a distinguished academic career out of doing so. 'I know I'm a dreary little puritan, but would you mind bringing a spot of sunshine into my tight-assed existence by making love to your sister in the privacy of your own home rather than in my front garden?' is not an unintelligible thing to say, even if it is not an everyday one.

It is striking how widespread this 'defamiliarising' case has been in modern times. The leading theoretician of the Prague school, Jan Mukařovský, attends to the innovative deviations of a work rather than to its reproduction of existing norms.[63] If this is also largely true of the aesthetics of Theodor Adorno, it is equally to be found in the semiotics of Umberto Eco, for whom literary texts occasion a reassessment of codes which issues in 'a new awareness about the world'.[64] Eco, to be sure, acknowledges that such texts can reinforce codes as well as challenge them: 'Every text threatens the codes [by which it is constituted] but at the same time gives them strength; it reveals unexpected possibilities in them, and thus changes the attitude of the user to them.'[65] In general, however, Eco the semiotician is here remarkably close to Iser the reception theorist. For him, too, the reader is forced, through the work of reading, to subject his spontaneous norms to a new kind of scrutiny. 'The addressee [of the text],' he writes, 'becomes aware of new semiosic [sic] possibilities and is thereby compelled to rethink the whole language, the entire inheritance of what has been said, can be said, and could or should be said.'[66] The hyperbole of the claim betrays it as an updated version of some more old-fashioned apologias for literary study. The reader has the universe at his or her feet – though now it is a universe of signs and codes, not one of cosmic energies and transcendent powers.

There is even a structuralist equivalent to this view of literature, despite the notorious anti-humanism of structuralism in general.

Claude Lévi-Strauss writes in *Tristes tropiques* that to understand other cultures is to understand one's own, since what we find in such cultures, in eye-catchingly unfamiliar guise, are the same unconscious laws which regulate our own symbolic universe. Myth is the way the Other or unconscious thinks in pre-modern peoples; but this same Other also thinks in us, and it is thus on the ground of this Otherness, paradoxically, that we and those who seem foreign to us can effect a genuine encounter. What we and they have in common is a signifying structure which is profoundly opaque to us both. Ironically, then, the fact of a universal unconscious means that apparently remote cultures are far more intimate with us than we may imagine; but it is also what gives rise to a certain self-estrangement, as we come to gaze upon ourselves with new eyes through a recognition of others as our kinsfolk. We must see ourselves, Lévi-Strauss remarks in a fine flourish in *Structural Anthropology*, as 'an other among others'.

It is thus that Lévi-Strauss makes a fetish neither of difference nor identity. On the one hand, the structuralism he founded in the anthropological field represents one of the last great surges of Enlightenment reason, with its faith in the fundamental unity of humankind. As a Jew and a foreigner in France, Lévi-Strauss writes in the wake of the orgy of unreason known as the Second World War, with its lethal cult of ethnic difference. Yet in his *Race and History* he also advocates cultural pluralism, and resists the reduction of diversity to sameness. Moreover, though the West and the 'savage mind' may share the same deep mental structures, this does not put the two camps on the same level. On the contrary, Lévi-Strauss finds much in pre-modern societies that is superior to modern civilisations, and from which we refuse to learn at our peril. The 'well-ordered' humanism he sees at work in tribal mythology is not the dominative humanism of the West; it is rather a humanism which 'does not begin with itself, but puts things back in their place. It puts the world before life, life before man, and the respect of others before love of self.'[67]

There is no question that structuralism, apparently the most value-free, technocratic of theoretical modes, is (at least in the hands of its now lamentably neglected founder) a profoundly ethical affair. Today, when everything that happened ten minutes ago is ancient history, even the mildest proposal that some features of the past were more estimable than some aspects of the present is likely to be derided as primitivist nostalgia. Despite the fact that Lévi-Strauss consistently elevated the cognitive power of science over that of myth, and was deeply engaged in the history of his own time, his admiration for tribal peoples can only appear like dewy-eyed sentimentalism to the traders in futures. Reading him after environmental politics, however, which scarcely existed in his day, it is possible to see a certain ecology, both natural and spiritual, as his abiding motif from start to finish. In his later writings, he concluded in elegiac spirit that it was too late for the world to be saved, and that the precious resources of la pensée sauvage were lost to us for ever.

The scepticism of the normative that marks the literary ethics I am examining is even more pronounced in the case of post-structuralism. For Roland Barthes and Jacques Derrida, value would seem to lie unequivocally in what gives the slip to structure and plays havoc with system, as though the marginal, aberrant and non-incorporable were always and everywhere dissident powers. It is possible see this universalist dogma as springing from a disen-chanted phase of recent political history, which can find no trace of merit in the norms and practices of everyday life. But it is also a form of left elitism, one with a long and discreditable history in French thought. If Wittgenstein has too credulous a trust in the commonplace, most French theorists of our time are too disdainful of it.[68] Few contemporary thinkers have taken their cue in this respect from Mikhail Bakhtin, whose Rabelais and his World pulls off the rare achievement of converting a poetics of estrangement into a mundane political force through the notion of carnival. In Bakhtin's work, astonishingly, a popular practice becomes a piece of avant-garde subversion. What deconstructs the arrogance of power is not a text but a festival of the common people. And since carnival is affirmative and utopian as well as satirical and debunking, it combines positive and negative aesthetics. The same can be said in a different sense of the theatre of Bertolt Brecht. Everyday life is no longer the opposite of the disruptive and defamiliarised. On the contrary, it is the very terrain on which they are to be discovered.

Even so, carnival is scarcely common life in its most workaday state. It is also a cautionary example of how playing havoc with one's everyday conventions is unlikely to dislodge them. On the morning after this orgy of irreverence, as the empty wine flagons and scraps of pork pie lie scattered around and dawn breaks on a thousand hangovers, those conventions are already slotting discreetly back into place, no doubt all the more authoritative because of the resilience they have displayed in the face of such pervasive mockery.

There is, finally, a Wittgensteinian wing to the doctrine that literary value lies in laying our routine assumptions open to critical inspection. David Schalkwyk has argued that works of literature 'make apparent the conditions of possibility of language itself', which is to say the practical forms of life with which language in Wittgenstein's eyes is so profoundly interwoven. Art in Schalkwyk's view 'effects a change of aspect that shows the degree to which what we are able to see is determined by *instituted* conceptual relations between the objects of our world ... the defamilarising power of the literary, which is the grain of truth in Formalism, enables it to *stage* historically specific modes of appropriating and reappropriating the world and entrenching it as "essence".'[69]

The literary, then, is a version of the grammatical investigation that Wittgenstein considered the only proper task of philosophy. In granting us images of the inseparable interweaving of language and the world, it reveals something that is already imperceptibly before our eyes. By laying bare the process by which certain entrenched conceptual relations determine our forms of seeing, works of literary art play a role in prising us loose from them, setting us free for other ways of perceiving. Literature, like any other language, assimilates the world into itself; but it does so with a peculiar kind of self-consciousness, allowing us to grasp the nature of our forms of life and language-games more vigilantly than usual. This case, too, assigns literature an inherently critical force. 'The literary,' Schalkwyk writes in a paraphrase of Stanley Cavell, 'can explore and shake the deepest levels of agreement upon which not only our language, but also our sense of ourselves and the world we share and struggle over, depend.'[70] But not all we call literature does anything quite so traumatic. Perhaps Schalkwyk is thinking more of Sholokhov or Dos Passos than 'Little Lamb, who made thee?'

If there is one critic who has stubbornly resisted the view that literary works seduce us into a spirit of self-criticism, it is Stanley Fish. In Fish's eyes, this whole conception is absurdly misconceived. Indeed, it is the ultimate epistemological fantasy. In his view, dredging your deepest assumptions into the light of day, even if it were possible, would achieve little or nothing. It is true that the result would probably be to stymie those assumptions, since beliefs as foundational as this work only when we are comfortably oblivious of them. Self-consciousness would be their undoing. All that would happen, however, is that we would slot another set of assumptions into place, which would then become familiarised in their turn.

In Fish's eyes, however, such a manoeuvre is not in fact possible. It would mean trying to leap out of your own skin or haul yourself up by your own bootstraps, since convictions that run this deep are what constitute one's identity in the first place. For the self to objectify what makes it what it is, it would need to stand outside itself in some metaphysical outer space, which is a rationalist delusion. The subject for Fish is effectively the prisoner of its beliefs, which exert upon it a rigorously deterministic power. We cannot ask where our beliefs come from, since the answer to that question would itself be determined by those beliefs. We cannot think ourselves outside our fundamental values and prejudices, since we can think only by virtue of them. We cannot call them into dispute because they themselves set the terms on which such disputes would be conducted. They are, in a word, transcendental. Whatever I think I can imagine beyond my familiar frame of reference must actually be a product of that frame, and thus cannot fall outside its scope at all. To hold one's values and principles at arm's length for critical inspection can only take place in a context, and that context is shaped by one's values and principles. One could only thoroughly objectify one's beliefs when one no longer held them, and thus when it would no longer be productive to do so. Once again, a radical epistemology turns out to have conservative consequences. Any Westerner who imagines he can subject the Western way of life to fundamental critique must be fooling himself. Where on earth could he be standing to do so?

How one can come to change one's convictions is thus bound to be something of a mystery. It cannot be on account of new evidence, since we have seen already that in Fish's world your convictions determine what will count for you as evidence in the first place, and so cannot be tested by it. Nor can it be through critical self-reflection, since this, too, will be a function of your current situation. There is no middle ground for this theory between being a helpless victim of one's world-view and the View from Nowhere. One is always in some sense inside one's culture, and hence complicit with it. Whatever may appear to be on the outside is either a fantasy projected from the inside, or another interpretive matrix altogether – one which, being radically incommensurable with one's own, can have no practical bearing on it, and certainly cannot subject it to a full-blooded critique.

Fish does not recognise that all cultures and belief systems have fuzzy frontiers and ambiguous categories, a view that might query his rigorous distinction between inside and outside. In fact, he has a deep aversion to the faintest whiff of indeterminacy, which would effectively spell the ruin of his theory. Nor does he see that there may be that within norms and conventions which has the power to undo them. He overlooks the fact that forms of life can generate forces which point beyond them. In fact, they may point in the end to their wholesale dissolution. As such, they are both 'inside' and 'outside' such life forms at the same time. It is this which has traditionally been known as an immanent critique, and for which a more recent name is deconstruction. Deconstruction occupies the logic of a regime (whether textual or political) from the inside in order to reveal how that system of sense is never entirely at one with itself, and how it is at its points of slippage and self-contradiction that it might begin to unravel. There is thus no need to suppose that any critique one can understand must be collusive with the given system, and that any other must be launched from some Archimedean point beyond all comprehension.

The period from Russian Formalism to the birth of reception theory was one in which the rise of new cultural theories coincided with the decline of older humanistic rationales for the study of literature. This is as true of Viktor Shklovsky as it is of the insurgents of 1968. It was becoming harder to claim that literature was a force for moral transformation, or that it put us in touch with transcendent truths. Some less implausibly direct role for it in repairing the human condition was called for; and one solution, as we have just seen, was that literary works did their moral work by unmasking the arbitrary nature of the codes, norms, conventions, ideologies and forms of culture by which we lived.

Jonathan Culler sees the study of literature as involving an 'expansion of the self'; but this is no longer a question of individual moral enrichment as it was for traditional literary humanism. Instead, it is a matter – once again – of nurturing 'an awareness of the *interpretive* models which inform one's culture'[71] – an aim which is far too intellectualist to satisfy the literary humanists, indeed which may be far too intellectualist *tout court*. Modernist or avant-garde texts are in this sense the most typical works of world literature, to steal a phrase from Viktor Shklovsky, since by putting their modes of sense-making so audaciously on show, they act out what is implicit in other literary artefacts. In suitably modernist style, literature improves us morally by making us more self-critical, self-conscious, flexible, provisional, open-minded and robustly sceptical of orthodoxies. The political function of literary works is not to lead an enraged theatre audience on the local town hall, but to protect us from the fascist within.

It is a largely negative function for literary studies, involving as it does a criticism of the actual rather than an image of the possible. It also fits supremely well with certain middle-class liberal assumptions. Holding one's convictions passionately would seem to be distinctly inferior to holding them at arm's length. (Though there are other possibilities: the historian A.J.P. Taylor once remarked that he had extreme convictions, but held them moderately.) The case retains some traces of the humanist legacy, albeit with a certain pathos. It says almost nothing about how we are to live once the doors of perception have been cleansed; but it allots the study of literature a modest role in altering our stance to the world, which is perhaps the best this residual humanism can muster in a deconstructive age.

Deconstruction marks the point at which the decline of the humanist heritage modulates into a militant anti-humanism. Accordingly, for a critic like Paul de Man, the literary work represents the truth of our condition not in its imaginative power or creative *élan* but in its bafflement and self-blindness, its ineluctable *mauvaise foi*, its inability to extricate its truth-claims from the ruses of figurative language and the snares of mystification.[72] The two terms in the phrase 'liberal humanist' are now starting to drift apart. Literature is the negative knowledge of human existence. There, at least, we can give a name to the groundlessness of our projects, the fictional nature of the self, our exile from reality, the rhetorical gestures we come to mistake for truth. Literary works may still be seen as events, but they are now ruined acts, botched performances. Since their medium is that bottomless duplicity known as language, they could scarcely be otherwise. 'Discourse' – the use of language for strategic ends in practical situations – is always liable to be undone and outrun by 'language', understood as the anonymous, textualising, deconstructive operations of the linguistic medium itself. Looking back, it is striking how the de Manian sensibility chimes so exactly with the climate of a politically disenchanted age.

Deconstruction may see the literary work as a symbolic act seeking to achieve certain effects in a determinate context; but it does so for the most part only to show with a certain ill-suppressed triumph how this act inevitably comes to grief – how its effects backfire, its truth-claims trip themselves up, its intentions fail to hit the mark and the determinacy of its context sags into shapelessness, and all this at the hands of that treacherous power known as language. It is not hard to see this literary ideology as part of a more widespread bafflement about the nature of constructive action in the wake of the late 1960s. For all its intellectual brio and fertility, deconstruction (indeed, post-structuralism in general) signified a certain loss of political nerve – a wariness of ambitious forms of action, for example, in the wake of a history in which such projects had too often bred monstrous consequences. Behind de Man's own nervousness of such politics lies a personal history of fascist fellow-travelling, for which the idea of the literary text as unmasking the groundlessness of all action and identity is perhaps, among other things, a symbolic compensation. In this sense, there is something that de Man's theory is trying to do, whatever his doubts about the efficacy of performatives.

CHAPTER 4

The Nature of Fiction

1

The theory of fiction is perhaps the most difficult aspect of the philosophy of literature, as well as the one that has attracted the most sustained scholarly attention. For some curious reason, commentary on the subject has produced not only some penetrating insights but also more than its fair share of embarrassing banalities. Gregory Currie, for example, informs us that 'we say that an inference is reasonable when it has a relatively high degree of reasonableness, unreasonable when its degree of reasonableness is very low'.[1] Peter Lamarque impresses on us the fact that 'fictional characters, like Mr. Allworthy or Miss Bridget, do not exist in the real world as persons'.[2] He also claims that 'what is fictional is what is made up', a proposition we shall be taking leave to doubt a little later.[3] One writer tells us that 'we are not forced to claim that a fictional statement like "Sherlock Holmes lived in Baker Street" must be understood literally, and is about Sherlock Holmes or Baker Street, respectively'.[4] Margaret Macdonald arrives hotfoot with the news that 'the novels of Jane Austen do exist'.[5] Lamarque and Olsen write that 'the interest which literature has for human beings, it has because it possesses a humanly interesting content, because what literature presents or says concerns readers as human beings'.[6] 'Fiction,' Grant Overton reveals, 'uses words, for the most part deprived of the aid of face, voice, and gesture.'[7] 'Proust,' we learn from Gregory Currie, 'could hardly have conveyed the full subtlety of *A La Recherche du Temps Perdu* without using words.'[8]

The banalities, however, are more than compensated for by the bizarrenesses. The philosophy of fiction is full of agreeable paradoxes and conundrums. Christopher New asks whether it is true that the planet Pluto exists in the Sherlock Holmes stories, even though it had not been discovered at the time.[9] He also inquires whether Ophelia has a determinate or indeterminate number of teeth, and whether it is true in the world of the *Iliad* that penicillin was going to be invented in the twentieth century. Peter van Inwagen defends the thesis that there are fictional creatures, and that every single one of them exists.[10]

In similar vein, R. Howell is thoroughly convinced that Sherlock Holmes exists.[11] A.P. Martinich and Avrum Stroll go one better and argue that he is a creature of flesh and blood.[12] David Lewis, in a classic essay, agrees with them wholeheartedly.[13] Thomas Pavel maintains that fictional characters are existent without existing.[14] Most philosophers of literature believe that Sherlock Holmes has a brain and a liver even though the tales make no reference to these organs, but the question of whether he has a mole on his back is famously moot. David Novitz believes that the starship *Enterprise* really does have a heat shield. He also thinks that Mr Pickwick is real, and that Sam Weller can see him even if we can't.[15] For the philosopher Alexius Meinong, a square circle is an object, though not an existent one, and so for some philosophers of literature is Heathcliff.[16] One's response to a fiction may even help to determine one's nationality. One of the questions in an examination for foreigners wishing to become British citizens was 'Where does Santa Claus live?' This is an example of Roy Bhaskar's claim that non-existent entities may produce real causal effects in the world of existing entities.[17]

Joseph Margolis declares that 'there are no sentences of a fiction that could be true of an actual person'.[18] If this is true, then there was no need for Raymond Williams to abandon a novel he was writing about a Labour MP pretending to have been drowned when a real Labour MP did precisely that. He would still have been writing a work of fiction. Gregory Currie believes that 'it is possible for two works to be alike in verbal structures – right down to the details of spelling and word order – yet for one to be fiction and the other not'.[19] David Lewis argues that there may be a man unknown to Arthur Conan Doyle whose adventures happened to coincide in every detail with those of his hero, and who might even have been called Sherlock Holmes, but that the stories are not about him.[20] Kendall Walton insists that when we experience fear while watching a horror movie, we are only 'fictionally', not actually, afraid.[21] He also thinks that we cannot have real feelings about non-existent people, only fictional ones.[22] 'In some cases [of narrative],' he tells us, 'it is fictional that the narrator speaks or writes nonfictionally, but in others it is fictional that he creates a fiction.'[23] Most of these comments, as the reader will have noted, reveal one remarkable fact about philosophers of literature. Their knowledge of literary works seems to consist entirely of the Sherlock Holmes stories, along with the first sentence of Tolstoy's *Anna Karenina*.[24]

Fiction and literature are not synonymous, despite Jonathan Culler's claim that 'to read a text as literature is to read it as fiction', and Morse Peckham's opinion that what makes a work literary is its fictional dimension.[25] Boswell's *Life of Johnson* and Hazlitt's *Spirit of the Age* are usually ranked as literature, but neither is fictional, or generally read as such. Nor are a great many other works that are classified as literary, from Cicero's speeches and Tacitus's history of Rome to Bacon's *Advancement of Learning*, La Rochefoucauld's maxims, Lessing's writings on theatre, Cobbett's *Rural Rides* and the essays of Emerson and Macaulay. We do not have to read these works as fiction in order to see them as literature. Literature is not confined to fiction, and fiction is not confined to literature. Eric Hobsbawm writes of Marx and Engels's *Communist Manifesto*, which some people admittedly regard as outrageously fictional, that 'as political rhetoric [it] has an almost biblical force. In short, it is impossible to deny its compelling power as literature.'[26]

'Whether or not a work is literature,' writes John Searle, 'is for the reader to decide, whether or not it is fiction is for the author to decide.'[27] Like many an aphorism, this is of dubious accuracy. It takes more than a reader to decide that a text is literary (Searle is clearly confining the word to the question of value judgement), while a 'fictionalising' reading may override an author's non-fictional intentions. Searle claims that the criterion for whether or not a text is a work of fiction must lie in the intentions of its author. Monroe Beardsley likewise maintains that the concept of art is genetic, including as it does a special reference to what the artist intends to do or thinks she is doing. Robert Brown and Martin Steinmann insist that 'a discourse is fictional because its speaker or writer intends it to be so'.[28] But if I write in a certain mode on a certain subject in a certain situation, I am probably going to be taken as writing fiction whatever I might intend. And inscribing 'A True Account' on the title page may make no difference. A sensational account of one's abduction by aliens which exploits all the familiar devices of science fiction and is placed next to Arthur C. Clarke in bookshops is likely to be taken as fiction, even if one wrote the novel in a spaceship speeding towards another galaxy.

Conversely, I may intend my account to be fictional only to see it universally taken as factual. It is not simply authorial intention that determines readerly uptake. Just as a 'fictionalising' reading can override an author's intention to produce non-fiction, so a reader may take a work intended as fiction as non-fictional. There is the case of the eighteenth-century bishop who threw *Gulliver's Travels* into the fire exclaiming indignantly that he didn't believe a word of it. The bishop was dismissing as fictional a text he believed was intended to be true but was in fact fiction. Stein Haugom Olsen is right to see that authorial intentions are themselves institutionally determined, which is true of a lot more than fiction.[29] A small girl cannot intend to become a brain surgeon if she lives in a society where the idea of girls becoming anything but housemaids is literally inconceivable. The objects of our desire, regret, shame, daydreaming and so on are set for us by our forms of social existence.

One might claim that taking a fictional text as factual does not alter the fact that it is fictional, since that is how the author conceived of it. The same goes for taking a factual text as fictional. But though the author of St John's Gospel no doubt intended his work to be true, many people today would rank it as fiction. And these people would presumably argue that their judgement on the issue trumps the author's. A writer knows, most of the time anyway, whether what he is writing is true or invented, but this settles the question of whether it is fiction or non-fiction only in the most technical of senses. Those who appeal to authorial intention here are generally afflicted by too narrow a notion of fictionality. We may choose to take an author's word as to whether his work is true; but even if he declares that it is, he can hardly dictate that we should not use it as an occasion for make-believe, or find some exemplary significance in it, or treat it non-pragmatically, all of which are aspects of what we call fiction. Neither can he prevent us from paying primary attention to its language, narrative structure and the like, treating its content in terms of its form, or ignoring the former altogether for the sake of the latter.

In this sense, to determine the work's fictional or non-fictional status by an appeal to its author's intention is drastically to over-simplify the meaning of fictionality. In any case, an original intention may be ousted over the course of time. I may have intended my pathetically incompetent sketch to represent an elephant, but it looks so much like the Duke of Edinburgh in a pair of fishnet stockings that everyone now refers to it as such, including myself. Frank McCourt did not intend *Angela's Ashes* to be a novel, but after millions of readers have treated it as just that, it seems both perverse and pedantic to withhold the title of fiction from it. This does not mean that what it records did not really happen. The work is fiction and memoir at the same time.

Olsen comments that 'it requires no great acumen to recognise that "fiction" and "literature" are different concepts', but this is because literature for him is a value term, and some fiction (popular genres, for example) is not to be invested with such merit.[30] He holds that all literature is fiction, but not vice versa. It is true that not all fiction is literature if one includes, say, jokes in the category of fiction. It is more contentious, however, to hold that not all fiction is literature because one should not include popular novels in the class. Neither is it the case that all literature is fiction, as we have just noted. One commentator notes that it is widely held that 'fictionality is a necessary (though not sufficient) feature of the definition of literature',[31] but in fact, like the other 'family resemblance' features we have examined, it is neither.

Culler thinks that fiction consists in 'telling stories',[32] but non-narrative literary forms such as lyric or elegy are fictional, too, not least in the sense that they provide material for make-believe. Joseph Margolis considers that nobody could correctly call Shakespeare's sonnets or Keats's odes fiction, but it is hard to see why not.[33] Fiction is an ontological category, not in the first place a literary genre. A passionately sincere lyric poem is as fictional as *Lolita*. Fiction is a question of how texts behave, and of how we treat them, not primarily of genre, and certainly not (as we shall see in a moment) of whether they are true or false. There is no good reason either to restrict the term to prose narrative, as some theorists do. Only in the nineteenth century did fiction become more or less synonymous with the novel. To confine the term to prose narrative simply means that you are likely to overlook some relevant aspects of poetry and drama, as well as some significant affinities between these forms. Fredric Jameson even proposes substituting the term 'narrative' for 'fiction', which it is hard to see as helpful.[34] It overlooks the existence of non-fictional narratives, as well as non-narrative fictions.

Bennison Gray, taking as usual the plain person's view, informs us that 'a fiction is a statement that refers to a made-up event, an event that has been invented or feigned rather than having actually happened'.[35] But the distinction between fact and fiction is by no means as stable as this suggests, and tends to blur as one moves back in time. Cicero considered that the historian must also be an artist, while Quintilian regarded historiography as a species of poetry in prose. Isocrates and some of his Ancient Greek colleagues viewed the writing of history as a branch of rhetoric. In ancient times, historiography could involve myth, legend, patriotic fervour, moral edification, political justification and a rare vein of stylistic virtuosity (Sallust, Livy, Tacitus). It was rarely just a question of the facts.

Most philosophers of fiction nowadays take the view, one at least as old as Sir Philip Sidney, that fictional propositions are neither true nor false because they are not meant to be genuine assertions in the first place. Like Kant's aesthetic judgements, or a good many ideological statements, they have the form of genuine reports on the world, but this is deceptive. The truth is that they function rhetorically, registering values and attitudes in the guise of describing the way things are. It is not, of course, that non-fiction is always assertoric whereas fiction never is. Fictional works quite often come up with genuine propositions, such as the fact that there was a world war raging in the 1940s, while non-fictional texts like security notices may be composed of warnings or commands. Examination papers are made up of non-assertoric speech acts known as questions. Only a small part of our everyday speech consists in describing the way things are. Jokes may make use of true statements while putting their truth-value temporarily in suspense. The status of statements may change as they shift from 'language' to 'discourse' – from general propositions about the world to features of specific utterances or acts of communication. A statement in a novel which might be seen as neither true nor false (because not intended as an assertion) may become true or false when spoken in a pub. Or an assertion may be untrue now but may become true later on. Eric Hobsbawm points out that what the

Communist Manifesto of 1848 has to say of the global reach of the middle classes was not true at the time, but has become true in our own day. The document characterises our own epoch better than it does its own.[36]

In any case, laying aside the question of a work's truth-value will not spontaneously convert it into fiction. You might simply not care whether an advertisement's claims are true, which is not necessarily to say that you treat it as fictional. You may not use it as an occasion for make-believe, or in any of the other ways we can 'fictionalise' a text. Conversely, you do not need to ignore the truth or falsehood of fictional statements, even if the term 'novel' on the title page invites you to do so. You can still note how grotesquely inaccurate the author's account of the manufacture of malt whisky is. And this, as we shall see later, can occasionally undermine the fictional effect. You can also value a text highly because its world-view strikes you as profoundly true, however much you are aware that the empirical statements which go to make up that view are either false, dubious or irrelevant to questions of truth and false-hood.

Nelson Goodman, unusually among philosophers of art, main-tains that 'all fiction is literal, literary falsehood', however 'meta-phorically' true it might be.[37] Bertrand Russell held much the same opinion. Gregory Currie is similarly at one with Plato in insisting that fictional works are typically false. He takes this view because he holds that truth and falsehood are a question of meaning rather than force, so that the non-assertoric force of a fictional text cannot dispense fictional statements from such judgements.[38] He also thinks that we 'dispositionally, rather than occurrently, disbelieve the propositions of a fiction',[39] meaning that we do not have their falseness vividly in mind while reading, but would no doubt declare that we disbelieved them were we to be asked. This, like Coleridge's 'suspension of disbelief', suggests the liminal nature of the act of reading fiction, caught as it is somewhere between arti-fice and reality. We shall see a similar ambivalence later, in the idea that it is possible to do a thing and pretend to do it at the same time. The fact that small children can slip so easily in and out of games of make-believe suggests something of the hair-thin frontier between fact and fantasy. This is scarcely surprising, given that for psychoanalytic thought a good deal of what we call reality is fantasy in the first place.

A work might be true in its every word but nevertheless fictional. Currie accepts this claim, but only in the rather toothless sense that a historical novel might fill in the gaps in the historical record with inventions that later turn out to be true. Fiction in his view can only ever be 'accidentally' true, in the sense that a made-up narrative might happen to coincide with a real course of events unknown to the author. As Currie observes, the *National Enquirer* ran a story not long ago reporting that Michael Jackson had only six weeks to live, which turned out to be almost exactly true. Even if readers do not believe what the *Enquirer* says is true, as many of them surely do not, they read it among other things because they like to make-believe that it is.

There are, however, more subtle senses in which a text can be factual and fictional at the same time. Shelley speaks in a memorable phrase in *A Defence of Poetry* of 'imagining that which we know'. To make-believe something you know to be true does not differ substantially from making-believe something you are aware is false. A writer may 'fictionalise' a factually true account, casting it in dramatic form, fashioning memorable characters, shaping it into an absorbing narrative and organising its features so as to highlight certain moral themes and general motifs. Norman Mailer's *The Executioner's Song* may serve as an example. So might *Angela's Ashes*. You might then read the book not for the sake of the empirical truth or falsehood of its account but precisely for these 'literary' qualities.

You may also take up a fictional stance to a work which is meant to be purely factual or pragmatic. It is possible to treat a pragmatic work non-pragmatically, 'refunctioning' it by (for example) searching it for some exemplary significance and thus detaching it from its intended function. You can read a non-pragmatic work pragmatically too, as when historians raid *Macbeth* for information about early seventeenth-century concepts of witchcraft. Peter McCormick thinks that works which invite a fictional reading are always marked as such, but you can read Mill's *Autobiography* or even *On the Origin of Species* fictionally even though the work clearly does not anticipate such a treatment.[40] In any case, as Mary Louise Pratt points out, 'nonfictional narrative accounts are world-creating in the same sense as are works of literature, and say, accounts of dreams'.[41]

Works can move in the course of time from fictional to non-fictional status, or vice versa. The Bible for most of the Western intelligentsia has moved from history to fiction. Or a text may be treated as fiction in one culture but not in another.[42] In any case, every work of fiction, as J.O. Urmson reminds us, comes with a whole hinterland of presuppositions that are actually true.[43] Richard Gale believes rather quaintly that you cannot have fiction if the major characters of a work are drawn from real life.[44] John Searle thinks that some bits of fiction genuinely refer while other bits only pretend to, and that the bits that really do refer must do so accurately. One must stick to the historical truth, for example, while writing about historical figures.[45]

This overlooks two points. First, fictional statements that do in some sense refer, such as those that proclaim that gobbling down whole stacks of cardboard will make you sick, do so within a context which 'fictionalises' them. I mean by this that it mobilises them as features within an overall rhetoric or way of looking. And this way of looking is often not itself subject to judgements of truth and falsehood, though we shall be qualifying this claim later on. There are plenty of factually true statements in almost all works of fiction, not least realist ones, but it is how they function strategically or rhetorically that counts, not their epistemological status. A statement, as Gale usefully puts it, 'can be true or false even if we do not care to ascribe any truth-value to it', rather as what someone says may be verifiable even though we might not bother to verify it.[46] This does not necessarily entail that we lose sight of the truth-value of such referential statements, simply that we inscribe those statements in a different context; and to do so is part of what we mean by fiction.[47]

Searle, to return to him, imagines in puritanical spirit that historical fiction must be loyal to the truth of the past, and thus fails to see that historical novels that take liberties with the facts may be in some sense truer than those that do not. Among other things, the point of fictionalising history is to reconfigure the facts in order to throw into relief what you take to be their underlying significance. This need not smack of a Stalinist ploy. It means that if you are writing a historical novel about Florence Nightingale, you might highlight just what a quintessentially Victorian figure she was by judiciously suppressing the fact that she survived well into the twentieth century. Instead, you might arrange a more symbolically satisfying death for her, perhaps in the arms of a young soldier she has just nursed back to life. Not long ago, an Egyptian government newspaper doctored a photograph of world leaders involved in the Middle East peace process by placing the Egyptian President in front of his US counterpart, on the grounds that the Egyptian leader had done more to advance the peace process than the American one. This is to allow moral truth sway over empirical truth, and is thus a classically fictionalising move, even if it was actually just a cynical piece of Orwellian manipulation.

Alasdair MacIntyre has suggested that you might improve a narrative by making it less true, or true in some different sense.[48] Works of fiction may be true to reality by being inventively false to it. History does not always get things in the right order, and can commit some unpardonable blunders. It passes up on the chance of some arresting symmetries and gratifying coincidences, kills off characters just as they are becoming interesting, trails off too often into bathos and farce, lavishes good fortune on the vicious, overloads the main narrative with a number of tedious subplots and allows some trifling accident to distract us from a crucial moment of truth. It is also a familiar fact that truth can not only be stranger than fiction but more fictional than it. No novelist concerned for his or her reputation would have had Henry Kissinger awarded the Nobel Peace Prize. There is a good deal in history that stretches one's credulity.

One reason why the category of fiction arose in the first place was to distinguish a form of imaginative writing that was becoming increasingly realistic from factual reports. You do not need the distinction as long as literary works are blatantly non-factual. Only unusually dim-witted readers need the word 'Fiction' appended to *Sir Gawain and the Green Knight* or the *Batman* comic. Initially, then, fiction was tacitly defined in relation to non-fiction, in a context in which the difference was becoming problematic. The instability of the distinction has lived on down the ages, as is evident from a number of critical muddles. Christopher New thinks that 'a work in which the number of nonfictional statements vastly outweighed the number of fictional ones would not qualify as a work of fiction',[49] but one wonders why not. A reader might still put aside the truth-value of the non-fictional utterances, or might still 'fictionalise' the whole work, fictional and non-fictional statements together, in the sense of assigning it some exemplary import, or using it as an occasion for make-believe. It is also possible for literary works to be fictional in one sense but not in another. A sermon or piece of political propaganda may want to be taken as true, unlike 'Gerontion' or *Le Père Goriot*; but they may also be fictional in the sense of inviting the reader to submit them to an act of make-believe or to a free play of imagination. A reader might hold both operations together in her mind. A realist novel which allows us to grasp characters in the round, snapping them so to speak from a number of angles simultaneously, can make such figures seem more real, in the sense of more intensely present and fully accessible, than a good many of the individuals who flit in and out of one's actual life. Iris Murdoch once remarked that we all live in the interstices of each other's lives, but this can cease to be the case in some kinds of fiction.

A reader might register the genuine cognitive force of certain propositions while using them as props in a game of make-believe. 'Imagining something,' writes Kendall Walton, 'is entirely compatible with knowing it to be true.'[50] Tolstoy tells us that Napoleon invaded Russia, and so he did; but by virtue of being called a novel, *War and Peace* also invites us to make-believe the fact, incorporate it into a fictional world. A couple in Jim Crace's novel *All That Follows* 'imagine making love while they are doing it'. Larry David was the creator of *Seinfeld* in real life and is also its creator in the television series *Curb Your Enthusiasm*. Oscar Wilde played himself far more skilfully than any subsequent actor. Reality can be the subject of fantasy, and a fantasy remains fiction even when it happens to correspond to a real set of events. Jean-Jacques Rousseau was both a paranoiac who really was persecuted and a hypochondriac who was always ill.

So something can be factual and fictional at the same time. To borrow one or two examples from Walton, someone can daydream that she enjoys warm climates and actually does. The Mississippi runs alongside Missouri in *Tom Sawyer* and really does. A child shouts 'Stop, thief!' in a fiction (a game) and also actually utters the words, so that it is both real and fictional that he does so. 'Fact can be fiction and fiction fact,' Walton claims, meaning that you can treat a fact fictionally, incorporating it into a game of make-believe, with the consequence that a fictional narrative can be composed entirely of empirical truths.[51] One might add that statements which are not literally true can become true in a different sense when transposed into a different verbal register. 'Workers of the world, unite! You have nothing to lose but your chains' is not literally true, since workers risk losing a great deal if they rebel against the state, not least, on occasion, their lives. Once the statement crops up in a political manifesto, however, the rules of that literary genre make it true in a different sense by converting it into a piece of rhetorical exhortation. It is now 'true' in the sense of helping to enforce a moral truth, namely that working people will achieve justice only by uniting and rebelling.

Let us return for a moment to the question of acts that are both factual and fictional. Imagine (to offer an example of my own, rather than one stolen from Walton) that you are rehearsing a drama and need someone to play the part of the archduke. By an extraordinary stroke of good fortune, a real archduke comes tottering along and blunders absent-mindedly into the rehearsal room. You hijack him instantly for the role. The dramatic illusion he creates is all the more convincing because he knows just how real archdukes behave. Reality has been pressed into the service of fantasy without ceasing to be itself. The same might apply to punching someone in a play. If you happen to harbour an intense aversion to your fellow actor, you may punch him as viciously as you like without stepping outside the fictional frame. Or you may have to sneeze in a play, find yourself sneezing for real and pass this off as part of the performance. You are thus sneezing both fiction-ally and for real. I might play a game in which the Queen of England is a North Korean spy, but also believe that she actually is. It may also be true that she is. There is a film called *Tropic Thunder* in which a group of Western actors making a movie in a far-flung country are pretending for the sake of the film to be at war with the local people, without realising that the local people actually are at war with them and are attacking them for real. But of course they are not, since all this is taking place in a movie.

Make-believe is not, of course, confined to fiction, and thus cannot be a sufficient definition of it. Even so, one of the several virtues of Walton's use of the concept is that it does not turn on some subjective fantasy. Make-believe in his sense is not primarily a state of mind but a social practice, conducted according to a determinate set of rules and conventions. In a game of make-believe, X (a teddy bear, let us say) stands for Y (daddy) and not for something else (though multiple meaning is always possible as well). What one is to imagine in such a game, and how one is to imagine it, is in this sense prescribed, not simply a matter of whim. This, then, is an agreeably non-Romantic conception of the imagination, which is supposed to brook no such prescription.

Joseph Margolis claims that 'one cannot pretend that a proposition is true when it is, and is known to be true'.[52] Gregory Currie writes in similar vein that 'you cannot do something and pretend to do it at the same time'.[53] But on certain meanings of pretence, if not perhaps on others, this is surely doubtful. Jean-Paul Sartre's waiter-playing-at-being-a-waiter in *Being and Nothingness* is a celebrated case in point. It is possible to play-act or perform what you actually are, as with those annoyingly bluff, forthright types who play self-indulgently to such an image of themselves. A good deal of human behaviour is marked by this duality: doing something yet performing it at the same time. If we are actors, we are also our own appreciative or censorious audiences. If Plato banished the theatre from his ideal republic, it was partly because it involved stage actors being both themselves and someone else, which struck at the stability of identity essential for a well-ordered society. If a cobbler starts to imagine not being a cobbler, politically corrosive consequences may follow.

This kind of doubled or divided consciousness belongs to the looseness of fit between ourselves and our surroundings. Being able to hold reality, including ourselves, at arm's length is part of the specifically human way we are bound up with the world. It is not a matter of standing outside it or floating above it. Our relation to the real is accordingly an ironic one. I really am furious, but at the same time I can see myself engaging in conventionally furious behaviour, conforming spontaneously to a certain script even though what I am feeling is entirely authentic. Observing the behaviour of dogs and rabbits, we have a sense that for better or for worse they do not share this ironic mode of consciousness.

Wittgenstein remarks that 'A dog cannot lie, but neither can he be sincere', to which we might add that he cannot live ironically. Neither can very small children, which is part of their charm. Some observers have reached this conclusion about whole nations. In this sense, at least, fictionality is part and parcel of reality. Fiction involves the reader in being both caught up in an illusion and sitting loose to it. It is thus a kind of irony, and as such writes large the nature of our everyday experience. We are dismayed by the death of Cordelia, even though, as Samuel Johnson observes, we never for a moment forget that we are in a theatre. Samuel Richardson writes in a letter of 'that kind of historical faith, which fiction is generally read [with], even tho' we know it to be fiction'.[54]

If, like Kendall Walton, you think of pretence as make-believe,[55] then it is clear that pretence and reality need not be at odds. Imagine a singer miming to the sound of her own voice who finds she can make the mime more convincing if she sings for real. She is still pretending to sing, in the sense of fitting her mouth movements to the sounds on the track, but she is also actually singing. I may drive my car while making believe that I am a famous racing driver like Michael Schumacher. But I may also actually be Michael Schumacher, driving his car while fantasising about the fact, narcissistically relishing images of his own celebrity. Or I may be struggling to wake up but also pretending that I am, in the sense of putting on a show of doing so. An old song entitled 'Only Make Believe' contains the lines 'Might as well make believe I love you,/ For to tell the truth, I do'.

One of the most astonishing cultural events of the twentieth century took place in November 1920 in Petrograd, when tens of thousands of workers, soldiers, students and artists re-enacted the storming of the Winter Palace. The performance, coordinated by both army officers and avant-garde artists, lasted for several days, using real guns and a real battleship. Many of the soldiers and sailors involved in this theatrical fiction had not only participated in the events they were commemorating, but were actively engaged at the time in the civil war in Russia. Revolutions, as Marx is aware in the *18th Brumaire of Louis Bonaparte,* seem to involve a curious crossing of fact and fiction, Something of the same is true of the Easter Rising in Ireland in 1916, as I have pointed out elsewhere.[56]

J. L. Austin offers as an example of pretending while doing something for real a party guest who behaves in an extravagantly 'vulgar' way simply to amuse himself, only to discover that even pretending to be vulgar is taken in this genteel setting as bona fide crassness.[57] It is the sign of a true gentleman that he is incapable even of mimicking vulgar behaviour. More dubiously, perhaps, Austin asks us to imagine two criminals engaged in an act of felony who seek to distract attention from what they are up to by sawing down a tree. They really are sawing away at the tree, but this, even so, is a show or pretence to deceive others. To saw away for real is to improve on the pretence. Pretending is not necessarily doing something without really feeling it. It might improve a show of sorrow if you can manage to work up a spot of genuine anguish. In any case, to pretend is not necessarily to appear sad without actually feeling sad. Plenty of people, by some quirk of temperament or physiognomy, look as though they are glum while feeling perfectly cheerful. What makes the difference between behaving respectfully at a funeral and merely appearing to is not always a matter of feeling. You can behave respectfully without feeling anything in particular.

Is it possible, Austin asks in world-shattering style, to pretend to cough? You can pretend to cough without actually coughing, as when you put a fist to your mouth and soundlessly heave your shoulders to deceive someone out of earshot. But you can make a coughing sound and still be feigning a cough. Does this mean making the sound deliberately, as opposed to being spontaneously seized by a rib-wrenching spasm? Not necessarily. Someone may cough deliberately just to clear his throat, whereas feigning is a social practice and a matter of context. ('Feigning' and fiction' have the same etymological root.) There must be someone you are trying to deceive, or to make a point to. Some Americans have taken to fake coughing when they encounter a smoker, in order to register their moral disapproval. Austin on coughing is a particularly blood-curdling instance of donnish whimsy. There have been more important issues in the history of philosophy. It would be hard to imagine Hegel or Heidegger wasting much sleep over the question. But it can cast useful light, for all that, on questions of fiction, reality, mimesis, performance, intention, experience and the like. It is no wonder that Jacques Derrida had a soft spot for Austin, in whose jokes, mischievous teasings, mock-solemnities and transgressions of scholarly decorum he no doubt glimpsed an Anglo-Saxon version of his own more Gallic style of anti-philosophy.

Stanley Cavell maintains that for Wittgenstein the difference between pretending and doing something for real is non-criterial.[58] He means by this that someone who is pretending to be lovesick is not someone who is trying but failing to satisfy the criteria for genuine lovesickness. Criteria tell us what something is, not whether any particular specimen of it is the genuine article. The criteria which determine what counts as being lovesick can be satisfied in cases where someone is merely making a plausible show of it.[59] This is why we can say that what she is pretending to be is lovesick, rather than in love, pain or despair. She fulfils all the usual criteria of lovesick behaviour. The concept of lovesickness, and the customary ways we apply it, come into play here just as much as they do in real cases of the condition. Grasping the concept of something is independent of whether it actually exists, and will not tell us whether it does or not. Someone can teach me what impatience is just as much by feigning impatience as by treating me to a sample of the real thing. I might get to know much more about sexual jealousy by reading Proust or *Othello* than I would in real life, and a lot more painlessly as well.

It would seem hard to pretend and not know it. But a Catholic nationalist in Belfast, cornered by loyalist paramilitaries during the

Troubles, might unwittingly slip into an English accent. There may be no sharp distinction between pretence and reality. To pretend, after all, is to do something for real.

Pretending to pretend is also possible. I may be seized by a genuine fit of coughing but suggest that I am only play-acting by theatrically clutching my throat. Or think of how, by making a ludicrously exaggerated show of being emotionally wounded, I may conceal the fact that I am actually cut to the quick. There is a sense in which a novelist is pretending to pretend, since he is supposed to convince us that certain fictional events actually took place, while knowing that we disbelieve that they did. Rather as an exaggerated show of hurt feelings is a pretence that deliberately gives itself away as one, so a literary work can signal the unreality of pretending that the story it records actually happened by the evident implausibility of its events, or by the highly wrought, hyperbolic nature of its language.

A.P. Martinich and Avrum Stroll maintain that a story beginning 'Once upon a time' would not be fictional if it went on 'in a big white house, a President of the United States named Bill Clinton was impeached for acting like an adolescent when he was half a century old'.[60] But the fact that we know this to be more or less true does not necessarily prevent us from treating it as fiction. We have already seen that when reading fiction, we regularly make-believe what we know to be true. The phrase 'Once upon a time' is a conventional generic marker which cues the reader not to worry too much over questions such as 'Did this actually happen?' It is designed to push the action back into a fabular, quasi-legendary domain so remote from the present that its truth or falsehood might not even be ascertainable, much less relevant to our reading.

Kendall Walton, in the most original and adventurous work on the theory of fiction to have appeared for many a decade, observes of a reader grieving over a pitiable historical figure portrayed in fiction that he or she may be grieving both 'fictionally' and for real.[61] 'What [a reader] actually knows to be fictional,' he comments, 'does not . . . affect what it is fictional that she knows to be true.'[62] He means that a reader may know that mermaids do not exist, but accepts the fact that it is true of a particular story that they do. Dickens's *A Tale of Two Cities*, Walton maintains, makes it fictional of Paris that it exists, in the sense that the reader is expected by the fiction to believe that Paris is a real city. One might also have a story in which it is fictional of the Scots that they are cunningly wrought automata. A statement may be true of a real person or place but also fictional, or it may be false but non-fictional. The name 'London' in a novel is fictional in the sense that the real city enters the text only under certain relevant aspects, edited, organised and 'focalised' (in Gérard Genette's term) in specific ways.

So it is not quite a case, as Marianne Moore remarks of poetry, of 'imaginary gardens with real toads in them'. It is more complicated than that. John Searle holds that fiction contains both true and false statements, and that an author can make 'serious' assertions in the course of writing fiction.[63] But he bypasses the problem of how to identify such assertions. A good many theorists regard the opening sentence of *Anna Karenina*, which declares that all happy families are happy in the same way, but that unhappy families are unhappy in their own distinctive ways, as a genuine assertion on the author's part. But how do we know? Literary artworks certainly make statements in the name of their narrators which the author himself does not credit. Even if Tolstoy did believe what he wrote, he may not have been intending to assert it as a truth. He may simply have been shaping a sentiment that pulled a certain weight in the moral and aesthetic economy of the novel. Or he may have believed it when he wrote it, but not ten minutes later. He may not have asked himself whether he believed it or not, or may have been genuinely agnostic about the fact. It is not at all uncommon not to know whether you believe something or not. Philosophers often tend to assume that beliefs are more clear-cut than they generally are.

Alternatively, Tolstoy may have believed that he believed the statement, but was in fact self-deceived. Or he may have granted the remark some provisional credence while reserving ultimate judgement. The reader, likewise, may have precious little idea whether she believes this claim or not, or whether she is meant to believe it, or whether it is to be treated on the same level as the opinions of the novel's characters. Or she may sign on for this view herself without necessarily believing that Tolstoy does, or that it matters whether he does or not.[64] As Nicolas Wolterstorff puts it, 'It is not necessary to a work of fiction that the states of affairs indicated be false, nor that the author believes them to be false. He may in fact believe them all to be true, and they may all *be* true. What makes him a fictioneer none the less is that he nothing affirmeth but something presenteth.'[65] An author of fiction in Wolterstorff's eyes is not pretending but presenting – offering something for our consideration rather than in the first place for the sake of its truth-value. Peter Lamarque rightly reminds us that this move is not peculiar to fiction.[66] I shall be suggesting some qualifications to this view in a moment.

An author may come out from behind his narrative persona and speak for a moment *in propria persona*. Thomas Mann does this rather poignantly towards the end of *Doctor Faustus*. But how are we to know that this is not simply another move in the fictional game, even if he insists that he is now addressing his readers directly and sincerely? How are we to be sure that breaking the rules of the game is not a rule of the game? Is Shakespeare being sincere when he appears to tell us in *Lear* that 'ripeness is all'? And how would we know? Such statements, after all, sometimes reflect the thoughts of an unreliable character or narrator. How much of Polonius's sententious advice to his son is mature Shakespearian wisdom, how much is bogus and how much lies somewhere in between? And how far did Shakespeare himself know the answer?

Moral discourse of this sort may or may not express authorial opinions, but this is not its main point. Its point is to be 'fictionalised', treated as an element in an overall design rather than abstracted from its context for isolated judgement. We may in fact find Polonius's counsel both true and useful, and this may enrich our response to the passage in question. Finding a work's moral outlook true and profound may deepen our response to it. But even if we do find it true and profound, we do so in terms of the way in which that way of seeing is formally constituted. And this is different from the way we might find Polonius's sentiments true and useful if we encountered them on a calendar.

'The vivacity of the reader's imaginings,' Walton writes, 'may be enhanced by the knowledge that what he imagines is true.'[67] The fact that we know Bucharest can be a dangerous city to stroll around may lend substance to our act of make-believe when we encounter this fact in fictional form. Imagination and reality can be in cahoots, not at daggers drawn. This may be true of the moral dimension of a work as well as its empirical one. According to speech-act theory, the most typical sort of fictional propositions can be neither verified nor falsified because they are really pseudo-propositions, such as 'Lok was running as fast as he could', which in the view of this theory only appears to make an assertion. Moral outlooks, however, can sometimes be judged to be true or false, at least if one is a moral realist. I say 'sometimes' because it is neither true nor false for a literary work to mourn the passing of time or hope for a brighter future. On the other hand, a novel might implicitly hold the view that some people are morally repulsive, which is undeniably true. If, however, it seemed to consider that this was the only truth about humanity worth noting, it might well be upbraided for its skewed moral vision. We might feel as certain that this was not true as we are sure that the weather in Montreal can be bitterly cold, or that Kerry is a more beautiful Irish county than Louth. W.G. Sebald is one of the most stunningly accomplished of all modern English-language writers, and as such the subject of remarkably little negative criticism; but one might wonder even so whether his unremittingly bleak portrayal of modern history is not seriously one-sided.

If that criticism is true, then it follows that we can still admire a piece of literary art even if we regard its overall vision as morally defective, an attitude which would have struck Samuel Johnson as somewhat disreputable. Johnson could not have enjoyed a piece of literature about which he had grave moral reservations. He could not have found a work aesthetically alluring yet morally objectionable. The contrast with the modern age is clear. Not many of those who rank Samuel Beckett as an artist of genius would subscribe to his glum estimate of human existence, and some might even regard it as morally debilitating. Yet few of these people are likely to be plagued by this conflict of opinions. If they found the Beckettian world-view really offensive, however, they might find themselves in the shoes of a Johnson and be unable to enjoy his work. During the first London production of *Waiting for Godot*, an outraged member of the audience shouted 'This is the kind of thing that lost us the Empire!'

So there are limits to this latitude. Lamarque and Olsen hold that the truth or falsehood of a literary work's moral vision does not enter into an appreciation of its quality, which I have just suggested is not always the case.[68] Literary works of art that advocate repugnant moral acts such as genocide are unlikely to redeem themselves by their formal splendour. A work may be all the more rhetorically effective because its moral values are sound – a point also overlooked by Monroe Beardsley, for whom literary value is entirely independent of the truth or falsehood of a work's ideas.[69] There are times when nothing convinces like the truth.

In the same way, we tend to allow an author a lot of rope empirically as well as morally, but not absolutely so. It might be claimed that literature is a place where it is well-nigh impossible either to lie or make a mistake. Because a literary work carries the implicit instruction 'Treat everything here as intended', an author's factual errors will tend to be interpreted as deliberate, and thus as integral to the text. Consistently misspelling the name 'Frankenstein', as W.B. Yeats would almost certainly have done had he ever used it,

will probably be taken to have some portentous symbolic significance. Even so, there can be self-evident errors. Not long ago, a
family in England mourning a murdered child erected a tombstone
to him carved with the words 'Not a day goes by /That we sit and
cry', which is presumably not what they meant. If you commit what
Arnold Isenberg calls a 'sensational' error,[70] your work may suffer
artistically for it. As it gradually dawns on the reader that the
author really does think that Spiderman is a real person, the
credibility of his novel is likely to take a knock.

2

One of the most pioneering accounts of fictionality in the philosophy of literature has been so-called speech-act theory. A vastly
influential early statement of the case is to be found in a classic
essay by Richard Ohmann.[71] On this theory, works of literary art
are 'not a particular kind of language but a particular kind of utterance'.[72] They are imitations of real-life speech acts, not least the
speech act of storytelling; but by violating the usual conditions of
a valid speech act, they imitate such utterances in a 'non-felicitous'
kind of way.[73] We do not ask a writer of fiction, for example,
whether she is in position to vouch for the truth of what she
reports, or whether she is being sincere, or is qualified to make
what assertions she does. Nor can the author know that readerly
'uptake' has been secured in any particular case, which J.L. Austin
regards as essential to the completion of an illocutionary act.

Fictional texts have often been seen as in some sense duplici-
tous. They are verbal illusions which pose as true accounts of the
world. Speech-act theory reformulates this duplicity in a suggestive
new way. What used to be thought of as a gap between language
and reality is now a difference between two uses of language. A
literary work is one that lacks the so-called illocutionary force that
would normally attach to the sentences of which it is made, and is
thus a deviant utterance. Like the Russian Formalists, speech-act

theorists deliver an essentially negative or aberrant account of literature, one which sees it as parasitic on so-called ordinary linguistic behaviour.

A reader, seeing the words 'novel' or 'short story', knows not to inquire whether the characters and events portrayed in the text actually exist, whether all the relevant information has been included, whether Hölderlin happened to be in sincere or truthful mood when he wrote *Hyperion* and so on. Instead, 'the writer pretends to report discourse and the reader pretends to accept the pretence'.[74] The rules governing genuine speech acts are suspended in the case of literature, though Ohmann acknowledges that this can be as true of jokes and other verbal forms as it is of Chekhov or Manzoni. It is not, then, a sufficient condition of the literary, and we shall see later that it is not a necessary one either.

For a particularly hard-nosed formulation of the theory we may turn to Gottlob Frege, who claims that 'assertions in fiction are not to be taken seriously, they are only mock assertions. Even the thoughts are not to be taken seriously, as in the sciences; they are only mock thoughts . . . The logician does not need to bother with mock thoughts, just as the physicist, who sets out to investigate thunder, will not pay any attention to stage thunder'.[75] Not many critics maintain that Milton's poignant lines in *Paradise Lost* about composing his verses while blind and encircled by his enemies are not to be taken seriously. We take them seriously even if we suspect that they are not factually true. They are not simply there to yield us aesthetic pleasure, even if they do that as well, and do so in a way inseparable from the plaintiveness and urgency of the thought itself. To call a statement a pseudo-proposition, if one feels that this is worth doing, is to characterise its epistemological status, not to dismiss it as hollow. So-called pseudo-propositions like 'The quality of mercy is not strain'd' have a lot more force than genuine propositions like 'This gerbil looks a bit off-colour'.

Just to endear himself to literary types even further, Frege remarks in the same classic essay, 'On Sense and Meaning', that 'the question of truth [when reading literature] would cause us to abandon aesthetic delight for an attitude of scientific investigation.[76] He is thus to be convicted of the scientistic prejudice that truth is synonymous with scientific truth. But there are other kinds of truth, as Frege himself was well aware, and other ways beside science of investigating them. You do not need a laboratory to establish whether Ophelia goes mad, or whether E.M. Forster's maxim 'It is more blessed to receive than to give' is slyly perceptive or merely glib. Jeremy Bentham writes in his essay 'The Rationale of Reward' that the purpose of art is to stimulate the passions, a project to which any hint of truth is fatal. He, too, thinks of truth simply as truth-to-fact. Even if we confine the term to that, however, it is not true that truth is the ruin of all passion. Bentham does not contemplate the possibility that nothing stimulates the passions like the truth.

There are relations between speech-act theory and what we have argued of literature so far. Consider, for example, the light it throws on what we have said of fictionality. From a speech act standpoint, literary works involve make-believe in the sense that readers must make-believe that certain conventions are operative while knowing they are not. Moreover, because a work's statements, being only imitations of genuine propositions, are not engaged in carrying on what Ohmann calls 'the world's business', they are non-pragmatic; and this induces us to bestow on them the kind of vigilant attention we would not generally grant to a circular informing us of changes to the times of garbage collection. It also invites us to generalise their significance in the way that such a circular generally does not, pondering their moral implications rather than treating them simply as an empirical report.

There are, then, complex relations between speech-act theory, fiction, make-believe, moral truth and the non-pragmatic. There is a relation, for example, between speech-act theory and the question of fictional truth. Literary speech acts belong to the larger class of verbal acts known as performatives, which do not describe the world but accomplish something in the act of saying. Greeting, cursing, begging, abusing, threatening, welcoming, promising and the like all fall into this category. To say you promise is to promise; to declare the new department store open is to open it. The meaning is incarnate in the act in the same way that the meaning is incarnate in a word. A work of fiction, likewise, consists of a set of realities which have no existence apart from in its act of enunciation. Or if they do, it is not all that important. Performatives are language at its most potently effective, but also at its most autonomous; and in this sense they have an interesting affinity with fiction. Fiction, too, accomplishes its ends simply in the act of saying. What is true in a novel is true simply by virtue of the discursive act itself. Yet it can have a palpable impact on reality.

Moreover, just as performative acts cannot be considered true or false since they are not assertions about the world, so fictional statements, being in speech-act theory merely mimes or parodies of such assertions, are not candidates for truth/falsehood judgements either. Sandy Petrey writes that 'truth and falsity are beside the point when we consider performative acts',[77] since such performatives – greeting, cursing, begging, denying and the like – are not propositional. Arthur C. Danto, rather similarly, sees a difference between 'sentences that miss the mark and those that have no mark to miss'.[78]

Yet reporting, depicting and describing are just as much performative acts as betting, denying or reviling. They, too, get something done. There is, in fact, no hard-and-fast line between the performative and what Austin calls the constative, meaning assertions about the world. In fact, Austin himself came to be aware of this, recognising that the difference between the two could depend on context. What may be constative in one situation may not be so in another. Moreover, constatives and performatives are interdependent not just in the sense that to make claims about how things are is itself a performative act, but because performatives tacitly involve accounts of how things are. If they can intervene in the world, changing the course of history by some momentous pledge or eleventh-hour warning, they must also submit themselves to the way the world is. Denouncing the government for planning to gas all senior citizens is pointless if it has now postponed the scheme as too messy and expensive. Promising you a purple-spotted lizard from the Isle of Man as a Christmas present is futile if there are no purple-spotted lizards on the Isle of Man, or for that matter anywhere else.

Part of what Austin came to see was that constatives have their appropriate conditions just as much as performatives. Propositions about the world can be as 'liable to infelicity' as performative acts, not just liable to falsehood.[79] Conversely, performatives like threatening or reviling can be felicitous only if their content is sound (is it an intelligible threat?), which involves an appeal to the facts. In the end, Austin allows the distinction between the two sorts of discourse to come apart in his hands. His book *How To Do Things With Words*, so Stanley Fish comments, is a 'self-consuming artifact'.[80] It is a *locus classicus* of deconstruction.[81] Very few statements we produce, Austin points out, are simply true or false. The literary critic Kenneth Burke, whom we shall encounter in the next chapter, calls the constative the 'scientistic' and the performative the 'dramatistic', but he, too, acknowledges that no absolute distinction can be drawn between them. Definitions are themselves a symbolic act, and all descriptive terminologies embody decisions, selections, exclusions, preferences and the like.[82]

That constatives and performatives can be hard to tell apart is clear from Jonathan Culler's claim that lying is not a performative like a promise but a statement of what is false, and so a constative.[83] But lies are not simply false statements. I may announce that Oliver Cromwell was a Zulu because I am genuinely convinced that he was, which does not amount to a lie. Nor does knowing one's statement to be false make the vital difference. It is not a lie to say 'My God, you're early!' when we both know you should have been here three months ago. Nor is it a lie to describe yourself in company as the reincarnation of Alexander the Great, since nobody would believe you intended the comment seriously. Lying is a matter of knowingly uttering a falsehood with the intention to deceive. And while this may not exactly be a performative in Austin's sense of the term, it certainly involves doing something. It is also possible, of course, to tell the truth in such a way as to suggest that what you say is false.

There is one fundamental sense in which constatives are dependent on performatives, as well as vice versa. We characterise, verify and falsify by deploying meanings, and meanings are bound up with a performance or social practice. This is the practice of assigning rule-governed meanings to things in the first place. And this practice underlies all our propositions about reality. P. F. Strawson reminds us that meaning or referring is not something that an expression does, but something that someone can use it to do.[84] In the beginning, then, was the performative. It is true that betting, blessing, baptising and so on are performatives which depend for their efficacy among other things on the veridical status of certain tacit claims about how it is with the world. There is no point in carrying on with the baptism if the baby beneath the expensive lacy shawl turns out to be a badger. In the end, however, these claims about the world are in turn dependent on what we do – on how we assign names and meanings, by what procedures we institute criteria of truth and falsehood in a specific form of social life, and so on. As Charles Altieri remarks, 'knowing how is logically prior to any specific claim that something is the case, for we must have mastered techniques before we can meaningfully point to objects and understand utterances'.[85] To say that signifiers are arbitrary is just to say that there is a level beneath which we cannot dig. There is no reason why a bottle should be called a bottle, or why one should measure in feet and inches, or why you can be caught and bowled in cricket. There is no need for one. To imagine that there is, to adopt a phrase of Richard Rorty's, is to scratch where it doesn't itch.

Speech-act theory gives a secular twist to an age-old tradition of viewing the human word as creative. The idea that we can affect the world purely by uttering a word is a staple element of magic. The priestly and powerful can get things done simply by breathing a sound. Shakespeare's *Richard II* broods on the limits and capacities of the kingly word, the times when it can create or undo reality as well as the times when it runs helplessly up against its brute recalcitrance. The idea can also be found in the Jewish Bible, where the Hebrew word *dabhar* can mean both word and deed. The idea of a sign that accomplishes what it signifies has the ancient theological name of sacrament. Sacraments are speech acts which achieve their ends simply by the act of saying: I baptise you, I confirm you, I ordain you, I grant you absolution from your sins, I marry you to this man, and so on. Like all performatives, they do what they proclaim, as both material acts and pieces of discourse. The sign and the reality are identical, as they are in the Catholic theology of the Eucharist. (In certain Protestant theologies, by contrast, the signs – the bread and wine – simply point to or commemorate the reality – the body of Christ.)

Sacraments are considered to work *ex opere operato*, meaning that they fulfil their ends simply by virtue of the actions they involve, not (for example) because of the sincerity or otherwise of the agents performing them. Those agents must be authorised ('ordained') to carry them out, but that is all. This is also true of fiction (though authors are self-authorising), where sincerity is no more to the point than insincerity. The sign is not dependent for its creative power on expressing the experience of a subject. If I promise to lend you fifty pounds, and as the words cross my lips have not the slightest intention of doing so, I have promised even so. To go through with a marriage ceremony and then exclaim with a horror-stricken countenance to the vicar that you didn't really mean to is probably not the most solid of grounds on which to secure a divorce, as well as not the best way to charm your newly acquired in-laws.

Conversely, buttonholing a total stranger on top of a bus and trying to marry her will not work from a performative viewpoint even if you are burningly sincere, feel yourself to be helplessly in love with her and enunciate all the correct phrases. This is because marriage, like sexuality as a whole, is not a private affair but a public (in the broad sense, political) institution in which the community as such has a stake; and to marry on top of a bus outside the usual context, and without a representative of the community being present, sets this fact aside. It turns marriage into a private pastime, thus helping to depoliticise it. There may well be civilisations in which the high streets are permanently jammed with buses on which people are marrying in droves. But this must be a conventional or institutional act, in the sense that, as with all social conventions and institutions, it must involve more people than myself and more considerations than my own personal wishes.

The doctrine of the creative word crops up again in Romanticism, as the poetic imagination brings whole new worlds into being. Kenneth Burke dreams of a purely creative act, original and gratuitous, beholden to nothing beyond itself, and as such an imitation of the divine act of creation.[86] Alain Badiou's notion of the 'event' has some family resemblance to this fantasy. These are secularised bits of theology, like so much that we know as aesthetics.

One could imagine a visitor from the planet Zog listening to our speech without grasping that it is supposed to do something. I mean 'do something' not in a narrowly practical sense, but in the broader sense of sharing a form of life. Perhaps he would hear human speech simply as a set of decorative sounds, like background music to our behaviour, without grasping that there were connections between what we said and what we did. Or perhaps he would imagine that language was some kind of ceremonial ritual, or just a way of keeping oneself awake. He might speculate that humans lapsed easily into states of torpor through sheer boredom or indolence, and that this continual spraying and blasting of noise at each other was intended to keep them on their mental toes.

In order to grasp the notion of verbal meaning, he would need to recognise that our utterances were purposive,[87] which is not the same as assuming that they are all commands or instructions or requests. Nor is it the same as imagining that they are all silently accompanied by some ghostly mental impulse known as an intention. The purposiveness is built into the shape of the discourse. You do not need to couple your words with an act of intending in order for them to have meaning, as E.D. Hirsch considers that poets and novelists need to do.[88] This would be rather like imagining that I perform an act of will every time I am about to do something. This may be true of getting myself out of bed, or out of the pub, but not of scratching my head or tapping you on the shoulder. A really brainy Zogian would probably be able to figure out that language is purposive by watching the way it interacted with our behaviour and arriving spontaneously at Wittgensteinian conclusions. A Zogian of genius might even work out for himself that certain bits of our discourse were intended to be non-functional in any very practical sense of the term – that such purposelessness was part of their purpose, and was part of what we meant by words like 'literary' and 'artistic'.

Fiction, then, like performatives as a whole, is an event inseparable from its act of utterance. It has no support from outside itself, in the sense that what it asserts cannot be checked off in any important way against some independent testimony. In this sense, it is more like swearing than reporting an armed robbery. Fiction manufactures the very objects to which it appears to refer. It covertly fashions what it purports to describe. It looks like a report, but is actually a piece of rhetoric. In Austinian jargon, it is a performative masquerading as a constative. As the German critic Karlheinz Stierle illuminatingly puts it, it is the auto-referential in referential form.[89] Its referent – a murder mystery, a political crisis, an adulterous affair – is purely internal, existing only in its own account of it. As Lamarque and Olsen put it, 'Fictive states of affairs owe their identity to their mode of presentation.[90] Fictional narratives project an apparent outside to themselves out of their own internal activities. Yet it is exactly this autonomous or self-referential quality that lends fiction its peculiar force. If it is 'creative', it is because it is by nature less constrained by the pressures of the real than a paper on the thyroid gland, and this applies just as much to spectacularly bad fiction as it does to the superbly good. 'Creative' here is thus more a descriptive than a normative term.

In this sense, all fiction is fundamentally about itself. Yet because it draws the materials for this self-fashioning from the world around it, the paradox of fiction is that it refers to reality in the act of referring to itself. Like Wittgenstein's forms of life, fictions are self-founding; but this is not to deny that they incorporate aspects of the world around them into their self-making, just as forms of life do. They could not be self-fashioning otherwise. Fredric Jameson remarks in *The Prison-House of Language* that for the Formalists and structuralists the literary work 'speaks only of its own coming into being, of its own construction',[91] but Terence Hawkes rightly adds that 'a work of fiction can only speak of its own coming into being against a background of speaking of something else'.[92]

There is a similar ambiguity at work in linguistic performatives like 'I swear' or 'I promise'. In one sense, these are purely self-referential phrases – autonomous verbal acts which do not denote a referent. In such a context, to adopt a phrase from Emile Benveniste, 'the word swears on itself, it itself becomes the fundamental fact'.[93] Yet such performative acts, as I have suggested already, can also be powerful interventions in the world, accomplishing momentous changes and producing tangible effects. It is through their peculiar force that fortunes are made, lifelong marriages contracted and pledges to serve the Führer sealed. By relating to themselves rather than reporting a state of affairs, performatives establish a productive relation to reality. And in this they have something of the paradoxical structure of fiction.

Pierre Macherey makes a similar point:

> The novelty of this [fictional] language derives from its self-constituting power. With nothing apparently before or behind it, untroubled by any alien presence, it is autonomous in so far as it is, in effect, lacking in depth, unfolded entirely on its own surface . . . [fiction is] language reduced to its thinness, devising a meaning within the narrow trajectory of its own development, opening a uniquely internal perspective; without an understudy, language repeats, reproduces, and prolongs itself, to the exclusion of everything else . . . the writer's work builds up its own horizon through the very labour that goes into producing it.[94]

Perhaps Macherey's Formalism has momentarily got the better of his Marxism here. Fictional discourse is indeed beholden to something outside itself, troubled by an alien presence, in the sense that the author of a realist narrative cannot place Times Square in Cairo. Where Macherey is right is that a writer is perfectly free to populate Times Square with whatever characters and events he chooses, and that how the place figures in his narrative will be determined by factors which are for the most part internal to the text.

Macherey does not mean to suggest that literary works of art stand magically aloof from the histories that give birth to them. On the contrary, they are the product of a great many historical factors: genre, language, history, ideology, semiotic codes, unconscious desires, institutional norms, everyday experience, literary modes of production, other literary works and the like. It is rather that these factors are combined in a way that allows the work to evolve according to its own internal logic. To call a piece of art self-determining is not to claim, absurdly, that it is free of determinations, but that it makes use of these determinations to fashion its own logic and give birth to itself. They provide the material for its self-making. The work of art does not simply reflect or reproduce the materials which go into its manufacture; instead, it actively reworks them, in the process of doing which it produces itself. Fiction is about the world by virtue of adhering to its own internal logic. Or – to change the terms round – it is about itself in a way that projects a world. Its inside and outside are reversible.

There is another sense in which literary works are self-consti- tuting. One of their features is that they are clearly snatches of 'discourse' rather than specimens of 'language', which is to say that they are language bound up with specific situations. In everyday life, such situations play a major role in how we make sense of signs. I can generally tell from the state of the traffic and the disposition of our two vehicles that when you flash your headlights you mean 'Go ahead!' rather than 'Watch it!', even though the action itself can conventionally mean either. The strangeness of literary works is not only that they lack such practical contexts, but that this absence helps to make them what they are. It is this that John Ellis seeks to capture with his notion of literature as contextually free-floating. Without a context, however, a work would risk being unintelligible, so its solution to this dilemma is to produce one for itself as it goes along. Each of a text's utterances is at once a verbal act in its own right and a contribution to the frame within which it is to be read. Rather as the work generates its own ideological subtext, as we shall see later, so it spins out of its own substance a good many of the terms of reference within which it can make sense. This is part of what we mean by a work's 'world'.

Comparisons between works of art and human beings are usually bogus. The literary work, *pace* Georges Poulet, is not a fellow subject with whom we can commune, but a set of marks on a page.[95] Even so, there is a parallel between the way in which fictional texts are self-determining and the way in which individ- uals are. Human freedom is not a question of being bereft of determinants but of making them one's own, turning them into the ground of one's self-constitution. This is one reason why art has sometimes been considered a paradigm of free activity. To act autonomously is not to dispense with laws but to be a law unto oneself, which is what the word 'autonomous' means. That there are crippling limits to any such project in real life is clear enough, which is doubtless one reason why art has been so idealised a phenomenon. Because it is less constricted by the real than we are, more radically self-constituting, it seems a peculiarly pure example of an autonomy which in our case can only ever be approximate.

In this aesthetic ideology, the work of art is a law unto itself in the sense that the principle which governs it springs purely from its own substance. It submits to no authority outside itself. Since every bit of the work is shaped by its general law or principle, with nothing contingent or extraneous, it forms a self-governing totality. Yet because this totality is simply the form taken by the relations of the work's various components to each other, these components can be said to submit to a law which they fashion themselves. And this, for republican thinkers like Rousseau and Kant, is what defines the ideal social order. Politically speaking, the work of art resembles a republic more than it does an authoritarian state, which is one reason why it can figure as a critique of the *ancien régimes* for the emergent middle classes of late eighteenth-century Europe. Republicanism means collective self-determination, which is also true of the cooperative commonwealth known as a work of art. As Friedrich Schlegel writes, 'poetry is republican speech: a speech which is its own law and end unto itself, one in which all the parts are free citizens and have the right to vote'.[96]

This, to be sure, is perfectly compatible with hierarchy, both in art and in life. Some features of the work of art are more dominant than others, just as some members of a republic are more powerful than others. To be a republican is not necessarily to be an egalitarian. We are not speaking here of socialist democracy. Charles Baudelaire denounces the kind of art in which the artist finds himself 'at the mercy of a riot of details, all clamouring for justice with the fury of a mob in love with absolute equality'.[97] It is just this kind of criticism, at once aesthetic and political, that will be aimed at Zola and his fellow naturalists. Yet the cooperative form of a poem or painting is entirely compatible with freedom, once freedom is understood positively as self-determination rather than negatively as freedom from constraint. Since each feature of the artefact works to enhance all the others, bringing them to their richest potential, the self-realisation of each (to adopt a phrase of Marx) is the condition for the self-realisation of all.

For this aesthetic, then, works of art correspond to reality less in their content than in their form. They incarnate the essence of human freedom not by pleading for national independence or promoting the struggle against slavery, but by virtue of the curious kind of entities they are. One should perhaps add that as images of self-determination, they reflect less the actual than the possible. They are exemplary of what men and women could be like under transformed political circumstances. If they point beyond themselves, what they point to is a redeemed future. In this view, all art is utopian.

There is a difference between a work of art being constrained by reality and reflecting that reality. A dancer is constrained by a whole set of factors – her body, the choreography, the material space in which she moves, her own artistic inventiveness and so on. But her dancing, rather than 'reflecting' these conditions, converts them into the stuff of her self-realisation. If she maintains a constant relation with the world, it is not for some practical end, as with labour or political activity, but for the sake of the internal, autonomous logic of her actions. Which is to say that dancing, unlike dish-washing, is a form of praxis whose goods are internal to it. Much the same can be said of a work of art.

To say that a work of fiction is self-fashioning, then, is not to suggest that it is unshackled. As we have argued already, it is restricted by the nature of its materials (not least if it is a realist work), just as it is by formal, generic and ideological factors. Yet art is a matter of internalising such constraints, incorporating them into its body, turning them into the stuff of its self-production and so restricting *itself*. There is a logic to its self-production, so that it is not free of a certain necessity. But it is a necessity which it creates itself as it goes along. If a realist novel decides to call its heroine Bridget on page 1, it cannot start calling her Gertrude on page 13 for no discernible reason, as a non-realist work might. This is a (supremely trivial) example of a text determining itself – creating its own necessity, conforming to its own self-constituting logic, being faithful to a law that it bestows on itself. That the heroine cannot be abruptly renamed is, of course, more than the author's decision. It is determined by generic conventions, and perhaps by ideological ones as well. A Victorian writer might feel it unchivalrous to take such liberties with his leading lady. But these conventions are not simply external limits on what texts can do. They are also raw material for its self-making.

Umberto Eco makes a similar point to Macherey's when he notes that 'semiosis explains itself; this continual circularity is the normal condition of signification and even allows communication to use signs in order to mention things'.[98] Just as he seems on the point of reducing language to a hermetically sealed system, Eco adds that this is precisely how it comes to communicate. It is by virtue of its circularity – the fact that one word refers us to another, and that to another – that semiosis opens itself up to the world. Eco can thus write in the same work, with no sense of incongruity, that 'semiotics is mainly concerned with signs as social forces'.[99] To complain that one never gets outside language would be like protesting that one can never break out of one's body. Bodies and languages are ways of being in the midst of things, rather than obstacles which shut us out from them. It is by being on the 'inside' of a body or language, not by over-leaping them as so many barriers, that we can encounter one another and intervene in what is misleadingly known as the outside world.

For speech-act theory, as we have seen, fiction represents a deviant sort of discourse, but one that is to that extent in (negative) relation to common speech. It is a non-pragmatic version of everyday acts. Yet because it brings a world of its own into existence, and does so by a self-referential act of language, it also has an autonomy which sets it apart from the quotidian. In this sense, speech-act theory captures in its own fashion a familiar ambivalence about fiction. It also pinpoints something of its freewheeling quality. If fictional speech acts are non-mimetic and non-pragmatic, then they have a potential playfulness about them. It is thus possible to bring together speech-act theory and the idea of the sportive, self-flaunting signifier, even if speech-act theorists themselves are generally silent on the subject of poetic language.[100] To do this is also to bring together an 'act' or communicative theory of the literary text with a view of it as a verbal object. We shall be looking at this convergence more closely in the next chapter.

Meanwhile, let us pursue the parallel between fiction and poetic language a little further. Monroe Beardsley points out that fiction and heightened language both help to set a discourse apart from the actual world – one, as he elegantly phrases it, 'by a deficiency of illocutionary force, the other by an excess of semantic display'.[101] We have seen that some critcs maintain that literary works are especially congenial to semantic ambiguity and richness of implication; and this claim has a bearing on the argument in hand. It is the slackness of the bond between sign and referent, as well as between fiction and the real world, that persuades us to see literary art as plural in meaning. In fact, some literary texts are less polyvalent than some non-literary ones. It is too simple to see the literary as the enemy of the univocal. Yet because fiction has no single direct referent against which it can be checked off, its meaning is likely to be more indeterminate and open-ended than a set of instructions for assembling a table lamp. In a similar way, the poetic sign is generally less constricted than the pragmatic one. Having less of a practical function to perform, it can revel in a surplus of meaning. It has more room to freewheel than a road sign.

There are other affinities between fiction and 'literary' language. In its circular nature, the structure of fiction bears a resemblance to the structure of the poetic sign, which broods similarly on its own being, denoting itself in the act of denoting something else. Indeed, the presence of such language in a text may be a microcosmic way of alerting us to its macrocosmic operations as a piece of fiction. Not all fiction is poetic. But when language signals to us like this, it may be alerting us to what questions not to ask, such as 'Did this really happen?' And this is also true when we see the words 'A Novel'.

For a critic like Paul de Man, the self-referential nature of literary language is where it is most faithful to reality, given that for this Nietzschean theorist the world itself is a linguistic construct.[102] Fiction reveals the truth of things, but not at all in the classical humanistic sense. Instead, it lets the ontological cat out of the bag, betraying the figurative nature of what we take to be unimpeachably real. In its awareness of itself as a set of tropes, its ability to know and name its own unavoidable mystification, literature represents the negative truth of everyday discourse. The modernist literary work, which puts its modes of signification candidly on show, gesturing ironically to its own inescapable artifice, thus represents the open secret of realist fiction, which dissembles its rhetorical nature in order to persuade us that we are in the presence of the real. Modernist fiction on this view is simply fiction as such writ large, its devices laid bare and its self-referential nature dragged centre-stage. If the nearest one can approach to authenticity in the late modern age is an ironic consciousness of one's own inescapable bad faith, then literature in de Man's world is the most authentic phenomenon of all.

If there is a kinship between fiction and the self-conscious sign, there is also one between fiction and morality. We have seen already that shaping a moral vision involves the kind of typifying, selecting and highlighting to which fiction is especially hospitable. It is one of the few places left in which the empirical is wholly under the sway of the moral. The real world is held at arm's length, transfigured, reorganised, granted an extraordinary degree of freedom and flexibility, so that certain moral truths about it may be more effectively brought to light. In fact, this may mean editing everyday reality as boldly as an avant-garde movie. Think, for example, of the idea of poetic justice, which constrains Henry Fielding to grant Tom Jones his reward when in reality he would probably have been hanged, or inspires Charlotte Brontë to plunge the hapless Bertha Mason off a blazing rooftop so that her heroine may be non-bigamously united with her now widowed lover.

Even the most lovingly particularised piece of fiction schematises the world, editing it according to the requirements of a way of seeing. I do not mean to suggest that the way of seeing comes first, and is then simply exemplified by the detail of the work. Nothing could be less true of the actual process of composition, not to speak of the event of reading. A novel in which every character and situation was set by a predetermined moral agenda (Samuel Johnson's *Rasselas* comes to mind) would not only have an implausible ring to it; it would also undermine the cogency of its own moral vision. Ironically, it is presence of contingency, not least in realist fiction, that makes a novel's outlook so convincing. It is as though, having sifted reality in its moral net, the work then conceals this fact by introducing a host of stray particulars. In this way, the non-necessary comes to the support of the necessary. The Lintons' residence in *Wuthering Heights* is called Thrushcross Grange, but the detail is quite arbitrary, as some other names in the novel are not. As those who have lectured on the work will be aware, the place could perfectly well have been called something slightly more pronounceable. A protagonist who is said to be five foot ten could probably have been six foot with little loss to the novel's purpose. It is in this way that a certain species of fiction produces what Roland Barthes calls the 'effect of the real'. Its carefully contrived arbitrariness gives it the rough-and-ready feel of everyday existence.

Speech acts do not only convey meaning, but are meaningful in themselves. We can speak of the meaning of an act of utterance, as well as the meaning of the utterance itself. 'Why is he telling me this?' I think to myself, as a total stranger buttonholes me at tedious length about the academic achievements of his various brats. As Denys Turner puts it, 'To say that human beings are "rational" is to say that human beings cannot help but that their grossest actions should speak, they cannot do anything meaninglessly. Hence, they cannot speak but that their action of speaking also says something.'[103] This kind of meaning, Turner considers, belongs to the domain of rhetoric. There is a sense in which people can indeed do meaningless things, such as tripping over a doorstep or absent-mindedly patting their hair. (I leave aside the question of unconscious meaning). But these are not acts in the sense that Turner has in mind. 'Saying something is never *merely* saying something,' as Stanley Cavell remarks.[104] So-called phatic speech acts, such as 'Well, here we are again, jawing away just like old times!', refer to the act of communication itself, so that the meaning of what is said is at one with the performance. In the case of realist fiction, by contrast, the meaning conveyed by the performance – 'this is a piece of fiction, not to be taken as true' – is at odds with the force of the individual statements.

Quentin Skinner claims that to understand the meaning of a text we need to grasp what the author was doing, and took herself as doing, in writing it, which is the equivalent of Austin's illocutionary force. In this sense at least, pragmatics takes precedence over semantics. What kind of *act* is this – ironic, polemical, satirical, informative, laudatory, apologetic or what? In Skinner's view, we cannot grasp the meaning of a piece of discourse from its words alone. Nor will putting the words in context automatically disclose their sense. Instead, we need to decipher not just the meaning of the utterance but its force – which is to say, what the act of speaking or writing is trying to achieve.[105]

Skinner distinguishes here between what he calls 'intention to do' and 'intention in doing'. The former refers to an aim on the part of the author, one which may or may not be realised, while the latter refers to the *point* of what he writes as realised in the writing. This is a fruitful distinction for literary criticism. There is a difference between 'What Turgenev has in mind here' and 'What *On the Eve* is trying to do here'. The latter is a more productive account of intentionality than the former. The first statement invokes intentions which may be irrecoverable, or recoverable but irrelevant; the second statement treats the text as a kind of strategy, an approach which we shall be considering more fully in the next chapter. As Noel Carroll puts it, 'The intention is evident in the work itself, and, in so far as the intention is identified as the purposive structure of the work, the intention is the focus of our interest in and attention to the artwork.'[106] This does not resolve the question of artistic intentionality, a notoriously thorny issue; but it places us on the right terrain.

There is also the case of what a writer intends *by* doing something. If a closet atheist writes a poem in praise of the Virgin Mary in 1608, tongue firmly in cheek, he is going to be taken as performing an act of religious devotion. Indeed, there is a sense in which he *has* performed an act of religious devotion, one which may spiritually enrich the lives of his readers. This might be so even though we are able to establish (from the author's private, luridly blasphemous letters, for example, recording among other things his exotic sexual fantasies about the Virgin Mary) that he felt no such piety at all. What he was doing *in* writing the piece, the point of it as determinable from what he wrote, was praising the Virgin Mary; what he was doing *by* writing the poem was trying to display his religious orthodoxy, hence saving himself from a charge of heresy and a particularly unpleasant death.

It is doubtful that one can identify an author's intentions with the illocutionary force of his text, since texts may have intentions of their own of which their authors know little or nothing. Turgenev may not have been aware of what *On the Eve* was trying to do at a particular point. What a writer is doing in writing may be determined as much if not more by the rules of genre or the historical context as by his personal intentions. To this extent, the intentions of his work, in the sense of what it is organised to achieve, cannot always be identified with what he himself has in mind, if indeed he had anything in mind at all. This is also true of much ideological discourse. What an author may be doing in writing – indirectly defending the interests of the propertied classes by celebrating a robust individualism of spirit, for example – might not even be intelligible to him in those terms. Like most middle-class Englishmen, Skinner is adamant in ruling this possibility out. There is also the case of what Freud calls unconscious intentions, a notion that makes the English even more nervous than talk of ideology. In the Freudian parapraxis or slip of the tongue, conscious and unconscious intentions collide in a piece of double talk.

The intentionality built into a genre, so to speak, may run counter to an author's intentions. She may take herself to be engaging in political polemic, but if this is set within a piece of fiction, its force is likely to be neutralised or transformed. However serious she may be about what she is doing, the fictional context will tend to override it. Similarly, you cannot produce ironic effects in a genre that excludes irony as unacceptable, since they will simply not be received as such. Regular readers of the *New York Times*, a journal which once told me that I was not allowed to use irony in a piece they commissioned from me, would probably take such ironic effects as non-ironic, familiar as they are with the paper's conventions. Readers of the *Guardian* might do the opposite. (I was also once informed by an American journal that I had to refer to the English newspaper *The Times* as the *London Times* in a piece I wrote for them, even though there is no such newspaper. It appears that US neocolonialism has now extended to telling other nations what the titles of their newspapers are.) In writing my autobiography, I may intend to reveal to the world how grace can abound even to the most wretched of sinners; but if I live in a culture which regards all autobiography as an exercise in egoism, this grovelling is likely to be interpreted as a devious way of blowing my own trumpet. What the genre is seen as doing will trump what I see myself as doing.

In most communicative situations, the meaning of the performance frames and orients the meaning of the utterances, determining the mode in which we are to take them. Once I grasp that you are telling me all this squirmingly self-deprecating stuff because you are pained by my opinion of you as arrogant and aloof, I can orient myself to your discourse all the better. To this extent, the rhetorical posture of a piece of language may help to determine its locutionary sense. To see a statement as sarcastic is to grasp that its locutionary meaning is the reverse of what it says. Once I perceive that your talk about setting fire to my overcoat while I am still inside it is fictional, belonging to the rhetorical mode known as *comédie noire*, I am able to understand your words in a different sense and lay down the iron bar I have been fumbling for. Something of the same goes for the speech acts of literary fiction, in which the performative (or act of saying) supervenes constantly on the constative (or what is said).

There is a dubiously logocentric air to the whole speech-act conception of literary works. Literary texts are not best thought of as acts of communication modelled on human speech, not even mimetic or aberrant ones. It is not as though everything in a work is subject to a unitary intention, as in utterances like 'Smear it with olive oil!' or 'Why does it keep turning puce?' At its most naive, the theory posits a self-transparent author in full possession of her intentions. We are not invited to inquire where this subject and its intentions sprang from. Instead, these things are taken as a point of origin. But texts are not best seen as vehicles of fiction-making intentions. In fact, there can be texts without intentions at all, such as the cracks in a rock that by a miraculous coincidence spell out the words 'Once upon a time there were three bears'. This means what it says even though nobody means it. The density of a literary work is not to be subordinated to the trajectory of an utterance. As

Joseph Margolis comments, 'there is good reason to believe that the subtle features of literary discourse ... will not yield in a productive way to speech-act analysis'.[107] In any case, the theory moves at too high a level of abstraction to be brought usefully to bear on such formal questions as viewpoint, subplot, peripeteia, the poetic sign and the like. Peter Lamarque comments perceptively in his *Fictional Points of View* on the way speech-act theory, along with much philosophy of literature, fails to take account of irony, unreliable narration, shifting point of view and other such devices.

Another of the theory's jejune habits is to posit a narrator who is enunciating a text even when there is no actual narrator around. Gregory Currie, for example, seems to think that when we encounter a literary work we always have to imagine a speaker. But this is surely not so. It does not help to imagine that Goethe's *Elective Affinities* or 'Little Boy Blue' is being recited to us by some shadowy character, perhaps an imaginary old crone squatting by an equally imaginary fireside. Not all stories depend on being identifiably authored. Who is speaking in *Finnegans Wake*? Who speaks *The Waste Land*? What do we do about polyphonic works? The concept of fiction attaches to texts and their contexts, not to the hypothetical intentions of a putative narrator. Even if the presence of such a narrator can be felt in a work, the fictional truths he presents may exceed or subvert her intentions.

One commentator writes that 'we are not told that the speaker in Gerard Manley Hopkins's "Felix Randal" is a priest, nor that he is speaking to a messenger. But if we do not infer this, the work will not be comprehensible to us'.[108] There is, in fact, no need to imagine that the poem's addressee is a messenger, and most of the piece would still be intelligible without realising that the speaker was a priest. The point, however, is that all literary works are treated by this approach as though they were dramatic monologues. The same critic goes on to observe rather astonishingly that we infer from Keats's Nightingale ode whether the speaker is a man or a woman. Richard Gale bizarrely takes as his paradigm case of fiction a storyteller narrating in the presence of an audience.[109] Texts, however, are not always the utterances of narrators, and as Walton points out there may be cultures which lack the concept of an implied narrator altogether. Texts speak themselves, as it were – a self-speaking which may include from time to time the presence of a fictional narrator.

Speech-act theory is meant to be an account of literature as such, but it is generally too dependent on the case of realist fiction. A lyric poem is fictional in the sense of inviting the reader to make-believe, to treat it non-pragmatically, and perhaps intimates this non-pragmatic status by foregrounding the signifier. But it may not take the form of a pseudo-report, as a realist narrative commonly does. Realist narrative, such as Wordsworth's 'Michael', is a minor part of what passes for poetry. Speech-act theory sometimes seems to assume that all literary texts are cast in the indicative mood, composed of statements like 'There were no photographs of the boy's father in the house upstate.' But what about 'Batter my heart, three-person'd God' or 'How can we know the dancer from the dance?' Poems are as fictional as novels in the sense that their empirical accuracy is not what is primarily at stake, as well as in the sense that what they say is meant to have general implications rather than a direct referent. But they are not necessarily fictions in the sense of consisting of quasi-assertions, since as Lamarque and Olsen point out, a literary work may contain no propositions at all.[110]

Speech-act theory assumes that authors of fiction do not intend to deceive since they do not assert, but some of them are surely out to fool us. Writers may want their readers to half believe that what they say is true, which is what Richardson may have meant by his comments on *Clarissa*. Or they may want them to believe it alto-gether, as with travellers' tall tales. Even if authors are not out to hoodwink their readers, it is doubtful whether pretending is the best way to describe what they are doing. It is true that a pretence which everyone recognises as a pretence is still a pretence, as when I masquerade ineptly as Groucho Marx before a group of secretly mocking friends. An actor on stage is not trying to bamboozle the audience into thinking she is somebody else, unless the auditorium is full of toddlers. She is representing how a fictional character feels and acts. We would not admire the representation so much if we thought she was identical with what she portrays. There is no particular skill involved in being oneself. But what she is doing could still be described as a pretence.

Even so, pretence does not seem the right word for fiction. As Gregory Currie argues in *The Nature of Fiction*, poets and novelists perform actual speech acts, inviting the reader to perform an act of make-believe. Lamarque and Olsen rightly point out that writers of fiction are doing something for real, namely engaging in the social institution of fiction-writing. Fiction is a social practice in its own right, and probably a universal one. It is not just a social parasite. In any case, one should not assume too univocal a model of so-called ordinary speech; and if one does not, there is less of a fixed standard from which fictional acts can be said to deviate. Moreover, when it comes to a sense of literature broader than fiction, authors may not be pretending at all. Laurence Sterne is not pretending to commend acts of charity in his sermons, and George Orwell is not pretending to admire miners in *The Road to Wigan Pier*. Speech-act theory works as a general theory of literature only if you restrict literature to fiction, and usually to realist fiction.

This is not to say that there is nothing to be learnt from it. Among other things, it casts fresh light on the self-referential quality of fiction. But we need to rethink the prejudice that literary works are creatively defective versions of something else. We have also seen that when it comes to literature in the broad sense, speech-act theory can be unhelpful. Literary works need not involve pseudo-propositions, which speech-act theory so often takes as exemplary. And even if writers are thought to be pretending, 'merely to pretend to perform the illocutionary act of asserting is no more to perform another type of illocutionary act than merely to pretend to commit the act of murder is to commit another type of crime', as Christopher New points out.[111]

In any case, it is not only in fiction that the rules governing 'normal' speech acts are suspended or transgressed. You can read non-fictional discourse without pausing to wonder whether the author is being truthful, sincere, knows what he is talking about, could brandish evidence to back up his claims and so on. Perhaps he is half sincere, or hasn't a clue how truthful he is being, or maybe it doesn't matter. For speech-act theory in general, speakers are supposed to 'commit' themselves in normal conditions to the truth of their utterances, taking them as valid, sincerely intended and so on; but as Thomas Pavel points out, we can sometimes be unsure whether we are committed to such statements or not. There are always cases on the part of both writer and reader of ambiguity, semi-scepticism, provisional commitment, taking statements on faith for the time being and so on.[112]

Speech-act theory springs from a historical era in which literary texts, like artworks in general, no longer seem to have much direct social function. So it is understandable to assume that all they can do is imitate other kinds of function, such as genuine acts of reportage. In this situation, the socially dysfunctional nature of literary works becomes almost part of their definition. Richard Gale sees fiction as the foe of the perlocutionary, in the sense of the actual impact that language can have on the world. 'To fictively listen to a use of language,' he writes, 'is to check, inhibit or sublimate the usual and appropriate response which the use of the language would elicit.'[113] Literary works, in short, resemble nothing quite so much as an agreeable narcotic or paralysing drug whereby, as in a dream, our practical life is put temporarily on hold. Alternatively, they are the equivalent of being rooted to the spot while being pursued by a monster in a nightmare. Literature is not a question of evoking our everyday responses, but of repressing them.

This is not quite how the ancient genealogist of the tribe regarded his role, or why Yeats wrote marching songs for the Irish fascist movement. It is not always true that poetry makes nothing happen. The ancient Jewish practitioners of *Midrash* held that you did not understand a text until you found a way of putting it into practice.[114] Or think of early twentieth-century agitprop theatre, where the audience might be invited to take a vote at the end of the play or discuss what political action should follow from it. In any case, what is the 'usual and appropriate' everyday response to 'That dolphin-torn, that gong-tormented sea' or 'Thou still unravished bride of quietness'? What are the real-world responses to these bits of language which are stymied and sublimated when we encounter them in literature?

3

In *Insight and Illusion*, a study of Wittgenstein's philosophy, P. M.S. Hacker argues that there is no connection in Wittgenstein's view between language and reality. They are not to be thought of as two domains between which certain general relations – of correspondence, construction, isomorphism and so on – can be said to hold. It is not that Wittgenstein is an inveterate sceptic who doubts that our thought can ever find a foothold in the real. On the contrary, his work advances some of the most arrestingly original arguments against scepticism that philosophy has ever come up with. He has no doubt that some of our claims about the world are true and some are false. It is just that he does not believe that how this comes about is best explained by the image of harmony, coherence, homology or correspondence between language and reality. In fact, he regards this as a piece of washed-up metaphysics that thwarts any real insight into the workings of truth and meaning. From this viewpoint, the case that language 'constructs' or 'constitutes' the world belongs just as much to this metaphysics as the idea that it reflects or corresponds to it. It, too, posits an invariant relation between two distinct realms. In Wittgenstein's eyes, however, language neither corresponds to nor constitutes reality. Instead, it provides us with the criteria for determining what kinds of things there are and how we are to speak of them.

His reflections on this topic turn on the idea of a grammar, meaning a set of rules that determine how expressions are to be used in a form of practical life. Grammars themselves cannot be true or false, as opposed to some of the statements they generate. It would not make sense to speak of the truth of Finnish or the falsity of Afrikaans. Grammars are not in this sense answerable to reality. They are antecedent to truth and falsehood, in the sense that they determine what it makes sense to say in a specific form of life. Whether, for example, a statement is of the kind that could count as being true or false is determined by the grammar itself, which is in this sense the matrix of all intelligibility.

A grammar asserts nothing about the facts. It will not tell us whether there actually are such creatures as elves. Establishing the facts is for Wittgenstein a matter of empirical inquiry to which philosophy itself has nothing to contribute. Instead, a grammar determines what might be intelligibly asserted about the facts. There are ways of talking about elves that make sense, and there are other ways, such as 'Light me an elf', that do not. A rule of grammar cannot be justified, any more than the rules of chess can be justified. In this sense it is arbitrary and self-grounding. It depends for its efficacy on nothing outside itself. 'Language remains self-contained and autonomous,' Wittgenstein writes in *On Certainty*. This is not to deny that a grammar is deeply interwoven with the world, simply to deny that it is grounded by the world, in the sense of being justified by an appeal to the way things are. A grammar does not mirror anything in reality, as Wittgenstein himself had once believed. It is an activity, not an image.

This is not to claim that the world has no hand at all in the business of truth and meaning. It is rather to claim that it has no hand in it in the way that some philosophers have considered it does, holding, for example, that the meaning of an expression is an object with which it can be correlated. As Wittgenstein sardonically characterises this view in the *Philosophical Investigations*: 'you think of the meaning as a thing of the same kind as the word, though also different from the word. Here the word, there the meaning. The money, and the cow you can buy with it. (But contrast: money, and its use).'[115] If you think of meaning as a 'signified', you may be tempted by the ruses of language to imagine it as something resembling a word or signifier, only rather more elusive – a dim picture in the mind, perhaps, one which lies behind the word and may flicker into life each time I speak or read it. Similarly, you might think of the value of money as determined by the object (the cow) you can buy with it – as involving some kind of correlation between the two. But the value of money is determined by its use in a form of life. And the same goes for words. The meaning of a word is the way it behaves. It is a social practice, not any kind of object.

To regard language as autonomous, then, is not a question of severing it from the real. Certain legal tribunals and official inquiries are autonomous, but this does not mean that they have no dealings with anything outside themselves. On the contrary, to take this view of language is to grant it its full materiality, rather than to treat it as a pale reflection of something else. Language and the world are related in the sense that the rules and criteria which govern the application of expressions are woven into our social practices – so much so that Wittgenstein can argue in *On Certainty* that what lies at the bottom of our language games is 'what we do'. Or, as Umberto Eco puts it, 'action is the place where the *haecceitas* ends the game of semiosis',[116] meaning that language comes to a temporary halt when it leads to changes of *habitus* or behavioural tendencies. Kenneth Burke speaks in similar vein of how works of art can alter attitudes and dispositions.[117] (He also notes in *A Grammar of*

Motives that attitudes can either lead to actions or act as substitutes for them, a distinction pertinent to the difference between materialism and idealism.) One might add that as a kind of permanent orientation to action, the Aristotelian idea of a disposition mediates between psyche and conduct, inner and outer.

In Wittgenstein's eyes, meaning and truth come down to questions of action, though not in any crudely pragmatist sense. They are rooted in the habitual activities of a shared form of social existence. For him as much as for Marx and Nietzsche, it is these activities which in the end determine how we go about carving up the world in concepts. Some of this behaviour reflects our common human nature – what Wittgenstein calls in Marxian style 'the natural history of human beings'. It is not peculiar to a particular culture. Wittgenstein is not in this sense a 'culturalist', in the sense of believing that culture in human affairs goes all the way down. He thinks quite properly that there are instinctive forms of bodily action, and that much of our behaviour is in this sense natural. It is partly on account of such abiding anthropological features, as well as on account of the relative stability of the physical world, that we can fashion the kinds of language-games we do. Creatures who were constantly mutating, or who inhabited a world which refused to stay still for a moment, would have nothing like our own rules and criteria of representation.

The consensus that a grammar embodies, then, is not in the end a matter of ideas or opinions, but of common ways of doing things. It is this that Wittgenstein means by a form of life – one that is foundational in the sense that though it can always be altered and even revolutionised, one cannot delve beneath it to something more fundamental. There is no turtle holding up the elephant. One might add that there are aspects of such life forms which must be always-already invisibly in place, and which cannot for the moment be dredged to consciousness, if we are to do the kinds of things we want to do (including changing those forms of life). Truth is a matter of language, but language is in the end a matter of what we do. It is thus that Wittgenstein can announce in *On Certainty*, in the illustrious wake of Goethe and Trotsky, that 'In the beginning was the deed'.

There are other ways, too, in which language is bound up with the real. Wittgenstein does not think that our concepts are rendered true or false by how the world is; but he does think that they have a point only against such a background, rather as a legal system makes sense only against the background of men and women who are keen on the idea of justice, occasionally felonious, morally frail, capable of suffering punishment, prepared to electrocute other people without being overcome by nausea in the process and so on. As Hacker puts it, making Wittgenstein sound more like Nietzsche than is usually the case, 'we create our forms of representation, prompted by our biological and psychological character, prodded by nature, restrained by society, and urged by our drive to master the world'.[118] These things form part of the material conditions of language-games, rather than being material to which such games 'correspond'. A grammar does not so much reflect the world as presuppose it.

One does not have to endorse this view unreservedly to appreciate the light it can shed on fiction.[119] We have seen that in Wittgenstein's eyes a form of life is a seamless weave of utterances and activities, and few things exemplify this more graphically than realist fiction. Many realist works convey the thickness of a specific form of life, a virtue they share with certain currents of sociology and anthropology. They act as a kind of phenomenology, reinvesting language with a wealth of experience which mainstream philosophy tends to abstract from it. It is not surprising that the lineage of what one might call anti-philosophy, from Kierkegaard, Marx, Nietzsche, Heidegger and Freud to Benjamin, Adorno, Wittgenstein and Derrida, is so intimately bound up with the aesthetic, as indeed is that most literary of philosophical movements, existentialism. The phrase 'existentialist novel' makes sense, as the phrase 'logical positivist novel' does not.

In reading realist fiction, we are able as in some controlled experiment to grasp the meaning of what is said against a background of experience and activity – a background which for Wittgenstein himself is in real life so complex, implicit and untotalisable as to be 'inexpressible', as he remarks in *Culture and Value*, but to which fiction can lend some more determinate shape. As Thomas Lewis puts it, 'Fictional reference inflects the perceptions of sign interpreters beyond explicitly represented entities towards the social practices out of which the various discourses about the world themselves emerge.'[120] There is a remote affinity here with the thought of Pierre Macherey. What Wittgenstein calls forms of life, Macherey calls ideology. There is also some kinship between Wittgenstein's sense of this taken-for-granted context, one which must be unconsciously in place for any sort of intelligibility to emerge, and Jacques Lacan's notion of the 'Other', which serves much the same purpose. So does what Hans-Georg Gadamer calls 'the fundamental non-definitiveness of the horizon in which understanding moves'.[121] In all these cases, we are speaking of what might be called the social unconscious.

Indeed, fiction presses the seamless interweaving of discourse and activity we know as a language-game to a parodic extreme, since its own 'reality' is nothing but a projection of its language. As J Hillis Miller puts it, 'We can only know of that world [of fiction] what the words tell us',[122] so that if a fact in a novel remains unestablished – if, say, we are not told the contents of a crucial letter, as in Henry James's *The Wings of the Dove* – it will remain a mystery to us for ever. This is because there is no fact to be discovered, rather as it is impossible to discover what Hamlet was doing before he first appears on stage because he was not doing anything. In a kind of magic or utopia of the creative word, reality in fiction is entirely responsive to language, but only because it is secretly language's own creation.

So there are parallels between Wittgenstein's idea of a grammar and fiction, not least of the realist variety. A grammar is a set of rules for organising a world of meaning, and this is also true of the techniques of fiction. Far from being the intriguing aberration of the speech-act theorists, then, fiction is a working model of grammars in general, a place where we can observe their operations in exceptionally graphic, condensed form. It is other language-games brought to a certain peak of self-reflexivity. This is why realist fiction is a sophisticated kind of magic. If it gives us images of the rough ground of everyday existence, its messiness and indeterminacy; it also eradicates the friction between word and world. It is both actuality and utopia. Seen in this light, it combines the early Wittgenstein's doctrine of a close fit between language and world with the later philosopher's sense of the fuzzy, makeshift quality of things, their cross-grained resistance to crystalline definition.

There are other ways in which fiction can cast light on the rest of our language-games. We have seen that Wittgenstein rejects the idea that the meaning of an expression is its referent, in the sense of some object in the world. To think in this way is to see meaning almost as a kind of verbal pointing. But pointing, as Wittgenstein begins the *Philosophical Investigations* by showing, needs a context in order to make sense. You could not teach someone the word 'stucco' by indicating a stretch of stucco and intoning the word unless she already had some conception of object, reference, naming, meaning, ostensive definition and the like. And what object does the word 'covetously' point to? If you point out someone who has been hiccuping for days to a small child and say 'hiccup', the child might spend the rest of his days believing that a hiccup means anyone with whom there is no point in trying to hold a conversation, and as such covers members of the British Nationalist Party as well as people in physiological difficulty. How is the child to know what you are pointing to? Anyway, what is the referent of 'Oh hell!', 'Hi there!' or 'Who are you staring at?'? Reference is not a ready-made hook-up between a sign and an object. It is a social activity with a diversity of modes, one which depends on the shared understandings built into a form of life. As

Paul O'Grady comments, 'Reference makes sense in the context of the employment of signs for certain purposes. Such employments occur in multiple ways and there is no unique connection between concepts and objects that stands out as the true one.'[123]

Ironically, the fact that fiction lacks a direct individual referent means that it can illuminate the nature of reference all the more instructively. In one sense of the word, fiction makes reference all the time – to wars and power struggles, sexuality and self-sacrifice, domestic affections and natural disasters. But since it accomplishes all this by portraying characters and events that do not exist, or whose real existence is beside the point, it is able to show up the act of referring as one dependent on contexts, criteria and the interrelations among signs, rather than as a straightforward connection. Fiction is thus a useful therapy for those with unduly reductive ideas of referentiality. We know how to use the name 'Julien Sorel' by grasping the conventions and procedures that govern the use of this name in *Le Rouge et le Noir*. As far as that goes, the fact that Julien does not exist is neither here nor there. By and large, we handle concepts and criteria in fiction, or decide that something in a work is fictionally true, in the same way as we do in everyday life.

Reference is not an act that secures itself. It poses a number of problems, and can be a fairly chancy affair. For some people, the language-game known as religion has a referent (God), while for other people it does not. But this begs the question of what would count as a referent here. A god who was seen as a supersized hero, even if he existed, could not count as the ultimate referent of the Judaeo-Christian language-game. If there happens to be a Supreme Being who is like us but infinitely more wise, good and powerful, he cannot be what the Jewish Bible calls Yahweh and the Christian Bible God. He would be ruled out by the prohibition on idolatry, as well as on a number of other theological grounds. To know what would count as a referent here, we need to look at the internal workings of the language-game.

The fact that there is no actual town of Middlemarch enriches the act of reference rather than impoverishing it. It encourages us to reflect on the mores of small provincial towns in general, not just to imagine that we are receiving a report on a specific early Victorian settlement in the English Midlands. Because Ahab does not exist but obsessional psychosis does, the depiction of him in *Moby-Dick* can be freed up from real-life constraints to stage that state of mind all the more resourcefully. Jan Mukařovský argues that the referential function of a work of art is weakened in the sense that it does not refer directly, but that it is enabled by this very weakness to refer in richer, deeper ways.[124]

Rather as phenomenology 'brackets' the referent in order to focus more closely on the act of intending it, so fiction draws our attention to the act of reference in its full complexity. The fact that it lacks a direct real-life referent, or that if it has one it is not important, is no different in principle from the fact that we can teach someone about the Gorgon or ancient drainage practices even though the former never existed and the latter no longer does. Non-existent objects also play a part in our real-life language-games, not just in our fictional ones. We hope and wish for things that have as yet no existence, just as we can celebrate or regret the past, which exists no more than the future does. Lying is by definition a piece of language without a referent. As Umberto Eco suggests, 'Every time there is signification there is the possibility of using it in order to lie'.[125] It is because we can speak the truth that we can also dissemble. If this is so, then the condition of being without a referent is built into language itself.

Fiction is the kind of language-game which must be able to operate in the absence of a referent. You may read out a poem lovingly dedicated to the Secretary for Work and Pensions in the presence of the Secretary for Work and Pensions, but his or her presence is not necessary for the poem to work as a poem. As David Schalkwyk points out, however, this is true of language in general: 'language requires no connection to any entity here and now to work as language'.[126] Or as Jacques Lacan puts it rather more portentously, the symbol is the death of the thing. Fiction is thus a more eye-catching example of an essential condition of all linguistic activity.

We have touched already on another way in which fiction is exemplary of language-games in general. It is clear in the case of fiction – a play, for example – that meaning does not depend on the experience of a subject. An actor does not have to feel at one with the psyche of a serial killer in order to represent him convincingly, unless he has been watching too much Marlon Brando. It is not that an actor lacks feelings, but that he has the feelings appropriate to what he is doing – to the techniques he deploys, the actions he performs and the words he articulates. 'Whoever asks a person in a play what he's experiencing when he's speaking?' Wittgenstein inquires.[127] The contexts of a sentence, he comments in the *Philosophical Investigations*, are best portrayed in a play. A poet does not need to have fallen down a mineshaft or violently in love for her words on these subjects to impress us as authentic. Meaning is not a mental or emotional process that shadows one's speech. It is not an experience, any more than promising, expecting or intending are experiences. These things may be accompanied by feelings (of affection, impatience, resoluteness, anticipation and so on), but that is a different matter. My mind may be aswirl with all kinds of intriguing mental images while reading Condorcet, but they cannot be part of the meaning of the work, and are of interest only to me and my psychoanalyst.

Rather as language-games need to place something provisionally beyond doubt in order to establish a backdrop against which to function, such provisional assent is also true of fiction. It is traditionally known as the suspension of disbelief. For the sake of playing the fictional game, we agree not to ask for the moment whether a gorilla could really be the size of King Kong, or anyone in real life could really be as preposterous as Goethe's Werther. Like a grammar, too, a piece of fiction contains a set of implicit rules and conventions for determining what can intelligibly be said and done within its compass, as well as what counts in these conditions as true or false. And these rules, like the rules of a Wittgensteinian language-game, are in some sense arbitrary and autonomous. This does not mean that they drop into our laps from outer space. In Wittgenstein's view, they are rules of representation or techniques for constituting fictional worlds, and such rules and techniques have a social history. For Wittgenstein, however, they are not spontaneously given by reality itself. The world does not naturally carve itself up into two main plots and a cluster of three subplots. In this sense, language-games are fictional in something like the sense that novels are.

It is true that in fiction, as in our other language-games, what can be intelligibly proposed is shaped by the way things stand with us and the world. In a realist narrative, an angel cannot put in an appearance in a Manhattan bar, as he might show up in a poem by Rilke. But it is not wrong in general to introduce an angel into a poem, if this seems a productive move within a certain kind of aesthetic grammar. It is no more wrong for *Jane Eyre* to end by marrying off its protagonist than it would have been for it to unmask her as a lesbian and pair her off with Grace Poole or Bertha Mason, or set all three up in a *ménage à trois*. Fiction draws upon other language-games, and in turn plays a part within them. For Wittgenstein, they play a vital role in the language-game of philosophy: 'Nothing is more important for understanding the concepts we have than constructing fictitious ones,' he remarks.[128]

Even so, the forms and techniques of fiction are autonomous of reality in the sense that if they did not stand at a distance from it, they could not carve the stuff up in so many different ways. Fiction is testimony to the fact that the world does not force us to depict it in a single way, which is not to say that we can depict it in any old way. We can take a lot more liberties with our portrayals of it in fiction than we can in real life, but even in fiction our imaginings are constrained. There are certain states of affairs that, given that we are a certain kind of material creature living in a certain kind of material world, we could not even in principle imagine. The imagination is nothing like as untrammelled as the romantics of this world would insist. This is one reason why almost all reports of aliens make them sound like green-coloured, multi-limbed, sulphurous-smelling versions of Tony Blair. Moreover, once we are inside a fictional world, as once we are inside a grammar or a game of chess, our freedom of thought and action is drastically curtailed. Rules that appear arbitrary from the outside then suddenly loom up as a lot more coercive. But a certain kind of philosophical therapy can help to free us from this rigid sense of coercion, rather as psychoanalysis seeks to free us from various paralytic constraints, and rather as fiction, despite its limits, can disclose possibilities beyond the actual.

CHAPTER 5

Strategies

1

It is now time to shift the question of whether things share a common nature from literature itself to the theories which investigate it. What, if anything, do literary theories have in common? What links semiotics and feminism, Formalism and psychoanalysis, Marxism and hermeneutics or post-structuralism and reception aesthetics?

One answer might be that they are all *theories*. This means that they have at least one (negative) feature in common: a shared opposition to empiricist or impressionistic criticism. Even so, the distinction between theoretical and other kinds of criticism is far from clear. It cannot be that the former deploys complex abstract concepts whereas the latter does not. So-called non-theoretical criticism goes in for such concepts all the time (symbol, allegory, character, metre, metaphor, catharsis and so on). It is just that it has ceased for the most part to recognise these abstract concepts for what they are. Ideas of character, plot or the iambic pentameter are supposed to be self-evident, whereas the unconscious, class struggle and the floating signifier are not. To this extent, critics who denounce so-called theory as excessively abstract are quite often in bad faith, however unwittingly. Perhaps they may legitimately object to it on other grounds, but scarcely on this one. It may be that the concepts employed by literary theorists are in some sense more abstract than those wielded by other kinds of critic, or drawn more often from non-literary sources. But this, too, is debatable. In what sense is the concept of litotes less abstract than images of emotionally retarded males?

The family-resemblance model would seem to apply as much to literary theory as to its object. There is no single feature or set of features that all literary theories share in common. There is, however, in Wittgenstein's words, 'a complicated network of similarities overlapping and criss-crossing'. Take as an example the idea that works of literature in some sense involve the unconscious. This is obviously the case for psychoanalytic criticism, and (to the extent that it draws upon it) a fair amount of feminist literary theory as well. But it is also true in a different way of structuralism, for which a literary work, rather like an individual, is generally unconscious of the 'deep structures' which govern it. Language, Claude Lévi-Strauss remarks, has its reasons of which man knows nothing. For post-structuralism, language involves the unconscious in a different sense, in so far as the boundless sprawl of signifiers into which any piece of discourse can be unravelled – 'textuality', in a word – can never be present as a whole to consciousness. In the case of political criticism such as Marxism, the unconscious of the text becomes the historical and ideological forces which shape it to its roots, but which are necessarily excluded from its self-knowledge. If the work were to be aware of these forces, it would not exist in the form it does.

Phenomenological criticism, by contrast, leaves little room for an unconscious, and neither do semiotics and reception theory. Even so, there are other parallels between these approaches and the ones we have just looked at. In its preoccupation with the sign, for example, semiotics belongs to the same world of discourse as structuralism. The family resemblances can be extended further. Phenomenology and reception theory both assign central importance to the experience of reading. Paul Ricoeur's notion of a 'hermeneutic of suspicion' is relevant to both political and psychoanalytic criticism. There is no essence to literary theory, but neither is it a random assemblage of ideas. In this respect, it resembles the phenomenon of literature itself.

It is possible, however, go one better than this. There may not be a single feature shared by all these theories of literature; but there is one concept in particular which can illuminate a good many of them, even if it is not always a concept they themselves employ. This is the idea of the literary work as a *strategy*. Since this is relevant to so many kinds of literary theory, we have here what with suitable modesty might be called a Theory Of (almost) Everything, a literary equivalent to the physicist's elusive TOE.

As Fredric Jameson has reminded us, it was Kenneth Burke more than anyone who added this term to the critical lexicon, even though Burke is nowadays probably the most neglected of the great twentieth-century critics.[1] It was he above all who taught us to think of literary works, indeed of language in general, in terms of ritual, drama, rhetoric, performance and symbolic action, as strategic responses to determinate situations, and whose catch-all word for this critical philosophy is dramatism.[2] One of the earliest pieces of literary theory we have, Aristotle's *Poetics*, sees tragedy as a symbolic act of purgation; and though the origins of the form are obscure, the name itself, which means 'goat song', may suggest that it is a symbolic act founded on another symbolic act, namely the expiatory sacrifice of the scapegoat. There are other genres with such origins. Epic and lyric begin life as oral performances. Satire is a symbolic flaying. Perhaps it is not until the emergence of the novel, aided by the arrival of mass printing technology, that the idea of the literary work as an object rather than a practice takes such firm root in the critical mind.

Jameson himself can be found drawing fruitfully on these staple Burkeian notions as early as *The Political Unconscious*, where he favours a mode of interpretation in which, in a double gesture, one rewrites the literary text in such a way as to reveal it as itself a rewriting of a prior historical or ideological subtext.[3] This subtext, however, to which the text proper can be seen as a response, has the curious quality of not actually existing apart from the text itself, and certainly not as some 'common-sense external reality'. It must rather be reconstructed after the fact – projected backwards, so to speak, from the work as such. The historical question the work addresses must be read off from the answers it delivers. As Paul Ricoeur puts it, works like *Oedipus the King* and *Hamlet* 'are not simple projections of the artist's conflicts but are outlines of their solutions'.[4] Paradoxically, the literary work of art projects out of its own innards the very historical and ideological subtext to which it is a strategic reply. This, then, is yet another sense in which there is a curiously circular or self-fashioning quality about literary artworks, over and above what we have said already about the structure of fiction, the nature of speech acts and the character of the poetic sign.

If this is such a resourceful model, it is largely because of the complex view it involves of the relations between text and ideology, or text and history. These things are no longer to be grasped, as in some mainstream Marxist aesthetics, as standing to each other in a relationship of reflection, reproduction, corre-spondence, homology and the like, but as alternative facets of a single symbolic practice. The work itself is to be seen not as a reflection of a history external to it, but as a strategic labour – as a way of setting to work on a reality which, in order to be accessible to it, must somehow be contained within it, and which conse-quently baffles any simple-minded dichotomy of inside and outside. Jameson writes of how the work, in order to act on the world, must have this world somehow inhere within it, 'as the content it has to take up into itself in order to submit it to the trans-formations of form'. 'The whole paradox of what we have here called the subtext,' he writes, 'may be summed up in this, that the literary work or cultural object, as though for the first time, brings into being that very situation to which it is also, at one and the same time, a reaction.'[5]

In a later essay on Burke's criticism, Jameson warms to this theme once again, writing of how 'the literary or aesthetic gesture thus always stands in some active relationship with the real ... Yet in order to act on the real, the text cannot simply allow reality to persevere in its being outside of itself, inertly, at a distance; it must draw the real into its own texture.' 'The symbolic act,' he goes on, 'therefore begins by producing its own context in the same moment of emergence in which it steps back over against it, measuring it with an eye to its own active project', thus fostering the illusion that the situation to which the work of art is a response did not pre-exist it – that there is, in short, nothing but the text. There are, then, two moments or aspects in question here, which are only analytically distinct: that of historical and ideological reality itself, now suitably 'textualised', worked up or 'produced' in a form on which the text can go to work; and this transformative project itself, which in Jameson's words represents the 'active, well-nigh instrumental stance of the text towards the new reality, the new situation, thus produced'.[6]

One might see the process Jameson describes here as an exemplary case of human practice in general. Human beings do not go to work on a raw, inert environment but on one always-already 'textualised', traced over with meaning like ancient palimpsests by countless previous or simultaneous human projects. By and large, the human species reacts to conditions that it has created itself. It is haunted by its own products, as well as occasionally hampered by them. If the world puts up such obdurate resistance to human endeavour, it is not so much because it is rough virgin terrain, but because it is already carved into determinate shape by the meanings and activities of others. The word 'labour' itself indicates this resistance on the world's part to our designs on it. Reality, to adapt a Jamesonian phrase, is what hurts.

This is not the case, however, with the literary work. It is not, of course, that the business of writing is magically free of toil, but that the act of evoking a context or subtext, and the process of working upon it, are aspects of the same (laborious) practice. To this extent, the literary work reveals a utopian unity of word and world, as we have seen already in the case of speech-act theory. If writing can be a displacement of other kinds of practice, it can also be a form of compensation for them. As Jameson phrases the point, it is 'the accomplishment of an act and the latter's substitute, a way of acting on the world and of compensating for the impossibility of such action all at once'.[7]

The technical term for a Freudian slip is parapraxis, meaning a bungled or substitute action or utterance, and this seems a fruitful way of seeing symbolic acts in general. John Henry Newman, perhaps the finest prose stylist of Victorian England, once complained in a sermon on 'Unreal Words' that literature is unreal 'almost in its essence' because it exhibits the disjoining of thought and practice. In another sermon, 'On the Danger of Accomplishments', he warns that imaginative literature, by severing feeling from acting, allows our sentiments to be stimulated to no purpose, and is therefore morally injurious.

Symbolic action, in short, would seem a crippled, emaciated form of action, a strange view for a devotee of the sacramental like Newman. We are a long way from Aristotle's catharsis, though not all that far from Plato's strictures on art. Literature would seem to depend for its existence on a certain loss or distancing of the real, and this absence is vitally constitutive of its presence. The same could be said of the human subject known to psychoanalysis. It is as though the work seeks to compensate for this loss of the real, one which is a condition of all symbolic practice, by repossessing it even more intimately in language; which is to say, in the very medium which placed it at a remove in the first place. All literature, like all language, is doomed to this perpetual ambiguity. It is forced to recreate the world in a medium which involves the loss of the world, at least in the form of sensuous immediacy. The symbol is the death of the thing. As such, writing is both a sign of the Fall and an attempt to redeem it.

Yet if the text is in this sense secondary and derivative, a mere metaphor or displacement of action proper, it is in another sense an action perfectly realised, fully consummated, one which cannot fall short of reality because the reality to which it is faithful is none other than one it fabricates itself. It is in this way that the classical literary work does away with the bunglings and contingencies to which all real-world action is subject, eradicating the accidental and wedding form harmoniously to content. As both displacement and compensation, symbolic acts capture something of the ambiguous potency and fragility of language as such. On the one hand, language is nothing but words. On the other hand, it is the power that makes human action possible in the first place, since there can be no such action without signification. It is only because we are linguistic animals that the back-and-forth motion of a hand can be seen as a gesture of farewell.

The idea of the text as answer should not be taken too literally. Literary works, not least modern ones, do not generally come up with textbook solutions to the problems they pose. We do not expect a work by Borges or Naipaul to conclude with an array of joyful marriages, the villains packed off empty-handed and the virtuous awarded their country estates. If there is the text of pleasure, in Roland Barthes's terms, with its courteous accommodation of our normative assumptions, there is also the text of jouissance, which is out to reap malicious, anti-superegoic delight from disrupting them. The typical Victorian novel ends on a note of reconciliation, which can be seen among other things as a psychical device. 'The motive force of fantasies,' remarks Freud, 'are unsatisfied wishes, and every single fantasy is the fulfilment of a wish, a correction of unsatisfying reality.'[8] In the traditional happy ending, the pleasure principle intervenes to soften the rigours of the reality principle, an operation sometimes known as comedy. By contrast, the typical modern novel, as Raymond Williams once remarked, ends with the protagonist walking off on his own, having extricated himself from some problematic situation.

'No literature in the world,' writes Roland Barthes, 'has ever answered the question it asked, and it is this very suspension which has always constituted it as literature: it is that very fragile language which men set between the violence of the question and the silence of the answer . . .'[9] The text is not bound to provide an answer in the sense that a medical diagnosis is meant to do. It may simply represent a response to the questions it poses, rather than a literal solution to them. If there are both acceptable and non-acceptable ways in which a work may resolve a problem, there are also acceptable and non-acceptable ways in which it may leave it unanswered.

Freud himself was aware that too blatant, full-blooded a wish-fulfilment on our own part tends to be repugnant to others, though this is hardly a pressing problem when it comes to modern literature. Too pat or predictable a closure would satisfy such a work's impulse to form only at the price of disrupting its clear-eyed realism. This is because happiness is not a plausible condition in the modern age. Even the word itself has a feeble ring to it, evocative as it is of manic grins and end-of-pier comedians. A comic ending in these disenchanted days can be as scandalously avant-garde as *The Tempest* would have been if it had married Miranda off to Caliban. The contrast with the Victorians is telling. *Bleak House* could not have killed off its protagonists in the final paragraph any more than it could have ended in mid-sentence. *Middlemarch* concludes on as muted, soberly disillusioned a note as a major Victorian novelist could decently get away with, while the defiantly tragic denouements of *Tess of the D'Urbervilles* and *Jude the Obscure* could still enrage a late Victorian readership. By contrast, we would be astonished and not a little unsettled if a work by Strindberg or Scott Fitzgerald were to end on a note of ecstatic affirmation.

Before Hardy, with one or two ambiguous exceptions such as *Wuthering Heights*, the only major tragic novel in England is *Clarissa*. After Hardy, with a few arguable exceptions such as *Ulysses*, it is comic endings that are ideologically impermissible.

Marxists detect a relation between this fact and the transition of the middle classes from their progressive to non-progressive phase. Yet a tragic response is still a constructive response. The death of Clarissa, for example, could be seen as the most appropriate riposte to the situation in which she finds herself. In any case, the response of a work to the situation it fashions does not lie simply in its conclusion. It is a question of its whole manner of treating it.

Nor should one confine the problem-and-solution model to individual literary texts. It may also work at the level of literary mode and genre. Elegy and tragedy inquire into how we are to make sense of our mortality, and even wrest some value from it, while pastoral puzzles over how we are to stay faithful to the humble sources of our sophisticated lives without losing what is precious about that hard-won civility. Comedy poses an abundance of questions, such as why there is something so uproariously funny about our frailty. Realism is among other things a response to the problem of how to respect the roughness of the empirical world while discerning in it a significant design. Naturalism is an answer inter alia to the question of whether literary art can also be a scientific sociology. Dramatic forms like Expressionism tend to arise when artists begin to ask how they are to put centre-stage spiritual or psychological realities which realism is forced to relegate to the wings. Like most currents of modernism, they are 'answers' to the problems of realism.

The literary work is perhaps a reply less to a question than to a cluster of questions. A good deal of light is thrown on the so-called New Testament, for example, if one reads it as a many-sided response to the destruction of the Jerusalem temple in AD 70 and the turbulence, hopes, divisions, disenchantments and intense anxieties that marked the Late Second Temple period. Aeschylus's *Oresteia* inquires how the self-perpetuating cycles of 'pre-civilised' vengeance can be transformed into the juridical order of a civilised state without denying what is serviceable in those more ancient systems of justice, and without emasculating a violence, or rationalising away a sense of reverence necessary for the survival of civilisation itself. George Eliot's *Middlemarch* struggles to reconcile a buoyant middle-class faith in progress, totality and grand narratives with a liberal wariness of such ambitious schemes, a nostalgia for the local and a tragic sense of human finitude, all of which can be seen as characteristic of a middle class whose high reformist hopes have been largely baffled. Yet all these issues bring other questions along with them, which in turn require other kinds of reply.

There is a relation between Jameson's view of the literary work as conjuring up the context to which it is a reaction, and the hermeneutical claim that to understand a text is to reconstruct the question to which it is an answer. In *Truth and Method*, Hans-Georg Gadamer acknowledges his indebtedness for this idea to the historian R.G. Collingwood, a rare instance of a German philosopher name-checking an English one.[10] Collingwood holds that every proposition can be understood as the answer to a question, and that all such questions involve a presupposition. Thus 'there is a baboon on my back' can be seen as an answer to the question 'what is that hideous, red-eyed thing with its hairy arms wrapped round your throat?', and involves the presupposition that there are hairy-armed creatures known as baboons.[11] 'You cannot tell what a proposition is,' Collingwood remarks, 'unless you know what question it is meant to answer.'[12] In the words of one commentator, what one needs to ask, hermeneutically speaking, is 'to what question did So-and-so intend this proposition for an answer?'[13] Knowing this will help to determine whether the proposition is true.

Collingwood accordingly wants to replace a propositional logic with a dialogical one, which in its constant dialectical unfolding seems to him more appropriate to the historical nature of human inquiry. Propositions then become implicit practices or performative acts. They are responses to questions which may no longer be identifiable as such, having been temporarily suppressed or set aside. There are also what Collingwood terms 'absolute presuppositions', which involve neither questions nor answers. Instead, they are transcendental, in the sense of representing the assumptions necessary for any particular dialectic of question and answer to get off the ground. According to one commentator on Collingwood's work, 'understanding the question a given statement is meant to answer involves uncovering the presupposition in the absence of which the question could not have arisen'.[14] One might say in similar vein that for Jameson, understanding a literary work is a matter of reconstructing the ideological context which poses the 'question' to which the work is a response.

There is an obvious relation between this hermeneutical model and the concept of the text as strategy. Grasping a literary work as a way of tackling an implicit question then becomes a special case of interpretation as such. Jameson begins his study *The Prison-House of Language* with the proposal that the history of thought is the history of its models, but he might also have claimed that it is the history of its questions. For the hermeneuticists, reality is what returns a coherent answer to a historically loaded question. A framework of acceptable questions – roughly speaking, what Louis Althusser names a problematic and Michel Foucault an episteme – determines what would count as a plausible or intelligible answer in a specific historical context. Perhaps this is what Marx had in mind when he remarked that human beings only ever set themselves such problems as they can resolve. If we have the means to raise a question in the first place, an answer may not be too far distant. The very terms in which we identify a problem may point us in the direction of a solution, or at least suggest what would count as one. Nietzsche remarks in *The Gay Science* that one only hears those questions to which one is in a position to come up with an answer.

Even so, questions do not come with their answers tied neatly to their tails. It is because we can occasionally receive arresting or unpredictable responses to our queries, *pace* Stanley Fish, that advances in knowledge are possible. It is in this capacity to be surprised that science arises. In much pre-modern thought, by contrast, learning something is for the most part confirming what one already knew. Most of what men and women encounter must already be familiar, since, for example, God would not have been so outrageously inconsiderate as not to reveal from the outset all the truths necessary for their salvation. It would have been unfair and irresponsible of him to have hidden the importance of not committing adultery from the ancient Etruscans while writing it in the skies above seventeenth-century France.

On this hermeneutical view, there can be no final answers, since answers give rise to new questions in their turn. What seems a solution turns out to pose a fresh problem. Only in myth can this process be brought to a close. When Oedipus answers the unsolvable riddle of the Sphinx, the beast kills itself. Yet as Claude Lévi-Strauss points out, disaster can also ensue in mythical thought if there is a failure to pose a question. Buddha dies because Ananda did not ask him to stay alive, while Gawain–Percival's failure to inquire after the nature of the Holy Grail will bring catastrophe to the Fisher King.[15]

Hermeneutical criticism, then, is a matter of reconstructing a question in order to shed light on an answer. Literary works reflect something of this circular, self-sustaining structure, one which we have had occasion to observe in other contexts. They appear to be at work on themselves, yet in doing so they are busy transforming historical materials into occasions for this self-activity. To grasp the meaning of a text is therefore to see it as an attempt to encompass a situation – an attempt which in Kenneth Burke's eyes always involves a certain mastery, and thus a certain will to power. Symbolic acts, from myth, magic, chanting and cursing to art, dream, prayer and religious ritual, are part of the way humanity subdues its environment to significance, and thus contribute to the way it manages to survive and flourish. Burke's comments on Milton's *Samson Agonistes* suggest something of his highly flavoured style and idiosyncratic approach, writing as he does of the poem as 'almost a kind of witchcraft, a wonder-working spell by a cantankerous old fighter-priest who would slay the enemy in effigy, and whose very translation of political controversy to high theologic [*sic*] terms helps, by such magnification, to sanction the ill-tempered obstinacy of his resistance'.[16]

Human labour is itself a mode of sense-making, a way of organising reality coherently enough to satisfy our needs; but for it to be truly effective we also need a mode of meta-sense-making, some more speculative form of reflection on the world our labour and language have opened up. This, all the way from myth and philosophy to art, religion and ideology, is the domain of the symbolic. If art is one of the ways we subdue the world to sense, or reflect on that process more generally, and if such sense-making is necessary for our survival, then the non-pragmatic is ultimately in the name of the pragmatic. Yet it may also be that the opposite is true – that historically speaking, the pragmatic (or realm of necessity) must be overtaken by the non-pragmatic (or domain of freedom). This, in a word, is the hope of Marxism. The most desirable future is one in which we would be less in thrall to practical necessity than we are at present. If this is more than a wistful yearning on Marx's part, it is because he believes that the resources accumulated by the drearily pragmatic narrative of class society might finally be made available for this end. The wealth which at present we toil to produce might be used to free us from toil. As strategy, the work of art belongs to the realm of necessity, or at least to that somewhat less constrained area of it known as the symbolic. As sport, it prefigures the domain of freedom.

To illustrate the idea of the text as strategy, let us take a brief glance at John Milton's *Paradise Lost*, a poem which asks among other things why it is that the high hopes of the Puritan revolutionaries have been dashed – why the Almighty seems to have turned his countenance from his chosen people and abandoned them to the tender mercies of the kings and priests. Is it because their project was misconceived, or because in their faithlessness they did not deserve to be victorious, or because of a mighty flaw at the very heart of humanity which tempts man to abandon his high moral purposes for ignoble ends (a flaw sometimes known as woman), or because the Lord in his unfathomable wisdom will still vindicate his own people, having plunged them into their present travails as part of his darkly inscrutable plan for their final salvation? Will the Fall from Eden turn out retrospectively to be an essential prelude to an even more magnificent form of human existence, as capitalism would seem for Marx to be an essential prelude to socialism? Or can one find in this calamity a kind of exculpation – a reason why men and women aspire and fail, but (as in classical tragic theory) are not entirely responsible for this debacle?

Since Milton's great epic is a poem rather than a political tract, it raises and responds to these questions in terms of narrative, plot, drama, rhetoric, image, character, emotional posture and the like, none of which can be grasped as the mere outward guise of an abstract inquiry. Yet though this *mise en scène* brings these issues home to us as lived experience, it also manages to complicate the whole business of textual strategy. The poem, for example, casts its sacred subject-matter in narrative form, but in doing so cannot help throwing into relief certain embarrassments inherent in the Biblical material, not least the way in which the whole story seems a singularly bad one for God. Once eternal truths are projected into temporal form, a number of moral and aesthetic difficulties inevitably arise. The form of the work, for example, cannot help cutting the Almighty down to size by presenting him as a coldly aloof character, even as it pursues its purpose of justifying his ways to an unregenerate nation. Milton is a Protestant poet of sense, discourse and reason, and needs to muster all these resources to justify a Supreme Being who would condemn our first parents for the crime of eating an apple. Yet this discursive, argumentative mode also risks undermining the sheer grandeur of the epic effect. Because Milton's God has a lot of arguing to do to rationalise his somewhat churlish conduct, the poem succeeds from time to time in making this majestically transcendent Creator sound like a buttoned-down bureaucrat or constipated civil servant.

There are also some telling discrepancies between what the epic shows and what it says; between, for example, the humanistic Milton's sympathetic portrayal of Adam and Eve, and the censorious moral stance the work officially takes up to the sinful pair. The poem's formal theological account is sometimes at odds with the dramatic representation. There are similar inconsistencies in the case of Satan. It is not true, as William Blake maintained, that Milton is of the devil's party without knowing it. The Satan depicted by this radical republican writer is a pompous princeling. Yet because he is brought so magnificently alive as a tragic figure, he steals the Almighty's thunder in a way which cuts to some extent against the work's ideological intentions. Making goodness seem attractive has become an uphill job since the days of Aristotle and Aquinas, and will become well-nigh impossible as modernity proceeds to unfold.

Like many a literary text, *Paradise Lost* continually throws up problems which it then seeks to resolve, sometimes creating yet more problems in the process. It involves a set of strategic compromises and negotiations, which involves a constant interplay of the 'aesthetic' and the 'ideological'. The opposition is in fact misleading, since the formal features of an artwork are quite as ideologically eloquent as its content; but it will have to stand for the moment. What happens in the evolving project of the text is a complex toing and froing between the two. An ideological contradiction, for example, may be provisionally resolved by a formal move; but this move may then generate a further problem at the ideological level, which in turn throws up a fresh formal dilemma, and so on.

It would take a study in itself to demonstrate this in the case of Milton's epic, but we might briefly consider a more tractable case like *Jane Eyre*. It is part of the novel's strategic project to bring Jane and Rochester together in the end; but it would violate the canons of realism, not to speak of representing too flagrant a wish-fulfilment on its own part, if it were to do so without first of all driving them apart. This narrative turn then fulfils a number of ideological ends. It satisfies the novel's belief (at once masochistic and puritanical) in the need for suffering and self-abnegation, at the same time as it protects its decorous heroine from the dangers of bigamy. It also allows her to confront in the austere St John Rivers a kind of alter ego which alerts her to the pitfalls as well as the allures of self-renunciation. Besides, abandoning the profligate aristocrat is one way in which the novel can punish him for his licentious designs on its heroine's virtue. Yet Rochester must not be chastised to the point where he can no longer function as the sublime object of Jane's desire. Rather, the narrative must unite the two lovers once more; but since there is no realist technique at hand to do so, it is forced to resort to the fabular device of Jane's hearing her master's cry for help from a long way off.

This risks furthering the book's ideological project only at the cost of undercutting its realism; but formally speaking the work is in any case a strikingly uneven mixture of realism, life-history, Gothic, romance, fairy tale, moral fable and the like, one of the effects of which is to suggest what secret affinities and monstrously improbable passions lie beneath the brittle surface of the everyday world. If this is a social text of the Hungry Forties, it is also a rerun of 'Beauty and the Beast'. The novel can thus (just about) get away with its anti-realist tactic, and Jane is restored to her afflicted lover. In the meantime, the work has cleared the path to the couple's marital union by killing off Rochester's crazed wife, in a move which requires another swerve from realism proper into melodrama and Gothic cameo.

Since Bertha Rochester figures in the novel's unconscious as an uncanny double of her husband (she is dark-complexioned like him, about the same height, transgressive, a dangerous alien, poten-tially destructive and full of animal passion), destroying her is also a displaced way of punishing him. More exactly, it is a way of punishing him without actually killing him, which would scarcely suit the benign conclusion the work has in store for its heroine. But this moral move is also a narrative mechanism for bestowing on Jane what she desires. Rochester has also been punished in his own person as well as through his spouse, blinded and crippled as the story unleashes upon him the full blast of its sadistic, scapegoating fury. This fulfils an ideological function, as Rochester is made to pay for his sins, and the aspiring petty-bourgeois woman brings low the predatory aristocratic male. But it also works as a plot device, cutting this overbearing patrician down to size and humanising or feminising him in the process, so that Jane the lowly governess can unite with her master as his spiritual equal. This, however, is achieved without emasculating the rogue, which, once more, would scarcely be in the interests of Jane herself. Indeed, there is something even more seductive about a wounded Rochester than one in rude health. If he is less dashing, he is also less alarming.

Jane, however, gains more than this. The blinding and crippling of Rochester allows her to exercise power over her master for the first time, as she leads this now broken hunk of manhood around by the hand. To act as his helpmeet, however, is also to fulfil the function of servant or meekly submissive wife, perpetuating Jane's previous role as well as repudiating it. This narrative shift, then, allows the book's heroine the status and sovereignty she unconsciously seeks without detriment to her piety, modesty and social conformity, not to speak of her sexual masochism. Jane's relationship with Rochester in the end is simultaneously one of submission, dominance and equality. In Charlotte Brontë's world, it is difficult to feel more fulfilled than that. It is no wonder that D.H. Lawrence thought the ending of the novel 'pornographic', as it guiltily savages the magnificent male beast it has created, cravenly delivering him into the hands of a mere woman. The project the novel has worked so hard to accomplish – to allow Jane her self-fulfilment, but securely within the social conventions – is finally complete.

So it is that *Jane Eyre*, like many a piece of realist fiction, seeks to provide an imaginary solution to certain pressing questions set for it by its historical context. It is in this sense that we can speak of the 'necessity' of the text, which is not to be mistaken for iron determinism. How is one to reconcile self-fulfilment and self-surrender, duty and desire, masculine power and feminine deference, the canniness of the common people and the enviable cultivation of the gentry, Romantic rebellion and a respect for social convention, thrusting social ambition and a petty-bourgeois suspicion of the haughty upper classes?[17] The textual strategies which address this task involve a constant movement across the frontier between 'form' and 'content', one which shows up the ultimate artifice of any such division. Like the morning and the evening star, form and content are analytically distinct but existentially identical.

Jane Eyre has to negotiate a trade-off between conflicting sets of values, but also between different narrative forms. In trying to resolve certain moral or social dilemmas, it also finds itself stitching together certain traditional literary modes with a militant, newly emergent realism, which as Raymond Williams has shown is seeking in the turbulent 1840s to register new strains of social experience.[18] When the narrative encounters problems to which no realist solution is on hand, however, it may choose to fall back on a more fabular or mythological device as a *deus ex machina*; and these – the timely inheritance, the discovery of the long-lost relative, the convenient sudden death, the miraculous change of heart – can be found everywhere in Victorian fiction. They point among other things to the limits of realist 'solutions'. Yet these lumbering bits of narrative machinery may throw up new problems in their own right, which then have to be 'processed' in their turn.

2

All this may seem complicated enough; but it becomes more so the moment we recognise that none of it can take place without a reader, and that reading is as much a strategic enterprise as the work itself. To read, then, is to engage in one set of strategies in order to decipher another set. It was the achievement of reception theory to turn the act of reading, for so long regarded as being as natural as sleeping or breathing, into a theoretical problem in its own right; and this was almost fated to happen in the wake of a literary modernism for which textual obscurity – the sheer sweat and toil of reading – is not simply a contingent affair but one central to the meaning of the work. The modernist text resists easy reading for a number of reasons: because it turns in on itself, troubled by the absence of an assured audience, and takes itself as its subject in a way that shuts it off from any easy access from outside; because it seeks to distil something of the fragmentation and ambiguity of modern existence, qualities which invade its form and language and risk rendering it opaque; because it turns its back contemptuously on the political, commercial, technical and bureaucratic discourses around it, which it feels are transparent only at the cost of being degraded, and seeks for itself a thicker, more subtle and elusive idiom; because it wants to avoid being treated as a commodity, and uses its obscurity as a way of preventing itself from being too easily consumed. In this sense, the obscurity of modernist art is rather like the defensive mechanisms with which Nature has thoughtfully equipped those animals in danger of being too easily snapped up by a predator.

James Joyce mischievously remarked that he wanted his readers to spend as long reading *Finnegans Wake* as he took to write it, and it is this high-modernist reader, confronted with a cryptic set of signifiers and a dearth or overload of information, who lies at the origin of reception theory. The reader, once the least privileged, most disregarded member of the holy trinity that includes author and work, treated as a mere skivvy or dogsbody by a disdainful caste of authors, finally comes into her own as co-creator of the literary work. Consumers are turned into collaborators. Wittgenstein has some interesting remarks in the *Philosophical*

Investigations about reading not as a 'mental process' but as the deployment of certain acquired techniques. The reader has certain experiences because she has learnt to do certain things, master certain strategies and manoeuvres, in the act of reading. If she could not deploy these techniques, she could not have the experiences characteristic of a skilled reader.

With reception theory, however, even more demands are piled on the hapless handler of texts. The reader is now obliged to engage in a strategic enterprise which would tax even the most manically energetic of individuals: connecting, revising, code-switching, synthesising, correlating, depragmatising, image-building, perspective-switching, inferring, normalising, recognising, ideating, negating, foregrounding, backgrounding, feeding back, contextualising, situation-building, coordinating, memory-transforming, expectation-modifying, illusion-building, gestalt-forming, image-breaking, blank-filling, concretising, consistency-building, structuring and anticipating. After an hour or two sweating over a book, there is nothing the reader needs more than a hot shower and a good night's sleep.

Wolfgang Iser, who gives an account of these activities in *The Act of Reading*, explicitly uses the word 'strategies' to describe the workings of the text. The 'repertoire' of the work consists of its themes, narrative contents and so on, but these must be structured and organised, and it is the task of the work's strategies to fulfil this function. These strategies, however, are not to be seen simply as structural features of the text, since as well as ordering its materials they create the conditions under which those materials become communicable.[19] They thus encompass both 'the immanent structure of the text and the acts of comprehension thereby triggered off in the reader'.[20] If they belong to the work as fact, they also belong to it as act.

Strategies, then, constitute the vital link between work and reader, as the cooperative activity which brings the literary work into being in the first place. They set off a 'series of different actions and interactions',[21] as part of the unfolding project that we know as the literary work. The text is a set of instructions for the production of meaning, rather like an orchestral score. 'As we read,' Iser comments, 'we oscillate to a greater or lesser degree between the building and breaking of illusions. In a process of trial and error, we organise and reorganise the various data offered us by the text . . . We look forward, we look back, we decide, we change our decisions, we form expectations, we are shocked by their nonfulfilment, we question, we muse, we accept, we reject . . . Elements of the repertoire are continually backgrounded or foregrounded with a resultant strategic overmagnification, trivialisation or even annihilation of the allusion.'[22]

In this potentially unending process, our initial interpretive hypotheses find themselves challenged by the gradual emergence of other possible readings. Areas of indeterminacy have to be filled in by the reader's imagination, connections forged, inferences drawn and imaginary situations assembled from the schemata offered us by the work. We are forced retrospectively to reconsider data we took at first to be unproblematic, and thus to reorient our preconceptions. The addressee of the text must intervene to fill in semantic gaps, choose her own preferred interpretive path from a multitude of possibilities and test out different, perhaps contradictory perspectives. The work can reformulate its own norms and conventions as it evolves, and this is a project in which the reader is a full participant, if not quite a co-author. Ownership of the work, so to speak, remains invested in the author – but this is a caring, liberal-minded author/employer with a lively social conscience, one who grants the reader/employee as much say in running the enterprise as is compatible with the necessarily asymmetrical relationship between them. The meaning of the text in this view is not an object but a practice. It emerges from a constant traffic between work and reader, so that (to put the matter in Lacanian idiom) the act of reading is a project in which one receives back one's own response from the other (the text) in transfigured or defamiliarised form.

There is something of Jameson's self-fashioning artefact here as well. 'As we read,' Iser remarks, 'we react to what we ourselves have produced, and it is this mode of reaction that, in fact, enables us to experience the text as an actual event.'[23] A literary work should be understood as 'a reaction to the thought systems which it has chosen and incorporated in its own repertoire', a formulation strikingly close to Jameson's own.[24] In common with most reception theorists, Iser shows scant awareness of the sphere of ideology, or indeed of much history other than literary history; but it is not hard to see in the way the Iserian work reacts to what it has produced a version of the case we have been examining. Indeed, at one point Iser casts the issue in explicitly Jamesonian terms, speaking as he does of the need for the literary work 'to comprise the complete historical situation to which it is reacting'.[25]

Stanley Fish, too, treats reading as a strategy, but like the campaign of an all-conquering general it is one which mows down everything in its path and meets with no resistance. This is because there is nothing there to resist it. 'Every component in such a [reception theory] account,' Fish insists, 'the determinacies or textual segments, the indeterminacies or gaps . . . will be the products of an interpretive strategy that demands them, and therefore no one of those components can constitute the independent given which serves to ground the interpretive process.'[26] Interpretation, then, like the works of fiction it deals with, is self-generating and self-legitimating. Since it produces what it purports to investigate, all interpretation is self-interpretation. The dim patch of light you glimpse down the microscope turns out to be your own eye.

Generally speaking, it is possible to distinguish between two ways of regarding literary works: as objects, and as events.[27] An exemplary case of the former is American New Criticism, for which the literary text is a closed system of signs to be dissected. It is an edifice or architectural structure, complete with various levels and sub-systems, which is supposed to exist in the reader's mind as a synchronic whole, rather than a dramatic or symbolic act with its own evolving history. The poem for the New Critics has the gem-like hardness of an urn or icon, cut loose from authorial intention, autotelic and unparaphrasable.

Ironically, then, the literary work could be said to imitate the commodity form in the very act of resisting it. Its sensory texture is a rebuke to the commodity's abstraction, the way it strips the world of its carnal being. Yet as a self-enclosed object, one which suppresses its own history and has no visible means of support, the work is an instance of reification in its own right. As a delicate balance of contending forces, the poem serves as a tacit critique of self-interest, dogmatic one-sidedness and over-specialisation. As such, it makes an implicit comment on the contemporary social order. Yet its supreme equipoise has a clinical, dispassionate air about it, which reflects the scientism of a technological age. It also reflects a liberal hostility to partisanship. The poem may be cut adrift from history, and thus from ideology; but if ideology is seen as an imaginary resolution of real contradictions, then the literary text becomes a model of the very phenomenon on which it casts so jaundiced an eye.

Russian Formalism is another case of treating the work as an object, though in the course of time it moves beyond a rather static view of it as an 'assemblage of devices' to a more integrated, dynamic conception of its operations.[28] The Prague structuralists inherit this theory of the text from their Russian counterparts, regarding it as a functional system and a structural totality. Yet a strategy is more than a matter of dynamic organisation. It is rather a structure with a certain built-in intentionality, one organised to achieve certain effects. It is a project, not simply a system. Its internal disposition is determined by its active relations to what it addresses. In the case of the Formalists, this is the process of 'de-automating' the reader's perceptions. In this sense, the poem's internal complexity exists for an 'external' end, which is to say that there is a tentative transition at work here from the text as object to the text as strategic act. Roman Jakobson writes of the literary work as 'a complex, multi-dimensional structure, integrated by the unity of aesthetic purpose'.[29] It is notable that the word 'design' means both a structure and a purpose it aims to achieve.

To this extent, the Formalist conception of the work as object is mildly at odds with the notion of estrangement. Estrangement, to be sure, can be specified in terms of the text's given features, and in this sense belongs to its objective structure. But it is also an event. It is language doing something to the reader, which is to say language as rhetoric. And that is considerably less easy to specify, depending as it does on more than the shape of the text itself. The Formalist work is accordingly suspended between object and event, with a decided tilt to the former; and this is largely because the strategic end of the poem – the modifying of perceptions – is so thoroughly immanent to it. Even so, the process of making-strange involves a transformative work on the reader, which is to say that the poem is both aesthetic system and moral practice.

The notion of the text as strategy is more evident in the Formalists' view of prose fiction. It is the habit of these critics to distinguish within literary narrative between 'story' and 'plot' – the former signifying the 'actual' sequence of events as they can be reconstructed from the narrative, the latter meaning the specific organisation of those events by the work itself. Plot, then, can be seen as a strategic operation on the materials of the story, reorganising them in a way which (through suspense, 'braking', 'retardation' and the like) renders them freshly perceptible.

What, then, of structuralism and semiotics, as far as the object/event distinction is concerned? There are strains of semiotics which treat the text as an object to be analysed, as in the writings of Yury Lotman or Michael Riffaterre.[30] But there are other semiotic currents – the work of Umberto Eco, for example – which are closer to what we have seen of reception theory, and for which the interpretation of signs is a complex strategic practice.[31] What Eco calls 'sign-production' is an activity on the part of the reader, who by abduction (hypothesis), induction, deduction, overcoding, undercoding and other such strategies, deciphers in the text a 'message' which is 'an empty form to which can be attributed various senses'.[32] The text is less a solid structure than 'a large labyrinthine garden' with criss-crossing paths that permit us to take many different routes. Reading is thus more like strolling through Hyde Park than it is like crossing Westminster Bridge. These routes or 'inferential walks' through the artefact involve the reader in sometimes endorsing and sometimes repudiating the author's codes, sometimes not knowing what the 'sender's' rules are, trying to extrapolate such interpretive guidelines from disconnected fragments of data, proposing certain tentative codes of her own to make sense of problematic segments of the work, and so on. Textual 'messages' are not simply to be read off from codes; they are events or semiotic acts irreducible to the codes which generate them. One thinks of Wittgenstein's comments on the creative nature of applying a rule. As Charles Altieri argues, performances cannot be reduced to verbal constructs.[33] And since codes themselves may be modified or transfigured by the reader's act of production, they can proceed to propose meanings radically different from those they have produced already.

The signs of the text for Eco are not stable units but the transient results of coding rules; and codes themselves are not fixed structures but momentary devices or working hypotheses posited by the reader to explain a 'message'. As such, they are constituted only in the performance of reading, pulling pieces of the text provisionally together to shed light on its modes of sense-making. The 'message' of the text is not a given either, but a 'network of constraints' which allows for 'fertile inferences' on the part of the reader, as well as for productive 'aberrations'. A work is less an order of meaning than a set of sometimes well-nigh illegible instructions for the production of such meanings; and this is true even of its individual signs, which are less the discrete, self-identical units of Saussure than 'microtexts' containing a diversity of semantic possibilities. At the level of both sign and text, semiosis finally shades off into infinity. Both the production and reception of signs, texts and messages are projects of byzantine complexity. And since this semiotic activity is in principle unlimited, as the meaning of a sign can be furnished only by another sign and that in turn by another, there is no natural resting-place for the toiling reader. We are dealing not with a stable structure but with a process of structuration. As Eco puts it, 'the aesthetic text continually transforms its denotations into new connotations, none of its items stop at their first interpretant, contents are never received for their own sake but rather as the sign-vehicle for something else'.[34]

In this process, each feature of the work is actualised by the reader, which then spurs her as a consequence into new interpretive activity. One actualises the structures of a text by applying certain provisional codes to the work, at the same time as one responds to what the work makes of the structures thus projected. This, one might claim, is Eco's own semiotic version of the Jamesonian model. The interaction of reader and text, in which the reader projects certain meanings to which she finds herself reacting, is akin to Jameson's view of the traffic between text and subtext. Eco's literary work is both structure and event, fact and act, and each of these in terms of the other. Textual codes and reader's codes ceaselessly interpenetrate. There is no literary work, as opposed to certain material objects known as books, without the 'actualisations' of a reader, but this activity is not self-determining. Though by no means prescribed by the structures of the texts themselves, it is nonetheless cued, guided and constrained by them. (This, one might note, is a key difference between Eco's approach and the bold-faced philosophical idealism of a Stanley Fish.) In decoding the work, the reader brings to bear on it a certain general competence; but this rule-governed set of capacities is realised in a unique and distinctive way through the actual performance of reading, to the point where competence and performance become hard to distinguish. The reader is not simply equipped with a set of fixed capabilities which she then obediently realises, any more than a tennis player at Wimbledon wins the championship by first mugging up on the techniques of the game in the dressing room, and then sallying forth to put them into practice.

Just as there are more and less strategic forms of semiotics, much the same distinction applies to structuralism. 'The [structuralist] inventory of [a work's] elements,' writes Wolfgang Iser, 'produces an order, the sum of its techniques relates the elements to one another, and there thus emerges a semantic dimension that constitutes the end product of the text – but all this sheds no light whatsoever on why such a product should emerge, how it functions, and who is to make use of it.' In response to this curiously sterile exercise, Iser quotes in Wittgensteinian mood the bon mot of a German colleague: 'One can only understand language if one understands more than language.'[35] Only by grasping the function of this textual structure – which is to say, grasping its relations to a context and seeing it as *performance* – can the structure itself be properly laid bare. In this sense, the structure of the text is not the final datum. This is also true more generally, since a structure could be foundational only if it was apodictic or self-interpreting. As long as it needs to be interpreted, there is something prior to it, namely the language in which this interpretation takes place.[36]

'The structures of the literary text,' Iser writes, 'only become relevant through the function of that text',[37] a claim which is equivalent to proposing that the text is best seen as a strategy. A strategy is precisely a structure which is broadly determined by its ends. In fact, Iser's claim is true not just of literary works, but of meaning as such. Meaning, to be sure, is in one sense a structural affair, as the structuralists are eager to insist; but the systemic difference between signs is a necessary rather than sufficient condition of making sense. I do not know how to use the word 'realty' simply by knowing that it does not mean the same thing as 'reality', indeed that in a certain sense it means exactly the opposite. I need instead to grasp its functions in a given form of life.

Historically speaking, the function of a literary work is a highly variable affair. Works, as we have seen already, may accomplish a whole gamut of purposes, from inspiring young warriors into battle to quadrupling one's bank balance. But we have also seen that the literary text has a kind of internal context as well, to which it has a kind of internal relation; and here, too, broadly speaking, it is function that determines structure. It is what the work is trying to do with this context that determines the devices it selects and the way it evolves. As Iser observes, 'If the literary text represents an act of intentionality directed towards a given world, than the world it approaches will not simply be repeated in the text; it will undergo various adjustments and corrections . . . In elucidating the relation of text to extratextual realities, [the concept of function] also elucidates the problems that the text sought to settle.'[38] The cautious bureaucratese of 'various adjustments and corrections' hardly does justice to the powerfully transformative process by which the world enters the text; but Iser is right to see that the concept of function and the notion of the work as problem-settling are closely linked.

There is a kind of structuralism that sets out to identify the rules by which texts combine their discrete elements into units of meaning, and this is a *locus classicus* of the work as object. The narratology of Gérard Genette and A.J. Greimas may be taken as exemplary here.[39] One thinks also of the literary taxonomies of Northrop Frye, who while not exactly a structuralist seems at times intent on the activity of classification as an end in itself. It is this strain of analysis that Jacques Derrida once criticised as animated 'only by a mechanics, never by an energetics'.[40] At its least inspiring, it fails to grasp a literary work as a piece of rhetoric – which is to say, as trying to do something. It is the view of literature from the planet Zog. Yet there is also a species of structuralism which has rather more in common with the notion of the text I have been proposing. It is one evident in Claude Lévi-Strauss's comment that 'mythical thought always progresses from the awareness of opposites towards their resolution.'[41] 'The purpose of the myth,' he writes 'is to provide a logical model capable of overcoming a contradiction.'[42] Seen in this light, myths are strategies which are 'good to think with', pre-modern machines for processing antinomies and contradictions. One does not need to subscribe wholeheartedly to this theory of mythology to recognise its value for literary analysis.

As with Iser's reception theory or Eco's semiotics, myths do not accomplish this task at a stroke but as a strategic process, as one set of antitheses is transformed into another and that into a third, one contradiction is mediated only to spring open a second, one element is displaced by another which is in turn dislodged and so on. There is also a ceaseless 'intertextuality' at work here, as one mythological text cannibalises another only to be recycled in turn by a third. The unconscious meaning of a myth, Lévi-Strauss observes, is the problem it seeks to resolve; and to achieve this resolution it deploys such conscious mechanisms as image, plot and narrative. We are warned, however, not to think of the relation between conscious and unconscious, plot and problem, as a mirror-image or homology, but as a transformation. Much the same may be said of the relation between textual strategies and their subtexts in Jameson's model.

Myths for Lévi-Strauss are a 'science of the concrete', prefiguring that later science of the concrete which will emerge at the heart of the Enlightenment as the aesthetic.[43] In one sense, as we shall see in a moment, they are about nothing but themselves, as symbolic forms in which the structure of the human mind can be found brooding on its own unfathomably intricate operations. In this sense, they are a kind of pre-modern version of the symbolist poem or (post) modernist novel. It is true that myths reveal these mental operations in the act of seeming to describing reality; but for the structuralist anthropologist, the world they purport to describe is also one they construct. Even so, by classifying that world with all the microscopic precision of a medieval schoolman, they allow men and women to feel more at home in it, and thus have their practical functions as well. They are forms of cognitive mapping as well as theoretical reflections or examples of aesthetic play. In all these ways, myths as the structuralists see them have an obvious parallel to literary fiction.

That this is so can be shown in the following passage from Lévi-Strauss, into which I have inserted my own alternative readings in parentheses:

> That the mythology of the shaman does not correspond to an objective reality [that the author's fiction does not have a direct referent] does not matter. The sick woman [reader] believes in the myth [fiction] and belongs to a society [literary institution] which believes in it. The tutelary spirits and malevolent spirits, the supernatural monsters and magic animals, are all part of an orderly, coherent system on which the natural conception of the universe is founded [ideology]. The sick woman [reader] accepts these mythical beings [suspends her disbelief] or, more accurately, she has never questioned their existence. What she does not accept are the incoherent and arbitrary pains [social oppressions and contradictions] which are an alien element in her system but which the shaman [author], calling upon myth [fiction], will reintegrate with a whole where everything is meaningful. Once the sick woman [reader] understands, however, she does more than resign herself; she gets well [resumes her practical role in social life].[44]

No doubt this parallel of myth and fiction might seem a touch reductive. Not every literary work operates as such a blunt ideological instrument. In fact, a good many 'canonical' literary works are deeply at odds with the ruling ideologies of their time, just as a good many popular or non-canonical works obediently reproduce it. One should not make the mistake of equating canonical with conservative and popular with progressive. Even so, there is something to be said for the crude transpositions of the above passage. Viewed in this light, myth is not just a machine to think with, but a symbolic act. It is a set of techniques for making sense of problems and contradictions that might otherwise prove intolerable.

Simon Clarke argues that whereas the early Lévi-Strauss treats myths as problem-solving devices, his later work views them in more rationalist spirit as disinterested intellectual exercises.[45] Now, shorn of their practical motivations, they are simply ways of organising the world according to a logic of parallelism, antithesis, inversion, homology and so on, and this almost obsessively meticulous ordering stands in need of no justification beyond itself. One might claim in Althusserian terms that myths have accordingly shifted in Lévi-Strauss's view from ideology to theory – from legitimating the social order by providing imaginary resolutions of its contradictions, to forms of pure cognition.

Yet such cognition, in so far as it satisfies a certain rage for order, is no more ideologically innocent than Althusser's concept of theory. Clarke speaks of Lévi-Strauss's *Mythologies* as practising a purely immanent form of analysis for which myths are coded expressions of the universal laws of the mind, and deal with nothing extraneous to themselves. In this sense, it is as though Lévi-Strauss's approach to myth has shifted not only from ideology to theory but from realism to modernism. Like some modernist or postmodernist texts, myths are self-referential. Indeed, it is possible to see structuralism itself as an incongruous combination of high French rationalism and an equally Gallic lineage of symbolism. The rationalism is present in the idea of universal mental structures; the symbolism lies in the fact that these structures are ultimately about nothing but themselves. The more 'realist' or pragmatic current in Lévi-Strauss's work, by contrast, sees myths as strategic operations on Nature and society, heuristic fictions that establish, mediate and transform oppositions. In doing so, they seek to resolve such conundrums as how humanity can be at once part of Nature and separate from it, or how men and women can be born both of the earth and of human parents.

As such, these tribal tales adopt concrete means to tackle abstract questions, which is another way in which they resemble literary works. We are speaking here of the myth-maker as *bricoleur* – as a craftsman who knocks together whatever scraps and leavings he finds to hand (the debris of events, recycled symbols, fragments of other myths and so on) for whatever symbolic task he is out to accomplish. (There is a parallel here with Freud's notion of the unconscious, which must similarly cobble together various off-the-peg bits and pieces to fabricate the texts we know as dreams.) The myth-maker of *Mythologies*, by contrast, is a more cerebral, aesthetic creature altogether, content as he is to gaze dispassionately on the human world for no other reason than to find in it an expression of the same laws which regulate his own mind, and which thus govern his own gazing. When Lévi-Strauss writes in *The Savage Mind* that Australians reveal a taste for erudition, speculation and even a sort of intellectual dandyism, it is not the surfers of Bondi beach but the Aboriginal peoples that he has in mind.

Symbolic thought of this kind seeks to restore unity to a world torn between Nature and culture. This is a paradoxical operation, since the very means by which such unity may be restored – thought, language, symbol – are themselves the product of this fissure. They are consequences of the schism they strive to repair.[46] The disruptive emergence of human culture poses a threat to the integrity of the world, but one that can be overcome in symbolic guise in the mediations of mythology. Not just in its content, in fact, but in its very form, which weds thing to thought, concrete phenomenon to general concept. In this sense, there is a secret utopian dimension to myth, rather as there is to literature. We have had occasion to note this magical or utopian quality of literary works already in the way they seem to reconcile language and reality, but only because the latter is secretly a product of the former. Literary works thus achieve in their form what they often enough fail to attain in their content, brooding as they do on the hiatus between desire and reality, the way human consciousness and its circumstances appear comically or tragically at odds. In the utopian aspect of its form, literary art seeks to compensate for the pathos of its content.

Myths may be structures built from the debris of events, yet for some thinkers they also offer a kind of resistance to events. 'Mythical history,' comments Paul Ricoeur, 'is itself in the service of the struggle of structure against events and represents an effort of societies to annul the disturbing action of historical factors; it represents a tactic of annulling history, of deadening the effect of events.'[47] For Lévi-Strauss, a different kind of relation between structure and event holds sway in art. Art, he remarks in *The Savage Mind*, involves a 'balance between structure and event'.[48] He means by this a balance between the artwork's general design or internal logic, and events in the sense of apparently extraneous accidents, things that happen in a story or painting that we feel could always have happened otherwise. The realist work, as we have seen, has a determinate design to it, but not one that is allowed to dragoon all the work's features into some rigorous order, or imbue them with an air of strict necessity.

This classical conception, of the form of the artwork containing but not subjugating its contents, is less suggestive than the concept of *structuration*. Structuration mediates between structure and event, in much the same sense that a strategy does. It signifies a structure, to be sure – but a structure in action, one constantly in the process of reconstituting itself according to the ends it seeks to achieve, along with the fresh purposes it keeps producing, and thus *eventual* in a way at odds with, say, the Saussurean conception of language or the early Formalist notion of the poem. To understand it demands a dialectical logic.

One might claim that a pure or total structure – what Paul Ricoeur calls an 'absolute formalism' – is empty. In reducing whatever happens within its bounds to its own unbending logic, it risks rendering such events arbitrary and interchangeable, meaningful only in so far as they exemplify its internal laws. Events can only instantiate the structure, not raise a hand against it. A pure event, by contrast, is blind: in being irreducible to any explanatory structure, it is as ineffable and enigmatic as a Dadist happening. (There is therefore something almost oxymoronic about a theory of the event, an idea central to the thought of the greatest living French philosopher.)[49]

The idea of a strategy or structuration, however, deconstructs the distinction between structure and event in an exact sense of the term 'deconstruction' – which is to say that rather than abolishing the difference between them, it demonstrates how it constantly undoes itself while retaining a certain undeniable force.[50] A strategy is the kind of structure that is forced to re-totalise itself from moment to moment in the light of the functions it has to perform. It is powered by an intention – but an intention in the sense of a purposeful design or set of designs inscribed within it, not in the sense of a ghostly force propelling it from the outside. Moreover, the structure of literary works generates events which can then react back on that structure and transform its terms; and to this extent such works have the form of a free human act. Since this two-way process is also true of so-called ordinary language, literary texts perform in a more dramatic, perceptible way what takes place in everyday speech.

Paul Ricoeur sees the word itself as lying at the juncture between structure and event. 'A trader between the system and the act', it is 'the point of crystallisation, the tying-together of all the exchanges between structure and function.'[51] On the one hand, it draws its value from the linguistic system to which it belongs; on the other hand, its 'semantic actuality' is identical with the 'actuality of the utterance', which is a perishable event. The word, however, 'survives the sentence', in both senses of 'sentence'. Rather than being doomed to die with the act of speaking, its iterablity allows it to resume its place in the structure of language, holding itself in readiness for whatever unpredictable new usages may happen along. But it does not return to its allotted position with quite the same virginal innocence as before. For it is now 'heavy with a new use-value'; and this means that in rejoining the linguistic system it changes the course of its history, however minutely.[52] Poetry is simply this dialectic writ large.

One of the paradoxes of the literary work is that it is 'structure' in the sense of being unalterable and self-complete, yet 'event' in the sense that this self-completion is perpetually in motion, real-ised as it is only in the act of reading. Not a word of the work can be changed, yet in the vicissitudes of its reception not a word stays dutifully in place. 'That which endures,' writes Jan Mukařovský, 'is only the identity of a structure in the course of time, whereas its internal composition – the correlation of its components – changes continually. In their interrelations, individual components constantly strive to dominate one another, each of them makes an effort to assert itself to the detriment of the others. In other words, the hierarchy – the mutual subordination and superordination of components ... is in a state of constant regrouping.'[53] Perhaps Mukařovský makes the literary work sound a little too much like Wall Street, but the kernel of truth in his case can survive its metaphorical husk.

We have seen that some types of structuralism and semiotics are more hospitable to the concept of strategy than others, and much the same is true of phenomenology. It would be hard to run such a notion to earth in the work of Georges Poulet or Jean-Pierre Richard, both luminaries of the so-called Geneva school, or the early J. Hillis Miller, who came under Poulet's influence at Johns Hopkins.[54] Reading for these critics represents an immersion of one's consciousness in the literary work, to the point where in a well-nigh mystical merging of subjectivities, one becomes the subject of thoughts and images other than one's own. There is a hint of Jacques Lacan's imaginary register about this mutual indwelling of text and reader, as the two pass ceaselessly in and out of each other in a sealed reciprocity of selves. In this constant interplay of intimacy and otherness, the work itself turns into 'a human being . . . a mind conscious of itself and constituting itself in me as the subject of its own objects'.[55] Reading becomes a blessed respite from alienation, allowing for a well-nigh erotic coupling of subject and object everywhere refused in commonplace reality.

This style of phenomenology, in which the critic's task is to recreate the inmost structures of the text's 'consciousness', extracting the very essence of the (always coherent) subjectivity incarnate in it, is a very different affair from the phenomenological approach of Roman Ingarden in *The Literary Work of Art*, with its stress on the reader's activity in 'concretising' various skeletal structures or abstract schemata implicit in the work. As one reads, one highlights textual aspects, fills in indeterminacies, establishes spatial and temporal contexts for various imaginary objects, raids one's past experience to make sense of the text, and thus builds up a total 'aesthetic object', one which is guided by the work itself but never entirely identical with it. If much of this has a familiar ring from the work of Wolfgang Iser, it is because Iser was much influenced by Ingarden's phenomenology, as his colleague Hans-Robert Jauss was by Gadamerian hermeneutics. Reception theory stands at the confluence of these two currents.

There is, however, another sense in which phenomenological thought, in its hermeneutical rather than transcendental guise, has a bearing on the idea of the literary work as strategy. One might suspect that as a way of thinking about art, the concept of strategy is altogether too instrumental. Is it not too much in thrall to just the means–ends rationality the aesthetic is out to question? What of the ludic, sensory, pleasurable, autotelic dimensions of the artwork?

Here, however, a phenomenological understanding of the human body, exemplified at its finest by Maurice Merleau-Ponty's *Phenomenology of Perception*, can come to our aid.[56] The human body itself is a form of practice, a point from which a world is organised. A body which is not a source of significations (a hot water bottle, for example) is not a human one. One may even speak of the body as a strategy, in the sense that it organises itself to achieve certain ends. It exists where there is something to be done. Indeed, it is in this self-organising power, as opposed to being organised like a jigsaw puzzle from the outside, that it differs most notably from material bodies like bassoons and scimitars, though not from bodies like stoats and aspidistras. Yet there is no contra- diction between conceiving of the body in this strategic way, and insisting in the teeth of an instrumental rationality that human beings do not exist 'for' anything. Their existence is indeed an end in itself, just like that of a pansy. Only megalomaniacs imagine that they were put on earth to fulfil some mighty purpose.

Some of what we do, like clearing a windscreen of ice or having one's wisdom teeth extracted, is indeed purely instrumental; but there are other activities which are undertaken primarily for their own sake, and these are arguably the most precious. Their point lies not in achieving ends outside ourselves (though they may involve this as well), but in being forms of self-realisation. Since such self-realisation involves organising oneself in specific ways, it is not at odds with the idea of the body as strategy. Kicking a ball into a net is a matter of fitting certain means to a certain end, so that a kind of instrumental rationality is internal to the activity. But the action as such may not be instrumental in the sense of being executed for the sake of an end beyond itself, unless one happens to be earning several million pounds a year for doing so. Even then, it may be a question of the activity figuring as an end in itself while also achieving an external purpose. One takes it that David Beckham does not *simply* play football for the money, or Brad Pitt star in movies simply for the celebrity.

One ancient name for this form of activity is *praxis*, meaning a practice whose ends are internal to it. For Aristotle, virtue is a supreme instance of such conduct. Virtuous men and women realise their powers and capacities not for any utilitarian motive but as a fulfilling end in itself. The concept thus dismantles the distinction between the functional and the autotelic.[57] One acts with an end in view, but this end is not distinct from the activity itself. The bearing of this idea on the literary work is surely evident. In fact, another traditional name for this type of self-grounding, self-fulfilling, self-validating form of practice is art.[58] This is not to deny that art has a function. In the instrumental sense of the word, as we have seen already, it has served many such goals, from massaging a monarch's ego to allaying the political anxieties of the middle classes. As with a millionaire footballer who delights in what he does, however, these external motives can coexist with functions internal to the practice itself. Art may generate profit or propaganda, but its point, as Marx understood, lies in its self-realising power.

Only those with too crude an understanding of the concept fail to see this as a function. The aesthete who scandalously proclaims that art has no function is in this sense the terrible twin of the philistine. Both share the same anaemic view of functionality. It is just that the philistine believes that anything without some instant utility is worthless, while the aesthete falsely assumes that being functional and being an end in oneself are necessarily at loggerheads. But a function fulfilled for its own sake is still a function. Besides, we have seen already how for the radical Romantic tradition the work of art has a function simply by existing as an end in itself, thereby prefiguring a political future in which this enviable condition might also be true of human beings.

If we refuse the false choice between a thing's function and its existence in itself, we no longer have to hold with the Formalists that we can bring the material body of the text into focus only by suspending its relations with the outside world. This is rather like supposing that we can attend to the materiality of the body only when the body itself has been 'depragmatised', retrieved from its instrumental context like Heidegger's broken hammer in *Being and*

Time and contemplated instead as a thing in itself. In both cases, the material density of a thing would seem at odds with its activities in the world. Yet it is part of the very idea of the 'poetic' that meaning and materiality work together, in the sense that the poem's material body opens on to a world beyond itself precisely by virtue of its internal workings. This is true of all language, but it is more obvious in the case of poetry. The more thickly textured the poem's language, the more it becomes a thing in its own right, yet the more it can gesture beyond itself.

Something similar can be said of the human body. Its material existence simply *is* its relations to a world, which is to say that it exists most fundamentally as a form of practice.[59] Practice is the life of the body in much the same sense that meaning (or use) is the life of a sign. This is one reason why Thomas Aquinas refused to speak of a dead body, a phrase which struck him as a contradiction in terms. Instead, he saw a corpse as simply the remains of a living body. Death is the haemorrhaging of sense from human flesh, leaving it a brute lump of matter. The fact that the phrase 'the body in the library' brings to mind a corpse rather than an assiduous reader is part of the malign influence of a dualism that Aquinas firmly rejected. The body for him was the principle of human identity. If Michael Jackson has a disembodied soul, this soul would not in Aquinas's view be Michael Jackson. So Michael Jackson is actually nowhere. Such are the consolations afforded by religion.

Art and humanity, then, can be seen as akin in that their function lies not outside themselves but in the activity of their self-realisation. So here is another way in which art exemplifies moral value in its very form, not simply in whatever worthy sentiments it might come up with from time to time. Like the body, art is a strategic practice, which is to say that it organises itself in order to accomplish certain ends. But as we have seen already, the materials on which it goes to work are internal to it. So what is in question here is not an instrumental rationality in the most customary sense of the term, any more than it is with the self-realising, self-determining activities of the human body. Besides, just as for Aristotle, Aquinas, Hegel and Marx the practice of self-realisation involves sensory pleasure, so it does in the case of art. As with the practice of virtue, however, the self-delight of the work is inseparable from its performance. It is not some kind of agreeable extra, but a pleasure inherent in and proper to its specific kind of self-realising practice. Pleasure is not an end that the activity is out to achieve, in the sense that buying a rail ticket may achieve the goal of landing you in Edinburgh. The savouring is inseparable from the strategy. Only hedonists pursue gratification as the Tory squires yearn to pursue foxes.

So the notion of strategy need not be excessively goal-oriented, as it is in the Pentagon or the boardroom of Microsoft. Instead, it can be in Kant's phrase a purposiveness without purpose. It is when the human body is incarnate in some piece of praxis like dance or sexual love that it is at its most materially present. In an older aesthetic idiom, doing and being are here at one. It is in activities like these that the flesh is consummated, in contrast to actions like hammering a nail or investing in real estate, where the sensuous stuff of the body is set aside for the sake of a pragmatic goal. What allows the material body to be at its most luminously meaningful is not a suspension of practice, but a suspension of particular forms of practice.

None of this should be allowed to suppress the fact that the body is also an object, despite the protests of those for whom such talk smacks of an offensive objectification. Human beings are fundamentally natural, material objects – outcroppings of Nature or pieces of biology. Unless they were objects, they would be unable to enter into relationship with one other. Individuals are only personal (as opposed to human), however, in so far as that objectivity comes gradually to be inscribed with meaning, which is to say in so far as the body becomes a sign. And this involves a sickeningly precarious evolution, which if Freud is to be credited is only ever a partial success. The body may come into its own through signs, but it is never entirely at home among them.

If the body is a sign, what is it a sign of? Of something beyond itself, or inside itself? What kind of semiotics of the body is at stake here? To call the body a sign is not to see it as standing in for something else, in which case it might be possible, as with the word 'marmalade', that another sign might serve just as well in its place. It is to describe the way its stuff is as intrinsically expressive of significance as a word is expressive of a meaning. A body is a piece of signifying matter, just as a word is. What the body signifies is itself, which is one way it resembles a work of art. Even before it can speak, a small child stretches out its hand to grasp a toy, and this action is intrinsically meaningful, not simply meaningful to an observer equipped with language. Human meaning is always carnal meaning. We think in the way we do because of the kind of bodies we have.

One might call this at a stretch a Dominican theory of meaning.[60] Swayed by Aristotle's doctrine that the soul is not separate from the body but the animating form of it, the thirteenth-century Dominican Order converted this into a theory of interpretation, with their claim that the 'spirit' of writing was not an esoteric mystery secreted within the text, but one to be found in its common literal and historical meaning. It is a pity that the Dominicans then went on to blot their copybook by running the Inquisition, which had a rather less enlightened attitude to human flesh and blood.

To call the human body rational is to say not that its conduct is always eminently reasonable but that it is suffused with sense.[61] The greatest of Dominicans, Thomas Aquinas, considers metaphor to be the most appropriate kind of language in which to discuss spiritual truths, since, being sensory, it is best suited to our corporeal nature. Human rationality, he believes, is a distinctively animal rationality. Our form of reasoning is incarnational, inseparable from the material nature of our bodies.[62] We think and understand as animals. If an angel could speak, we would not be able to understand what he said.[63]

To see human flesh as intrinsically expressive is another way of saying that the body is not simply an object but a purposive form of practice. Its actions are a kind of eloquence. (Though one should not entertain too virile, red-faced an image of purposive action here, one drawn from the playing fields of Eton. Tasting a peach, smelling lavender, arguing about whether it will rain and listening to a jazz saxophonist are also activities.) Simply by virtue of its material structure, and the practices to which this gives rise, the body generates an enormous range of tacit assumptions and implicit understandings, which is why individuals who speak mutually incomprehensible languages can easily collaborate on the same practical tasks. The body is a mode of intelligibility in itself.

Some theorists, as we have seen, regard literary works as acts or events, and some as structures or objects. The same goes for ways of regarding the body. A surgeon necessarily treats the body beneath her scalpel as an object. It would betray a lack of compassion to do otherwise. It would be of no benefit to the patient for her to indulge in lurid daydreams about his private life while delving into his guts. Phenomenology, by contrast, treats the stuff of the body as a disclosure of subjectivity, though always ambiguously so. The human body does not thereby slip from opaque matter to transparent meaning. It remains something of an object even for oneself. I can properly speak of using my body, as when I selflessly turn myself into a human carpet to allow Tom Cruise to descend from his limousine without getting mud on his shoes. The body hovers in an indeterminate space between subject and object, rather as our talk about it tends to hover between 'having' a body and 'being' one. Because it is both meaning and materiality (the word 'sense' covers both), caught perpetually on the hop between the two, the body resists that dream of unity between them which is known among other things as the work of art.

Or, more exactly, a certain classical conception of the artwork. The doctrine of the unity of form and content means that there is no particle of the work's material body that is non-signifying, no feature that does not assume its place within a unified pattern of sense. This is the artwork as redeemed or risen body, the word made flesh, its material being as transparently expressive of significance as a smile or a wave of the hand. It is a utopian transfiguration of our common-or-garden flesh, which is usually forced to conduct its signifying business against a perpetual background rumble of biological non-sense, and whose gestures may occlude meaning in the very act of articulating it.

The fragmented body of the modernist or postmodernist work represents a riposte to this noble lie. Meaning and materiality are now beginning to drift apart, as things no longer seem to secrete their sense within themselves. The high-modernist work is aware of its own material body, forcing us to wonder in the case of writing how a set of humble black marks on a page can possibly be the bearers of something as momentous as meaning. Yet the more its material medium looms large, the more spectral and elusive its signs seem to grow. It is as though the work interposes its bulk between the reader and its meanings. It can no more be fully present in any one of its significations than a human body can be in any one of its actions. We have left behind the Romantic fantasy of the single action that would say it all, the one pure event that would manifest the truth of the self in a single flash or epiphany, the word of words that would compress a whole complex history in its mute yet eloquent presence. We have, in a word, put paid to the symbol, in which meaning and materiality are reconciled.

Like the body, literary works are suspended between fact and act, structure and practice, the material and the semantic. If a body is not so much an object within the world as a point from which a world is organised, much the same is true of the literary text. Bodies and texts are both self-determining, which is not to say that they exist in a void. On the contrary, this self-determining activity is inseparable from the way they go to work on their surroundings. We have seen that for Jameson those surroundings are not simply external to the work, but are installed as a subtext on its inside; and the same is true in a different sense of the body, which does not exist in a world which is 'external' to it. The world is a place we are in, not a place outside us. It would be odd to speak of beer as 'external' to the cask that contains it. Only if my real self is secreted inside my body, as a ghost in the machine, could reality be said to be external to it. The body would then become external to the self as well, as it is for Descartes. Wittgenstein, no doubt with a touch of *faux naïveté*, once professed himself puzzled by the phrase 'the external world'. He was surely quite right to think it strange. In any case, most of the world around us is an extension of the body itself. Castles, banks, television stations and the like are all ways in which the human body stretches beyond its limits to constitute a civilisation.

3

Nowhere is the idea of what is accomplished in an act of saying more vital than in the scene of psychoanalysis.[64] Discourse for the science of human discontent, as one might dub psychoanalytic theory, is both meaning and force, rather as the unconscious can be seen both as a semantic field and a cockpit of contending powers. To the question of what we are doing in our saying, psychoanalysis adds the question of what we are doing in our non-saying. There are many ways of not saying something, some of them considerably more loquacious than others. Rather as the literary critic treats what a work says in the light of how it says it, thus marking a difference between how we read poems and how we read road signs, so the analyst attends to the discourse of the analysand as a performance rather than as a set of propositions. It is what the patient is doing in the act of utterance – repressing, resisting, displacing, rationalising, disavowing, denegating, projecting, transferring, sublimating, idealising, aggressing, regressing, placating, seducing and so on – that is the key to the transactions between the two parties.

In all these stratagems and devices, what the analyst is attuned to is the anonymous murmuring of desire; and desire has the effect of skewing meaning out of true, disrupting narrative coherence, conflating one signifier with another, hijacking speech for its own devious ends with a certain cavalier disregard for empirical truth. Truth in this analytic scene is as performative an affair as it is in fiction. It is not a theory or proposition but a species of action. It consists above all in the drama of transference, in which the analysand comes to reorganise his or her psychical reality around the signifying figure of the analyst. In Kenneth Burke's term, nothing could be more 'dramatistic' and less theoretical than this encounter, in which, as in a lyric poem, empirical or conceptual material is of value only in so far as it can be assigned a role in a scenario which is itself neither empirical nor theoretical. The interpretation that counts in this situation is one that might disclose the truth of the subject, and in doing so prove to be life-transformative. Once again, something similar could be claimed of poems and novels. As Philip Rieff points out, 'As a strategist in the wars of truth, Freud habitually insisted that theory and therapy are really the same'.[65]

Interpretations are strategic forces in the drama of transference, to be modified, elaborated or discarded according to how far they 'take' or 'stick'. The same might be said of a playwright revising his script each morning in the light of the audience's reactions to it on the previous evening. Interpretations are to be judged in terms of the sense they allow the patient to make of her experience, which is to say the extent to which they permit her to deliver a coherent narrative of herself. The patient's discourse is treated strategically, as a set of moves in a game, a piece of rhetoric alive with the stirrings of power and desire. As with fiction, what look like constatives are unmasked as performatives. In this sense, the scene of analysis, in which theory is constantly turning into practice and practice perpetually in the process of modifying theory, is more like a site of political struggle than an academic seminar.

No doubt the analyst may be intrigued to hear that her patient has just slaughtered all five of her children before taking the bus to her thrice-weekly session. What counts psychoanalytically

speaking, however, is what this action signifies for the unconscious, and how this figures in the transferential process. What
matters is the role it plays in the fictional world on which the two
parties are busy collaborating as co-authors – how it resonates or
fails to resonate in the intimate, cloistered, profoundly impersonal
dialogue between the two. In the same way, a critic may be mildly
interested to learn that the poet really did run naked down
Tunbridge Wells High Street shouting that he was Joan of Arc, but
the revelation will not alter his account of the poem. In the scene
of analysis, the question of whether an event really happened may
be nothing like as important as it is in the scene of a crime. In one
sense, the scene of analysis is exactly that; but the crime in question
is nameless, anonymous, timeless, unlocatable, of uncertain agency,
buried in oblivion, never reducible to an actual event, and not one
for which we are in any case truly responsible. In this, it has a good
deal in common with what theologians know as original sin.

The psychoanalyst's consulting room is a species of fiction in a
number of senses. For one thing, the content of the discourse there
is always to be grasped under the sign of form and force. For
another thing, truth is less a question of direct reference than of a
statement's function within a wider, artificially fabricated context
(the scene of analysis itself), one which has its own peculiar
internal dynamic. It is this entire context, not any single proposition that can be plucked from it, that has a bearing upon truth,
which is to say on the Real of the patient's desire.

Real-life events and emotions make their way into the scene of
analysis, just as they do into a poem or novel. As with the literary
text, however, the everyday world is 'depragmatised' on entering
this theatre of the psyche, its characters and events prised loose
from their familiar functions and lifted into another domain
altogether, a symbolic sphere in which they can be seen in the
transfigurative light of the unconscious. They enter upon the
psychoanalytic stage only to be altered, sometimes out of recognition, by the demands of its inner logic. They are grist to the mill of

its self-sustaining project, rather as wars, games of croquet and adulterous liaisons are the materials upon which a literary fiction seizes in order to evolve in accordance with its own rigorous internal requirements. The scene of analysis is deliberately insulated from the world outside: an analyst would not dream of dropping in to her patient's apartment for a chat, or offer him tea and biscuits after their session as though he had just given blood. Talking to someone who is permanently out of sight, mostly silent, and who will interrupt a patient in full confessional flight with the curt instruction 'Time's up!' is scarcely the stuff of everyday living. Like art, the scene of analysis is elaborately ritualised. Both are insulated by virtue of their procedures from the workaday world. Yet rather as it is precisely fiction's distance from the real, the outrageous liberties it can take with it, that allows it to disclose truths beyond the empirical, so one may say the same of the so-called talking cure, which has something like the oblique relation to the real world of a poem or a play.

Besides, just as a literary work, in the act of unfolding a specific fable or motif, gestures to a broader context of meaning, so the discourse of the scene of analysis is always in some sense doubled. If it is a dialogue between two individuals, it is one informed by a larger, more anonymous narrative of trauma, desire, repression and so on, which it is the aim of Freud's theoretical work to recount. As with a realist literary work, what the patient has to say is irreducibly specific, yet resounds with certain 'typical', impersonal, transindividual topics. When Freud was told that his great rival Jung had just discovered something called the collective unconscious, he remarked sardonically that the unconscious is collective anyway.

There is a sense in which psychoanalysis treats the body as a text. In neurosis, for example, the body itself becomes a kind of script, traced with a set of symptoms or signifiers which, as with some obscure modernist work, must be deciphered to lay bare the meanings they half reveal and half conceal. Criticism inverts this act, treating a text as among other things a material body. For phenomenological thought, as we have seen, meaning and materiality never slot smoothly together, and much the same is true for psychoanalysis. The body is half in and half out of meaning at the same time. It is not just a brute object in the world, but neither can it be reduced to a representation. 'The mode of being of the body,' writes Paul Ricoeur, 'neither representation in me nor thing outside of me, is the ontic model for any conceivable unconscious.'[66] In Freud's view, the drive lies on the frontier between the psychical and the somatic. It represents the body for the mind, and is therefore cusped between flesh and sign. It is not a meaningful force in itself, springing as it does from the depths of our somatic being; but we can grasp it only through the semantic, rather as the force of an utterance can be grasped only through its meaning.

The unconscious for Freud is thus both a sphere of signifiers and an economy of forces, which is to say that it is semantic and somatic together. As Paul Ricoeur remarks, 'we are ceaselessly at the juncture of the erotic and the semantic'.[67] But these twin domains cannot be neatly mapped on to each other; and though desire seizes continually on this or that meaning, generating among other things those sign-saturated texts we call dreams, it is not meaningful in itself. Desire for Freud is not a question of teleology, as it is, say, for St Augustine, who finds in human longing a dim foreshadowing of the God in whom alone it can come to rest. Desire for psychoanalysis comes to rest only in death – a death dimly foreshadowed by the vacuity at its heart.

The body, then, is written, traced over with signifiers; but it will never be entirely at home in language, and the running battle between the two is the point from which desire wells up unstaunchably. All human flesh must be inserted into some symbolic order of meaning, but this proves a traumatic event from which we will be reeling for the rest of our days. For Freud himself it involves a symbolic castration, as we pay the forfeit of a pound of flesh for our access to the human world. Language hollows our being into desire and pitches us into temporality, shattering the imaginary unity for which we continue to hanker. And the Real – the place where desire, the vengeful Law and the death drive knot together to constitute the monstrously alien core of the self – is as far beyond the reach of the signifier as the taste of peaches.

It is sometimes jocularly claimed that nobody walks out of the psychoanalyst's consulting room cured of the affliction with which they walked in. This is because what has intervened between the walking in and walking out is a transformative work, in which real-life conflicts are recast by the drama of transference in terms of their potential resolution. In this sense, what the analyst seeks to unravel is not exactly a real-world problem but a fictionalised version of it, one which trades in image, narrative, symbolism, rhetoric and the like. Since it is this reworked version of her problems of which the patient is finally unburdened, it is indeed true that the psychoanalyst's couch bears scant resemblance to a hospital bed. In the analyst's consulting room, the stuff of the patient's everyday life is reorganised and reinterpreted; and this means that the process of analysis in some sense produces the very materials on which it goes to work. It has a hand in constituting the problems to which it offers a solution. The problems resolved in the consulting room are ones that have been in large measure manufactured there. The parallel with Jameson's theory of the literary text is evident. When the Viennese satirist Karl Kraus caustically remarked that psychoanalysis represented the problem to which it offered a solution, he would have been dismayed to know how orthodox a Freudian he was being.

The idea of a subtext has another bearing on psychoanalytic theory. In an essay entitled 'The Unconscious', Freud points out that we can know this submerged region of the self only through conscious experience; and this means knowing it only after it has undergone translation and transformation in the light of day. In reality, the ego is a mere outcrop of the unconscious, that part of it with the unenviable assignment of coping with the 'external' world. In the sphere of interpretation, however, this hierarchy is reversed, as consciousness becomes a form of access to the deeper forces that determine it. It is not, to be sure, the royal road to the unconscious. That, Freud insists, is the dream. But dreams must be interpreted by the waking mind. And the dream as we know it is the product of what Freud calls secondary revision, the process by which the dreamer, once awake, rationalises his dream into a more coherent text than it actually is. In effect, then, the unconscious is always a subtext crafted by the conscious mind. Like the history and ideology which enter the literary work as subtext, it can never be known in the raw. We know it only in the form in which the ego has strategically shaped it.

If the scene of analysis reconstitutes the problem to which it is a response, something of the same question-and-answer structure can be found in neurosis. This is because neurosis is a symbolic act with a dual structure. In Freud's view, it signifies a problem, but also represents a strategic attempt to resolve it. Both features can be found in the neurotic symptom, which expresses a desire at the same time as it registers its repression. The symptom represents a deadlock or aporia, as the irresistible force of unconscious desire meets the immovable objection of the censorious superego. In this sense, the neurotic symptom is a kind of problem-and-response situation in itself. Because it aims at a working compromise between the desire and its prohibition, it is a constructive response to the condition that it signifies. It is as though, on Jameson's model, the unconscious wish is the subtext to which our attention is drawn only by the strategic act of trying to master it.

The neurotic for Freud is someone who keeps symbolically summoning a problem into existence in order to master it. It is just that, as with writers of fiction, mastery can only ever take an imaginary form. Once the problem is resolved in real-life terms, the neurotic symptom should disappear. As soon as real conflicts have vanished, there is no longer the need for a displaced or symbolic resolution of them. Similarly, some rather upbeat Marxists have held that once historical contradictions have been successfully tackled, ideology, in the sense of an imaginary resolution of them, will no longer be necessary. We might equally predict that with the disappearance of human conflict all together, literature will wither away. It is because no such condition is possible that it continues. This is one sense in which literary art plucks a virtue from necessity.

If the discourse between patient and analyst lies at the juncture of meaning and force, so do the dreams on which it goes to work. The interpretation of dreams for Freud involves a dynamics and a semantics together. One must decipher the dream's representations, but in doing so find in their distortions, elisions and displacements a warring of unconscious forces. These forces stamp their impress on meaning, but they do so in ways which bend it violently out of true. Within the dream's economy, meaning must strike a compromise with power, as the censoring superego intervenes to soften, repress, condense, displace or disguise the dream's representations. The gaps, elisions, falterings, evasions and narrative leaps which result from this censorship then provide the analyst with vital clues to the operations of the unconscious. In a similar way, a Marxist critic like Pierre Macherey seeks to throw light on the literary work's relations to ideology by attending to what it compulsively, loquaciously and repetitively fails to say.

If dreams involve a dynamics and a semantics together, it is clear that neither an 'energetics' nor a hermeneutics is enough in itself to make sense of them.[68] The former is too mechanistic a method, while the latter is too idealist. What we need instead is a type of analysis which grasps the dream-text as both event and structure – as, in a word, structuration. It is this that Freud has in mind when he speaks of the 'dream-work', which represents a dynamic process of generating, condensing, repressing, deforming, displacing, disguising and transfiguring the dream's materials. All this can be seen as an unfathomably complex strategy on the part of desire. The dream is not so much a structure as a structure-in-action. In some of its favourite devices (storytelling, metaphorical substitution, metonymic displacement, the over-determination of its imagery and so on), it bears a striking resemblance to the poetic text.

Condensation, displacement, disguise, censorship, distortion: all these mechanisms, which belong to the dream-work, are so many strategic operations on the 'latent content' of the dream; and the result of their labours is what Freud calls the 'manifest content' or dream-text itself. This is the dream as we recall it once we are awake, and with which we then proceed to bore our friends and family. Because the transformations of the dream-work intervene between latent content and manifest content, it would be a mistake to posit one-to-one correspondences between these latter two, rather as it would be naive to assume such direct correspondences between a work of fiction and reality. To do so would be to see fiction as a mirror rather than as a work.

The role of the analyst, rather like that of *Ideologiekritik*, is not so much to reveal the meaning of a distorted text as to expose the meaning of the text-distortion itself, unmasking it as an effect of power. Psychoanalysis is that rare kind of hermeneutics which takes the workings of power with intense seriousness, which could scarcely be said of the work of Wilhelm Dilthey, Hans-Georg Gadamer or E.D. Hirsch. Beneath the coherent, continuous dream-text produced by secondary revision lies the true, shapeless, mutilated text of the dream itself, with its blanks, enigmas and surreal absurdities, its canny attempts to dodge the censor and smuggle a scandalous meaning past it. And all this wily, resourceful, strategic activity on the part of the censor, in its encounter with the equally devious stratagems of desire, has the most embarrassingly banal of goals: to allow us to sleep peacefully on. Otherwise we might wake in alarm, disturbed by too stark an encounter with the traumatic core of the dream. In this, too, perhaps, the dream-text has an affinity with ideology: both are symbolic acts that stand in for an 'impossible' confrontation with the psychical or political Real.

A dream for Freud is a disguised wish-fulfilment, which is to say that it contains both a real wish and an imaginary fulfilment.[69]

He speaks in his *Introductory Lectures on Psychoanalysis* of the dreamer's *relation* to his unconscious wishes, which he may repress or repudiate as unpleasant. In this sense, the relation between wish and fulfilment can be recast as one between problem and solution. In dreaming, one gets to indulge a wish which in waking life would be forbidden; and one does so because the wish is processed by the work of the unconscious, tempered, disguised and redacted until it can present itself in reasonably civilised form. In a similar way, Charlotte Brontë cannot grant Jane Eyre her fulfilment in the novel's first paragraph. If she did, there would be no novel. If *Jane Eyre* presents the reader with a narrative, it is partly because its heroine's desire must be deferred, deflected, modulated, rebuffed, displaced from one object to another, until it can be realised on terms acceptable to the social censor. Like the neurotic symptom, then, the dream is a compromise-formation. Both are substitute or symbolic ways of gratifying a prohibited desire, one which would provoke an excess of anxiety if denied outright. Both dream and symptom are strategies for managing and containing unconscious forces as well as giving vent to them.

If both dream and symptom display a circular structure, provoking into existence the very problems they seek to master, this is also true for Freud of the relation between Law and desire. The austere edicts of the Law or superego, by reminding us of what is forbidden, tend to provoke the very desires they deny, thus providing the insanely vindictive Law with something to repress. The grim news, however, is that what we have here is less a problem-and-solution structure than a problem-and-problem one, as the Law (itself the cause of so much of our misery) generates a desire that is also a source of unhappiness, and as this desire then incites the Law to yet more gratuitous savagery. To twist the knife even further, we also desire the Law, craving its punishment in order to expiate our guilt; but this masochistic delight in being chastised breeds more guilt in its turn, which brings the Law once more gleefully down on our heads. On this conception, we live not in a progressive evolution of question and answer, but in a stalled dialectic, pitched from one source of sorrow to another.

We have seen that the dream tempers an otherwise fearful confrontation with the Real; and what also aims for this goal is art. Art for Freud is a form of substitute satisfaction or wish-fulfilment, but of a suitably non-neurotic kind – one which allows us to indulge our fantasises without shame or self-reproach, and thus to avoid the sadistic fury of the superego. It modifies our illicit fantasises to what is socially acceptable, striking a compromise between desire and necessity, pleasure principle and reality principle. For some psychoanalytic critics, art is a case of the pleasure principle coming under the judicious management of the reality principle, as the ego, in the guise of literary form, intervenes to shape a desire that might otherwise get out of hand. Rather as for some Marxist critics, form distances ideology to the point where it becomes newly perceptible and thus open to challenge, so the literary work can be seen as objectifying unconscious fantasies, converting this shapeless, sublimely terrifying stuff into tangible images. Once objectified in this way, conflicts can be confronted and the distress they evoke relieved.[70] Form thus acts as a mode of psychical defence, as well as a kind of mastery. It assuages the guilt involved in indulging our fantasy, as well as satisfies a certain infantile need to make things whole. Art, in short, is a kind of therapy, and a much cheaper one than psychoanalysis. One might add that one word for gratifying one's fantasies in a socially acceptable form is fiction.

This whole style of psychoanalytic criticism, suggestive though it can prove, involves a simplistic form/content dichotomy, terms which correlate roughly with ego and unconscious. Its view of form as ordering and unifying is more relevant to the classical work of art than to the (post)modernist one. Moreover, rather as vulgar Marxist criticism fails to grasp form as itself a central medium of ideology, so this brand of theory largely fails to recognise how form can collude in the construction of fantasy, not only in defending the ego against its perilous excesses.

A more sophisticated approach, one in which form is itself the medium of desire, can be found in Peter Brooks's psychoanalytic reflections on the nature of narrative. Brooks comments in his *Reading for the Plot* that plot is 'perhaps best conceived as an activity, a structuring operation', which is to say as a strategy.[71] Reading reveals a 'passion for meaning' driven by the unconscious. 'Narratives,' he writes, '. . . lay bare the nature of narration as a form of human desire: the need to tell as a primary human drive that seeks to seduce and to subjugate the listener, to implicate him in the thrust of a desire that can never quite speak its name – never can quite come to the point – but that insists on speaking over and over again its movement towards that name.'[72] Moreover, rather as Eros in general builds up larger and larger complex unities (families, cities, nations), the reader of narrative seeks to construct meanings into ever larger wholes. Narrative desire is totalising, and (since it will come to rest only in the narrative's ending) is among other things a desire *for* an ending.

This, however, links narrative as much to Thanatos or the death drive as to Eros, since Thanatos is similarly in hot pursuit of its own self-delighting demise. Within the story itself, this passion for closure can be found in Brooks's view in its repetitions, its continual recircling upon itself, its stalling of its own restless movement. In this way, Thanatos seeks to suspend time, defeat the relentless forward motion of Eros and regress to some more primitive, prehistorical condition before the painful emergence of the ego. Yet these compulsive textual repetitions – these sameness-in-differences in which one can detect the presence of the demonic and uncanny – also serve to 'bind' the otherwise diffuse energies of the text, and in mastering them in this way prepares them for their pleasurable release. In this sense, then, Thanatos is harnessed to the service of Eros. It is also in the service of Eros in the sense that desire yearns for its own consummation, but (since that consummation will also spell its extinction) demands it in a way that also defers it. It needs to find its own circuitous path to closure, and when it enters narrative makes use of various repetitions and deviations to delay its own fulfilment. This deviance or divergence has the name of plot, which postpones the ultimate discharge of desire in the quiescence of a conclusion. In non-literary terms, this wandering of lost, unhappy souls between their origin and their end is known to Freud as human existence.

'What could be more profoundly rhetorical,' inquires Kenneth Burke, 'than Freud's notion of a dream that attains expression by stylistic subterfuges designed to evade the inhibitions of a moralistic censor?' [73] Burke is thinking of rhetoric here as a political act, and thus seeing psychoanalysis in political terms as well. Like radical politics, it is an inquiry into why we are robbed of our fulfilment, or granted it only on the alienating terms of the Law. If the psyche is the place where a repressive force does violence to meaning, so is ideology, as the neuralgic point where power impacts upon discourse and bends it out of true. The literary has sometimes been seen as an antidote to ideology, seeking as it does to retrieve the rich ambiguity of language from the monistic and manipulative. The assumption is surely naive. But the case also involves too reductive a view of ideology itself, which is well capable of mobilising the resources of ambiguity, indeterminacy, polyvalence and the like for its ends.[74]

Both psychoanalysis and political criticism are also studies in how we reap a certain obscene pleasure from our very subjugation, in a primary masochism which threatens to deliver us into the hands of the ruling powers. The safest way for any such power to ensure an easy ride for itself is to persuade its citizens to relish the process of their own self-violation. In political terms, this is known as hegemony; in psychoanalytic ones, it is the act of internalising the Law. The good news is that both procedures are fraught with peril, likely to achieve only partial success. If there is that in us which desires the Law, there is also that which rejoices to see it brought low. Tragedy is one name for the former impulse, and comedy for the latter.

What, finally, of political criticism? In an essay entitled 'On Literature as an Ideological Form', Etienne Balibar and Pierre Macherey speak in traditional Marxist terms of literary works as symbolic acts – imaginary resolutions of real contradictions – but add a theoretical twist to this otherwise familiar notion. 'It would be pointless,' they declare, 'to look in the texts for the original "bare" discourse of these ideological positions, as they were "before" their "literary" realisations, for these ideological positions can only be formed in the materiality of the literary text. That is, they can only appear in a form which provides their imaginary resolution, or better still, which displaces them by substituting imaginary contradictions soluble within the ideological practice of religion, politics, morality, aesthetics and psychology'.[75] The parallel with the Jamesonian model is once again clear. The contradictions on which the text goes to work appear not in the raw, so to speak, but in the form of their potential resolution, or in displaced guise. One can therefore speak of such problems only 'as formed in the materiality of the literary text' – only in the form in which the text works them up into a subtext, one which is also the object of its operations.

Once more, the literary work is grasped as a solution to the question which is itself. For political criticism, as for so many other brands of literary theory, the work is a kind of strategy. Unlike a military campaign, however, it addresses a world outside itself in a way which allows it to be self-fashioning. In assimilating what it seeks to resolve into its own substance, it constructs a relation to reality by establishing a relation to itself. As a result, an age-old dilemma – is art autonomous or is it referential? – is lit up from a new angle.

There are several difficulties with this hypothesis. Are all literary works from Catullus to Coetzee problem-solving devices? It is not, of course, a matter of how either Catullus or Coetzee saw what they were doing, any more than Shakespeare was aware that he was a sophisticated semiotician. We are speaking of a set of techniques, not of an authorial intention. Yet the theory has its limits, just like any other. Is every literary work the handmaiden of a governing ideology, resolving conflicts in ways it finds convenient? To imagine so is to take far too negative a view of them. The work of art, whatever its capacity to collude in forms of oppression, is an example of human praxis, and therefore of how to live well. In this sense, political criticism should involve more than a hermeneutic of suspicion. It should also be mindful of William Blake's image of the good life: 'The arts, and all things in common'.

What of works that resist a sovereign power? What, too, of modernist or postmodernist texts which shun the seductions of closure, flaunting dissonance and contradiction rather than fore-closing them? We are not speaking in such cases of a self-divided content being contained by a unity of form. It is rather a question of such conflicts infiltrating the very language and structure of the work, dissolving it into fragments which may not even be determinate enough to enter into mutual antagonism. A work like *The Waste Land* seeks to resolve certain problems of modernity by recourse to the death-and-rebirth cycles of mythology; but this centripetal subtext, which seeks to gather the poem's heap of broken images into a coherent design, has to fight hard against the centrifugal force of its fragmentary surface.

The concept of strategy, however, is not exhausted by Balibar and Macherey's version of it. It need not be confined to works with fairy-tale endings. It is not just a question of how certain conflicts may be resolved, but how they may be left fruitfully unresolved, or how they are treated as a whole. One advantage of the concept lies in the fact that it avoids too unified a view of the artwork on the one hand, while on the other hand granting it enough identity for it to make sense to say that a particular feature of it is a feature of *this* text. Strategies are loose-jointed, internally differentiated affairs, powered by a set of general purposes but with semi-autonomous parts, between which there can be frictions and conflicts. If they have their own complex logic, it is one which can be reduced neither to a single informing intention nor to the anonymous functioning of a structure. In this sense, neither a phenomenology centred on consciousness, nor a structuralist objectivism, is enough to account for them.

Strategies are purposive projects, but not the intentional utterances of a single subject. A non-literary example of this is the kind of power Antonio Gramsci names hegemony, which is oriented to certain goals, but which cannot be grasped as the act of a single subject (such as a governing class). Strategies are neither objects nor unitary acts. If they are thoroughly worldly affairs, it is not because they 'reflect' or 'correspond to' reality but because, rather in the manner of a Wittgensteinian grammar, they organise it into significant shape by deploying certain rule-governed techniques.

The concept of strategy has also allowed us to find parallels between different forms of literary theory. And making such connections is always gratifying to philosophy, which as Freud once observed resembles nothing quite so much as paranoia.

Notes

Chapter 1: Realists and Nominalists

1. Terry Eagleton, *After Theory* (London, 2003), Ch. 2.
2. For this debate in general, see M.H. Carré, *Realists and Nominalists* (Oxford, 1946); D.M. Armstrong, *Universals and Scientific Realism, vol. 1: Nominalism and Realism* (Cambridge, 1978); and Michael Williams, 'Realism: What's Left?', in P. Greenough and Michael P. Lynch (eds), *Truth and Realism* (Oxford, 2006).
3. For Scotus, see M.B. Ingham and Mechthild Dreyer, *The Philosophical Vision of John Duns Scotus* (Washington, DC, 2004). More advanced studies are Thomas Williams (ed.), *The Cambridge Companion to Duns Scotus* (Cambridge, 2003) and Antonie Vos, *The Philosophy of John Duns Scotus* (Edinburgh, 2006). See also Alasdair MacIntyre, *God, Philosophy, Universities* (Lanham, Md., 2009), Ch.12.
4. For a magisterial study, see Gordon Leff, *William of Ockham* (Manchester, 1975). An equally informative discussion is to be found in Marilyn Adams, *William Ockham* (South Bend, Ind., 1989). There is also some useful material in Julius R. Weinberg, *Ockham, Descartes, and Hume* (Madison, Wis., 1977).
5. Antonie Vos, *The Philosophy of John Duns Scotus*, p. 402.
6. Charles Hartshorne and Paul Weiss (eds), *Collected Papers of Charles Sanders Peirce*, vol. 1 (Cambridge, Mass., 1982), para. 458. See also James K. Feibleman, *An Introduction to the Philosophy of Charles Sanders Peirce* (Cambridge, Mass., 1970), p. 55.
7. Charles Taylor, *A Secular Age* (Cambridge, Mass. and London, 2007), p. 94.
8. See Fernando Cervantes, 'Phronesis vs Scepticism: An Early Modernist Perspective', *New Blackfriars* vol. 91, no. 1036 (November, 2010).
9. See Terry Eagleton, *The Ideology of the Aesthetic* (Oxford, 1991), Ch. 1.
10. Carl Schmitt, *Political Romanticism* (Cambridge, Mass. and London, 1986), p. 17.
11. There is a useful discussion of this theological view in Hans Blumenberg, *The Legitimacy of the Modern Age* (Cambridge, Mass. and London, 1983), pp. 152–5.
12. Quoted by Carré, *Realists and Nominalists*, p. 40.
13. See Frank Farrell, *Subjectivity, Realism and Postmodernism* (Cambridge, 1994).
14. A paradox noted by Conor Cunningham in 'Wittgenstein after Theology', in John Milbank, Catherine Pickstock and Graham Ward (eds), *Radical Orthodoxy: A New Theology* (London and New York, 1999), p. 82.

15. For an excellent study of Scotus's contemporary relevance, see Catherine Pickstock, 'Duns Scotus: His Historical and Contemporary Significance', *Modern Theology* vol. 21, no. 4 (October, 2005).

16. Fergus Kerr, *Thomas Aquinas* (Oxford, 2009), pp. 69 and 48.

17. John Milbank, *The Future of Love* (London, 2009), p. 62. For Milbank and his Radical Orthodoxy colleagues, Scotus really represents the moment of the Fall, a reading of him which has been strongly challenged by other scholars. He stands on the brink of a disastrous lapse into modernity – a lapse which is not for these comentators a *felix culpa* or Happy Fall, as it is for Marxism.

18. See Eagleton, *The Ideology of the Aesthetic* Ch. 1.

19. Not all of them, however. Graham Hough tells us in *An Essay on Criticism* (London, 1966) that we all know what we mean by literature even if we cannot define it (p. 9). The English do not need to bother with definitions, bearing as they do such knowledge in their bones.

20. Tony Bennett, *Formalism and Marxism* (London, 1979), p.174.

21. Tragedy in the artistic sense known to the West would seem to have no precise equivalent in Eastern civilisations, and thus is not exactly universal in scope. But its presence across a whole range of Western cultures and a lengthy time-span is notable even so. See my *Sweet Violence: The Idea of the Tragic* (Oxford, 2003), p. 71.

22. Simon Clarke, *The Foundations of Structuralism* (Brighton, 1981), p. 191.

Chapter 2: What is Literature? (1)

1. See Terry Eagleton, *Literary Theory: An Introduction* (Oxford, 1983), Introduction.

2. Stanley Fish, *Is There A Text In This Class?* (Cambridge, Mass., 1980), p. 236. For Fish's general case, see also his essays 'What Is Stylistics and Why Are They Saying Such Terrible Things About It?', in Seymour Chatman (ed.), *Approaches to Poetics* (New York, 1973), and 'Literature in the Reader: Affective Stylistics', *New Literary History* vol. 2, no. 1 (1970).

3. E.D. Hirsch Jr, *The Aims of Criticism* (Chicago, 1976), p. 135.

4. Ludwig Wittgenstein, *Philosophical Investigations* (Oxford, 1963), para. 66. One might claim that what all games have in common is the fact that they are played for their own sake. It could be objected to this that some games, like football, are played for profit. But this is not a necessary feature of football, any more than the fact that some volumes of poetry make a profit is a necessary feature of poetry.

5. Charles L. Stevenson, 'On "What is a Poem?"', *Philosophical Review* vol. 66, no. 3 (July, 1957).

6. Morris Weitz, 'The Role of Theory in Aesthetics', in Francis J. Coleman (ed.), *Contemporary Studies in Aesthetics* (New York, 1968).

7. Robert L. Brown and Martin Steinmann, Jr., 'Native Renders of Fiction: 4 Speech-Act and Genre-Rule Approach to Defining Literature', in Paul Hernadi (ed.), *What is Literature?* (Bloomington, Ind. and London, 1978), p. 142.

8. Colin A. Lyas, 'The Semantic Definition of Literature', *Journal of Philosophy* vol. 66, no. 3 (1969).

9. John R. Searle, *Expression and Meaning* (Cambridge, 1979), p. 59.

10. Christopher New, *Philosophy of Literature: An Introduction* (London, 1999), p. 19.

11. Peter Lamarque, *Fictional Points of View* (Ithaca, NY and London, 1996), p. 215.

12. Stanley Cavell, *The Claim of Reason* (Oxford, 1979), p. 186. Cavell also holds that Wittgenstein is not advancing the family-resemblance idea as an alternative to

those who believe in universal natures (since for one thing a universalist might ask for the essential meaning of this very idea). Nor is he proposing that this model is enough to explain naming, meaning and so on. In Cavell's view, he wants rather to wean us off universals and persuade us that they are neither useful nor necessary (ibid., pp. 186–7). One does not need to endorse this more general view to appreciate the force of the family-resemblance concept.

13. See John Dupré, *The Disorder of Things* (Cambridge, Mass. and London, 1993), p. 64.
14. See Terry Eagleton, *The Illusions of Postmodernism* (Oxford, 1996).
15. Peter Lamarque, *The Philosophy of Literature* (Oxford, 2009), p. 34. For other critics of the concept, see Maurice Mandelbaum, 'Family Resemblances and Generalisations concerning the Arts', *American Philosophical Quarterly* vol. 2, no. 3 (1965), and Anthony R. Manser, 'Games and Family Relationships', *Philosophy*, vol. 42, no. 161 (1967).
16. Stein Haugom Olsen, *The End of Literary Theory* (Cambridge, 1987), p. 74.
17. See Robert Stecker, *Artworks: Definition, Meaning, Value* (Pennsylvania, 1997), p. 22.
18. Stephen Davies, *Definitions of Art* (Ithaca, NY and London, 1991), p. 37.
19. See Terry Eagleton, 'Brecht and Rhetoric', in Terry Eagleton, *Against the Grain: Essays, 1975–1985* (London, 1986).
20. For institutional accounts of art, see George Dickie, *Art and the Aesthetic* (Ithaca, NY 1974) and Davies, *Definitions of Art*.
21. See R. Wellek and A. Warren, *Theory of Literature* (Harmondsworth, 1982), p. 25.
22. See Bennett, *Formalism and Marxism*.
23. Jan Mukařovský, 'Standard Language and Poetic Language', in Paul L. Garvin (ed.), *A Prague School Reader on Esthetics, Literary Structure, and Style* (Washington, DC, 1964), p. 19.
24. Bennison Gray, *The Phenomenon of Literature* (The Hague, 1975), p. 80.
25. Thomas C. Pollock, *The Nature of Literature* (Princeton, 1942), *passim*.
26. Jan Mukařovský, 'The Esthetics of Language', in Garvin (ed.), *A Prague School Reader on Esthetics, Literary Structure, and Style*.
27. See Jacques Rancière, *La Parole muette: essai sur les contradictions de la littérature* (Paris, 1998).
28. See Philippe Lacoue-Labarthe and Jean-Luc Nancy, *The Literary Absolute* (New York, 1988), p. 11.
29. Grant Overton, *The Philosophy of Fiction* (New York and London, 1928), p. 23.
30. Dorothy Walsh, *Literature and Knowledge* (Middletown, Conn., 1969), p. 33.
31. Monroe Beardsley, *Aesthetics* (New York, 1958), p. 126. The case is also advanced in Beardsley's *Literary Theory and Structure* (New Haven, 1973).
32. See Fredric Jameson, *The Modernist Papers* (London, 2007), Part 1.
33. F. E. Sparshott, 'On the Possibility of Saying What Literature Is', in Hernadi (ed.), *What is Literature?*, p. 5.
34. Fish, *Is There A Text In This Class?*, p. 108. See also his 'How Ordinary Is Ordinary Language?', *New Literary History* vol. 5, no. 1 (autumn, 1973).
35. Fish, *Is There a Text In This Class?*, p. 478.
36. Ibid., p. 12.
37. Robert C. Holub, *Reception Theory* (London and New York, 1984), p. 104.
38. See J.L. Austin, *Sense and Sensibilia* (Oxford, 1962), pp. 84–142.

39. For Fish on interpretation, see Martin Stone, 'On the Old Saw, "Every Reading of a Text is an Interpretation"', in John Gibson and Wolfgang Huemer (eds), *The Literary Wittgenstein* (London and New York, 2004).

40. See Louis Hjelmslev, *Prolegomena to a Theory of Language* (Madison, Wis. 1961). See also Fredric Jameson's critical use of this concept in *The Political Unconscious* (London, 1981), Ch. 1.

41. Lamarque, *Philosophy of Literature*, p. 221.

42. Victor Erlich, *Russian Formalism – History and Doctrine* (The Hague, 1980), p. 206.

43. Lamarque, *Philosophy of Liturature*, p. 263.

44. See Terry Eagleton, *How To Read A Poem* (Oxford, 2007), Ch. 4.

45. Charles Altieri, 'A Procedural Definition of Literature', in Hernadi (ed.), *What is Literature?*, p. 69.

46. In fact, the verse may not be as trite as it seems. According to one theory, it concerns the raiding of the homes of the recusant Catholic nobility by Cromwellian troops. 'Goosey goosey gander' is an allusion to their goose-stepping march as they rudely invade the bedroom of a Catholic gentlewoman and put to the sword the elderly Catholic chaplain who refuses to pray in the newly prescribed manner.

47. Stein Haugom Olsen, 'Criticism and Appreciation', in P. Lamarque (ed.), *Philosophy and Fiction* (Oxford, 1994), pp. 38–40. See also Stein Haugom Olsen, *The Structure of Literary Understanding* (Cambridge, 1978), and Peter Lamarque and Stein Haugom. Olsen, *Truth, Fiction and Literature* (Oxford, 1994).

48. Olsen, *The End of Literary Theory*, p. 53.

49. Only the most masochistic of critics have been drawn to write on the insufferably tedious Knowles. See Terry Eagleton, 'Cork and the Carnivalesque', in Terry Eagleton, *Crazy John and the Bishop* (Cork, 1998), pp. 178–9.

50. E.D. Hirsch Jr, 'What Isn't Literature?', in Hernadi, (ed.), *What is Literature?*, p. 30.

51. William Ray, *Literary Meaning* (Oxford, 1984), p. 129.

52. Quoted in Raymond Williams, *Keywords* (London, 1983), p. 185.

53. Richard Ohmann, 'Speech Acts and the Definition of Literature', *Philosophy and Rhetoric*, vol. 4 (1971), p. 6.

54. Berys Gaut, '"Art" as a Cluster Concept', in N. Carroll (ed.), *Theories of Art Today* (Madison, Wis., 2000), p. 56.

55. Richard Gale, 'The Fictive Use of Language', *Philosophy*, vol. 46, no. 178 (October, 1971).

56. Charles Altieri, 'A Procedural Definition of Literature', in Hernadi (ed.), *What is Literature?*, p. 73.

57. On this question see Pierre Macherey, *A Theory of Literary Production* (London, 1978), Part 1.

Chapter 3: What is Literature? (2)

1. This sense of the word contrasts with its use in John Gardner's *On Moral Fiction* (New York, 1977), where in upbeat, perennially optimistic, American style it is used to mean 'edifying' or 'life-enhancing'. Moral works seek to improve life rather than debase it. There is something of this in Arnold and Leavis, too, if rather less crassly.

2. See Eagleton, *The Ideology of the Aesthetic*, Ch. 1.

3. David Lee Clark (ed.), *Shelley's Prose* (New York, 1988), p. 283.

4. Catherine Wilson, 'Literature and Knowledge', *Philosophy* vol. 58, no. 226 (1983).

5. Monroe Beardsley, *Aesthetics* (New York, 1958), p. 383.

6. See Terry Eagleton, *Literary Theory: An Introduction* (Oxford, 1983), Ch. 1.

7. For virtue ethics, see Rosalind Hursthouse, *On Virtue Ethics* (Oxford, 1999).

8. Searle, *Expression and Meaning*, p. 74.

9. Lamarque, *Philosophy of Literature*, p. 240.

10. David Novitz, *Knowledge, Fiction and Imagination* (Philadelphia, 1987), p. 140.

11. Gale, 'The Fictive Use of Language', p. 338.

12. Hilary Putnam, 'Reflections on Goodman's *Ways of Worldmaking*', *Journal of Philosophy* vol. 76, no. 11 (1979). See also James O. Young, *Art and Knowledge* (London, 2001).

13. See John Hospers, 'Implied Truths in Literature', *Journal of Aesthetics and Art Criticism*, vol. 19, no. 1 (autumn, 1960).

14. See Peter Jones, *Philosophy and the Novel* (Oxford, 1975), p. 196.

15. Jerome Stolnitz, 'On the Cognitive Triviality of Art', *British Journal of Aesthetics* vol. 32, no. 3 (1992).

16. See, for example, Martha Nussbaum, *Love's Knowledge* (Oxford, 1990). The book contains a rewarding account of James's *The Golden Bowl*, though one which takes a decidedly angelic view of Adam and Maggie Verver.

17. Lamarque, *Philosophy of Literature*, p. 254. See also C.G. Prado, *Making Believe* (London, 1984), Ch. 1.

18. See Elias Schwartz, 'Notes on Linguistics and Literature', *College Literature* no. 32 (1970).

19. New, *Philosophy of Literature*, p. 32.

20. E.D. Hirsch Jr, 'What Isn't Literature', in Hernadi, *What is Literature?*, p. 32.

21. John M. Ellis, *The Theory of Literary Criticism* (Berkeley, 1974), p. 44.

22. This brief description of Ellis's position perhaps makes it sound rather more akin to post-structuralist theory than he would, as a conservative critic, presumably welcome. But there are parallels even so.

23. W.K. Wimsatt and M.C. Beardsley, 'The Intentional Fallacy', in David Lodge (ed.), *Twentieth Century Literary Criticism* (London, 1973), p. 339.

24. See Karen Armstrong, *The Bible: The Biography* (London, 2007), Ch. 4.

25. Plato, *Phaedrus* (Oxford, 2002), p. 70.

26. Karlheinz Stierle, 'The Reading of Fictional Texts', in Susan R. Suleiman and Inge Crosman (eds), *The Reader in the Text* (Princeton, 1980), p. 87.

27. Ellis, *Theory of Literacy Criticism*, p. 51.

28. Ibid., pp. 51 and 93.

29. Ibid., p. 84.

30. Some philosophers of literature have a problem about how general truths are to be derived from the kind of non-assertoric statements that constitute fiction. See, for example, L. B. Cebik, *Fictional Narrative and Truth* (Lanham, Md., 1984), who claims that fiction can produce no new truth. See also D.H. Mellor, 'On Literary Truth', *Ratio*, vol. 10, no. 2 (1968), and Thomas G. Pavel, *Fictional Worlds* (Cambridge, Mass., 1986), who argues that the truth of a literary text as a whole is not recursively definable starting from the truth of the individual sentences that compose it (p. 179). See also Mary Sirridge, 'Truth from Fiction?', *Philosophy and Phenomenological Research*, vol. 35, no. 4 (1975).

31. Robert Stecker, 'What is Literature?', *Revue internationale de philosophie*, no. 50 (1996).

32. Lamarque, *Philosophy of Literature*, p. 208.

33. Jacques Derrida, *Acts of Literature* (New York and London, 1992), p. 43.
34. See Maurice Merleau-Ponty, *The Visible and the Invisible* (Evanston, Ill., 1968).
35. Gale, 'The Fictive Use of Language', p. 335.
36. Gerald Graff, 'Literature as Assertions', in Ira Konigsberg (ed.), *American Criticism in the Post-Structuralist Age* (Ann Arbor, Mich., 1981), p. 147.
37. Olsen, *The End of Literary Theory*, p. 152.
38. Lyas, 'The Semantic Definition of Literature', p. 83.
39. Stevenson, 'On "What is a Poem?"'.
40. Gregory Currie, *The Nature of Fiction* (Cambridge, 1990), p. 67.
41. New, *Philosophy of Literature*, p. 3.
42. Ibid.
43. Paul Crowther, *Critical Aesthetics and Postmodernism* (Oxford, 1993), p. 54.
44. Williams, *Keywords*, p. 184.
45. Raymond Williams, *Marxism and Literature* (Oxford, 1977), p. 51.
46. Derek Attridge, 'Singular Events: Literature, Invention, and Performance', in Elizabeth Beaumont Bissell (ed.), *The Question of Literature* (Manchester, 2002), p. 62. See also his *Peculiar Language: Literature as Difference from the Renaissance to James Joyce* (London, 1988).
47. See Hans Robert Jauss, *Toward an Aesthetic of Reception* (Minneapolis, 1982), pp. 3–45. Several of Jauss's key positions are anticipated by the Prague structuralist Felix Vodicka, whose work Jauss was not aware of when he first set out. See in particular Felix Vodicka, 'The History of the Echo of Literary Works', in Paul L. Garvin (ed.), *A Prague School Reader on Esthetics, Literary Structure, and Style* (Washington, DC, 1964).
48. See Theodor Adorno, *Aesthetic Theory* (London, 1984).
49. Quoted by Holub, *Reception Theory*, p. 72.
50. There have indeed been Marxist critics who have sailed close to this conception. Pierre Macherey, as we shall see, is one of them. But it is not characteristic of Marxist aesthetics as a whole.
51. See Holub, *Reception Theory*, Ch. 2. See also Terry Eagleton, 'The Revolt of the Reader', in Terry Eagleton, *Against the Grain* (London, 1986), Ch. 13.
52. See Wolfgang Iser, *The Act of Reading* (Baltimore, Md. and London, 1978), p. 61.
53. See Roman Ingarden, *The Literary Work of Art* (Evanston, Ill., 1973), and *The Cognition of the Literary Work of Art* (Evanston, Ill., 1973).
54. Iser, *The Act of Reading*, pp. 77–8.
55. Wolfgang Iser, *Prospecting: From Reader Response to Literary Anthropology* (Baltimore, Md. and London, 1989), p. 213.
56. Ibid, p. 73.
57. See Macherey, *A Theory of Literary Production*.
58. Ibid., p. 271.
59. See Louis Althusser, 'A Letter on Art in Reply to André Daspre', in *Lenin and Philosophy* (London, 1971).
60. See Terry Eagleton, *Criticism and Ideology* (London, 1976), Ch. 5.
61. Iser, *The Act of Reading*, p. 87.
62. See Terry Eagleton, *Ideology: An Introduction* (London, 1991), p. 58.
63. See Jurij Striedter, *Literary Structure, Evolution and Value* (Cambridge, Mass., 1989), p. 161.
64. Umberto Eco, *A Theory of Semiotics* (London, 1977), p. 261.
65. Ibid., p. 274.

66. Ibid., p. 274.
67. Claude Lévi-Strauss, *Structural Anthropology* (London, 1972), pp. 366–7.
68. See Terry Eagleton, *Trouble with Strangers: A Study of Ethics* (Oxford, 2009), Part 3.
69. David Schalkwyk, *Literature and the Touch of the Real* (Newark, Del., 2004), p. 219.
70. Ibid., p. 220.
71. Jonathan Culler, *Structuralist Poetics* (London and Ithaca, NY, 1975), p. 130.
72. See Paul de Man, *Blindness and Insight* (New York, 1971) and *Allegories of Reading* (New Haven and London, 1979). See also his key essay 'The Rhetoric of emporality', in C. Singleton (ed.), *Interpretation: Theory and Practice* (Baltimore, Md., 1969).

Chapter 4: The Nature of Fiction

1. Currie, *The Nature of Fiction*, p. 92.
2. Lamarque, *Philosophy and Fiction*, p. 60.
3. Lamarque, *The Philosophy of Literature*, p. 185.
4. Alex Burri, 'Facts and Fiction', in John Gibson and Wolfgang Huemer (eds), *The Literary Wittgenstein* (London and New York, 2004), p. 292.
5. Margaret Macdonald, 'The Language of Fiction', in Joseph Margolis (ed.), *Philosophy Looks at the Arts* (Philadelphia, 1978), p. 424.
6. Lamarque and Olsen, *Truth, Fiction, and Literature*, p. 267.
7. Overton, *The Philosophy of Fiction*, p. 4.
8. Currie, *The Nature of Fiction*, p. 31.
9. Christopher New, 'A Note on Truth and Fiction', *Journal of Aesthetics and Art Criticism*, vol. 55, no. 4 (1997).
10. Peter van Inwagen, 'Creatures of Fiction', *American Philosophical Quarterly*, vol. 14 (1977).
11. R. Howell, 'Fictional Objects', *Poetics* no. 8 (1979). See also Stuart Brock and Edwin Mares, *Realism and Anti-Realism* (London, 2007), Ch. 12.
12. A.P. Martinich and Avrum Stroll, *Much Ado about Nonexistence* (Lanham, Md., 2007), p. 39.
13. David Lewis, 'Truth in Fiction', *American Philosophical Quarterly* vol. 15 (1978), p. 37.
14. Pavel, *Fictional Worlds*, p. 31.
15. Novitz, *Knowledge, Fiction, and Imagination*, p. 123.
16. See A. Meinong, 'The Theory of Objects', in R.M. Chisholm (ed.), *Realism and the Background of Phenomenology* (New York, 1960). See also Terence Parsons, *Nonexistent Objects* (New Haven and London, 1980), Graham Dunstan Martin, *Language, Truth and Poetry* (Edinburgh, 1975) and John Woods, *The Logic of Fiction* (The Hague, 1974), Ch. 2. Amie L. Thomasson regards literary characters as fictional objects rather as 'marriages, contracts, and promises may be created through the performance of linguistic acts that represent them as existing' (*Fiction and Metaphysics*, Cambridge, 1999, p. 13). See also G.D. Martin, 'A New Look at Fictional Reference', *Philosophy* no. 57 (1982). Richard Rorty has a useful summary and critique of some debates about fictional reference in his 'Is There a Problem about Fictional Discourse?', in Richard Rorty, *The Consequences of Pragmatism* (Brighton, 1982), Ch. 7.

17. Roy Bhaskar, *Reclaiming Reality* (London and New York, 1989), p. 126.
18. Joseph Margolis, *Art and Philosophy* (Brighton, 1980), p. 269.
19. Currie, *The Nature of Fiction*, p. 2.
20. Lewis, 'Truth in Fiction', p. 39.
21. Kendall L. Walton, *Mimesis as Make-Believe* (Cambridge, Mass., 1990), p. 196.
22. Ibid., p. 271.
23. Ibid., p. 368.
24. The Russian Formalist Viktor Shklovsky is also keen on quoting Conan Doyle.
25. Jonathan Culler, *Structuralist Poetics* (London, 1975), p. 128; Morse Peckham, '"Literature": Disjunction and Redundancy', in Hernadi (ed.), *What is Literature?*, p. 225.
26. Eric Hobsbawm, *How to Change the World* (London, 2011), p. 110.
27. John R. Searle, *Expression and Meaning: Studies in the Theory of Speech-Acts* (Cambridge, 1979), p. 58.
28. Robert L. Brown and Martin Steinmann, 'Native Readers of Fiction: A Speech-Act and Genre-Rule Approach to Defining Literature', in Hernadi (ed.), *What is Literature?*, p. 149.
29. Olsen, *The Structure of Literary Understanding*, p. 46.
30. Olsen, *The End of Literary Theory*, p. 59.
31. Siegfried J. Schmidt, 'Towards a Pragmatic Interpretation of Fictionality', in Teun A. van Dijk (ed.), *Pragmatics of Language and Literature* (Amsterdam, 1976), p. 161.
32. Culler, *Structuralist Poetics*, p. 24.
33. Margolis, *Philosophy Looks at the Arts*, p. 427.
34. Fredric Jameson, *The Ideologies of Theory* (London, 2009), p. 146.
35. Bennison Gray, *The Phenomenon of Literature*, p. 117.
36. Hobsbawm, *How to Change the World*, pp. 111–12.
37. Nelson Goodman, *Of Mind and Other Matters* (Cambridge, Mass., 1984), p. 124.
38. Currie, *The Nature of Fiction*, pp. 4–9.
39. Ibid., p. 8.
40. Peter J. McCormick, *Fiction, Philosophy, and the Problems of Poetics* (Ithaca, NY and London, 1988), p. 41.
41. Mary Louise Pratt, *Towards a Speech Act Theory of Literature* (Bloomington, Ind., 1977), p. 95.
42. Ibid., p. 124.
43. J.O. Urmson, 'Fiction', *American Philosophical Quarterly*, vol. 13, no. 2 (1976), p. 154.
44. Richard M. Gale, 'The Fictive Use of Language', p. 325.
45. John R. Searle, 'The Logical Status of Fictional Discourse', in *Expression and Meaning*. See also Marie-Laure Ryan, 'Fiction, Non-Factuals, and the Principle of Minimal Departure', *Poetics* no. 9 (1980).
46. Gale, 'The Fictive Use of Language', p. 327.
47. Some philosophers like Searle hold that fictional statements do not actually refer, since everything referred to must exist. Others like Martinich and Stroll maintain that 'if a fictional name is accepted by a community, then it has a referent' (Martinich and Stroll, *Much Ado about Nonexistence*, p. 28). See also Charles Crittenden, *Unreality: The Metaphysics of Fictional Objects* (New York, 1991). Graham Dunstan Martin is among those theorists who argue that there can be non-existent referents (*Language, Truth, and Poetry*, p. 76). Teun van Dijk, by

contrast, regards the referential value of a literary work as irrelevant (*Some Aspects of Text Grammars*, The Hague, 1972, p. 337).

48. In personal conversation with the author.
49. New, *Philosophy of Literature*, p. 40.
50. Walton, *Mimesis as Make-Believe*, p. 73.
51. Ibid, p. 74.
52. Margolis, *Philosophy Looks at the Arts*, p. 429.
53. Currie, *The Nature of Fiction*, p. 51.
54. John Carroll (ed.), *Selected Letters of Samuel Richardson* (Oxford, 1964), p. 85.
55. A meaning licensed by the *Oxford English Dictionary*, which defines 'pretend' as 'to engage in an imaginative game or fantasy', as well as 'to act so as to make it appear that something is the case when it fact it is not'.
56. See Terry Eagleton, *Heathcliff and the Great Hunger* (London, 1995), p. 304. An illuminating account of Austin on pretending is to be found in Malcolm Bull, *Seeing Things Hidden* (London, 1999), Ch. 1.
57. J.L. Austin, 'Pretending', in J.L. Austin, *Philosophical Papers* (Oxford, 1970), p. 259n.
58. Stanley Cavell, *A Pitch of Philosophy* (Cambridge, Mass., 1994), pp. 91–2.
59. Stanley Cavell, *The Claim of Reason* (New York and Oxford, 1979), p. 43.
60. Martinich and Stroll, *Much Ado about Nonexistence*, p. 15.
61. Walton, *Mimesis as Make-Believe*, p. 253.
62. Ibid., p. 261.
63. See Searle, 'The Logical Status of Fictional Discourse', *passim*.
64. On belief in fiction, see Arnold Isenberg, 'The Problem of Belief', in Francis J. Coleman (ed.), *Contemporary Studies in Aesthetics* (New York, 1968).
65. Nicholas Wolterstorff, *Works and Worlds of Art* (Oxford, 1980), p. 234.
66. Lamarque, *The Philosophy of Literature*, p. 180.
67. Walton, *Mimesis as Make-Believe*, p. 93.
68. Lamarque and Olsen, *Truth, Fiction, and Literature*, p. 325.
69. See Beardsley, *Aesthetics*, pp. 422–3.
70. Isenberg quoted in F. Coleman (ed.), *Contemporary Studies in Aesthetics*, p. 251.
71. Richard Ohmann, 'Speech Acts and the Definition of Literature', *Philosophy and Rhetoric*, vol. 4 (1971).
72. Lamarque and Olsen, *Truth, Fiction, and Literature*, p. 32. I should add that these authors usefully criticise the whole speech-act model.
73. On speech-act theory in general, see J.L. Austin, *How To Do Things With Words* (Oxford, 1962).
74. Ohmann, 'Speech Acts and the Definition of Literature', p. 14.
75. Peter Geach and Max Black (eds), *Translations from the Philosophical Writings of Gottlob Frege* (Totowa, NJ, 1980), p. 130.
76. Ibid, p. 132.
77. Sandy Petrey, *Speech Acts and Literary Theory* (New York and London, 1990), p. 11.
78. Arthur C. Danto, 'Philosophy as/and/of Literature', in Anthony J. Cascardi (ed.), *Literature and the Question of Philosophy* (Baltimore, Md. and London, 1987), p. 8.
79. J.L. Austin, 'Performative Utterances', in *Philosophical Papers* (Oxford, 1970), p. 248.
80. Fish, *Is There A Text In This Class?*, p. 231.
81. See Schalkwyk, *Literature and the Touch of the Real*, pp. 104–13.

82. See Kenneth Burke, *Language as Symbolic Action* (Berkeley and Los Angeles, 1966), p. 45.
83. Culler, *Structuralist Poetics*, p. 108.
84. P.F. Strawson, 'On Referring', Mind, vol. 59, no. 235 (1950).
85. Charles Altieri, *Act and Quality* (Brighton, 1981), p.45.
86. Kenneth Burke, *A Grammar of Motives* (Berkeley, 1969), p. 66.
87. A point made by Peter Jones, *Philosophy and the Novel* (Oxford, 1975), p. 183.
88. See E.D. Hirsch Jr, *Validity in Interpretation* (New Haven, 1967).
89. See Stierle, 'The Reading of Fictional Texts', pp. 111–12.
90. Lamarque and Olsen, *Truth, Fiction, and Literature*, p. 88.
91. Fredric Jameson, *The Prison-House of Language* (Princeton, 1972), p. 89.
92. Terence Hawkes, *Structuralism and Semiotics* (London, 2003), p. 51.
93. Quoted by Giorgio Agamben, *The Time that Remains* (Stanford, 2005), p. 133.
94. Macherey, *A Theory of Literary Production*, p. 434.
95. For Poulet's phenomenological criticism, see Georges Poulet, 'Phenomenology of Reading', *New Literary History*, vol. 1, no. 1 (October, 1969).
96. Friedrich Schlegel, *'Lucinde' and the Fragments* (Minneapolis, 1971), p. 150.
97. Quoted by Antoine Compagnon, *The Five Paradoxes of Modernity* (New York, 1994), p. 20.
98. Eco, *A Theory of Semiotics*, p. 71.
99. Ibid., p. 65. The statement is italicised in the original.
100. Monroe Beardsley makes this connection in 'The Concept of Literature', in Frank Brady, John Palmer and Martin Price (eds), *Literary Theory and Structure* (New Haven and London, 1973), p. 135.
101. Beardsley, *Literary Theory and Structure*, p. 39.
102. See de Man, *Allegories of Reading*.
103. Denys Turner, *Faith, Reason and the Existence of God* (Cambridge, 2004), pp. 98–9.
104. Stanley Cavell, *Must We Mean What We Say?* (New York, 1969), p. 66.
105. See Quentin Skinner, 'Meaning and Understanding in the History of Ideas', in James Tully (ed.), *Meaning and Context: Quentin Skinner and his Critics* (Cambridge, 1988). For a strongly intentionalist approach to literary works, see Stephen Knapp and Walter Benn Michaels, 'Against Theory', in W.J.T. Mitchell, *Against-Theory: Literary Studies and the New Pragmatism* (Berkeley, 1985).
106. Noel Carroll, *Beyond Aesthetics* (Cambridge, 2001), p. 160.
107. Margolis, *Art and Philosophy*, p. 237.
108. Gray, *The Phenomenon of Literature*, p. 156.
109. Gale, 'The Fictive Use of Language', p. 337.
110. Lamarque and Olsen, *Truth, Fiction and Literature*, p. 9.
111. New, *Philosophy of Literature*, p. 26.
112. Pavel, *Fictional Worlds*, p. 21.
113. Gale, 'The Fictive Use of Language', p. 337.
114. See Gerald L. Bruns, 'Midrash and Allegory: The Beginnings of Scriptural Interpretation', in Robert Alter and Frank Kermode (eds), *The Literary Guide to the Bible* (London, 1978), p. 629.
115. Wittgenstein, *Philosophical Investigations*, para. 120.
116. Umberto Eco, *The Role of the Reader* (London, 1971), p. 195.
117. Kenneth Burke, *A Rhetoric of Motives* (Berkeley and Los Angeles, 1969), p. 50.
118. P.M.S. Hacker, *Insight and Illusion* (Oxford, 1986), p. 195.

119. Nor should my use of Wittgenstein throughout this book be taken as an uncritical endorsement of his thought, much as I have benefited from it. For a more general evaluation on my part see Terry Eagleton, 'Wittgenstein's Friends', *New Left Review* no. 135 (September–October, 1982).

120. Thomas E. Lewis, *Fiction and Reference* (London, 1986), p. 180.

121. Hans-Georg Gadamer, *Truth and Method* (London, 1975), p. 336.

122. J. Hillis Miller, *On Literature* (London and New York, 2002).

123. Paul O'Grady, *Relativism* (Chesham, Bucks, 2002), p. 71.

124. Jan Mukařovský, *Aesthetic Function, Norm and Value as Social Facts* (Ann Arbor, Mich. 1970), p. 75.

125. Umberto Eco, *A Theory of Semiotics* (Bloomington and London, 1976), p. 59.

126. Schalkwyk, *Literature and the Touch of the Real*, p. 114.

127. G.H. von Wright and Heikki Nyman (eds), Ludwig Wittgenstein, *Last Writings*, vol. 1 (Oxford, 1982), 38.

128. Ibid., p. 19.

Chapter 5: Strategies

1. See Jameson, *The Ideologies of Theory*, p. 150.

2. See, for example, Kenneth Burke, *The Philosophy of Literary Form: Studies in Symbolic Action* (Baton Rouge, 1941); Kenneth Burke, *A Grammar of Motives* (Berkeley, 1969); Kenneth Burke, *Language as Symbolic Action* (Berkeley, 1968). For a valuable commentary on Burke, see Frank Lentricchia, *Criticism and Social Change* (Chicago and London, 1983), Parts 2–5.

3. Fredric Jameson, *The Political Unconscious* (London, 1981), p. 81.

4. Paul Ricoeur, *The Conflict of Interpretations* (Evanston, Ill., 1974), p. 140.

5. Ibid., pp. 81–2.

6. Jameson, *The Ideologies of Theory*, p. 148. There are some parallels between this theory of textual production and the one I develop in *Criticism and Ideology*, Ch. 3.

7. Jameson, *The Ideologies of Theory*, p. 158.

8. *Standard Edition of the Work of Sigmund Freud* (London, 1953), vol. 9, p. 146.

9. Roland Barthes, *Critical Essays* (Evanston, Ill., 1972), pp. 202–3.

10. Gadamer, *Truth and Method*, p. 333. There are, to be sure, some celebrated examples of German philosophers acknowledging their debts to English ones. Kant on Hume and Carnap and Frege on Russell come to mind.

11. See R.G. Collingwood, *An Autobiography* (London, 1939), Ch.5, and *An Essay on Metaphysics* (London, 1940). The baboon example is my own.

12. Collingwood, *An Autobiography*, p. 33.

13. Richard Murphy, *Collingwood and the Crisis of Western Civilisation* (Exeter, 2008), p. 115. See also Giuseppina d'Oro, *Collingwood and the Metaphysics of Experience* (London and New York, 2002), p. 64.

14. Peter Johnson, *R.C. Collingwood: An Introduction* (Bristol, 1998), p. 72.

15. See Edmund Leach, *Lévi-Strauss* (London, 1970), p. 82.

16. Burke, *A Rhetoric of Motives* 1969, p. 5.

17. I have examined these issues in more detail in Terry Eagleton, *Myths of Power: A Marxist Study of the Brontës* (London, 1975).

18. Raymond Williams, *The English Novel from Dickens to Lawrence* (London, 1970), pp. 32–3.

19. See Holub, *Reception Theory*, p. 88.
20. Iser, *The Act of Reading*, p. 86.
21. Ibid., p. 95.
22. Wolfgang Iser, *The Implied Reader* (Baltimore, Md. and London, 1974), p. 288.
23. Iser, *The Act of Reading*, pp. 128–9.
24. Ibid., p. 72.
25. Ibid., p. 80.
26. Stanley Fish, 'Why No One's Afraid of Wolfgang Iser', *Diacritics*, vol. 11, no. 3 (1981), p. 7.
27. For literature as event, see Derek Attridge, *The Singularity of Literature* (London and New York, 2004), pp. 58–62.
28. For formalist writings, see L.T. Lemon and M.J. Reis (eds), *Russian Formalist Criticism: Four Essays* (Lincoln, Nebr., 1965), and for a fuller anthology L. Matejka and K. Pomorska (eds), *Readings in Russian Poetics* (Cambridge, Mass., 1971). See also Viktor Erlich, *Russian Formalism: History – Doctrine* (The Hague, 1980) and Jameson, *The Prison-House of Language*.
29. Quoted in Erlich, *Russian Formalism: History – Doctrine*, p. 198.
30. For Lotman, see *Analysis of the Poetic Text* (Ann Arbor, Mich., 1976) and *The Structure of the Artistic Text* (Ann Arbor, Mich., 1977). For Riffaterre, see *Semiotics of Poetry* (London, 1980).
31. There are still other brands of semiotics which seize on the concept of strategy in ways rather different from the author of *The Name of the Rose*. There is a work by Jean-Marie Floch entitled *Semiotics, Marketing and Communication: Behind the Signs, the Strategies* (Basingstoke, 2001). French theory has certainly come on apace since the days of Michel Foucault.
32. Umberto Eco, *A Theory of Semiotics* (London, 1977), p. 139. See also his *The Role of the Reader* (Bloomington, Ind., 1979).
33. Altieri, *Act and Quality*, p. 234.
34. Eco, *Theory of Semiotics*, p. 274.
35. Iser, *Prospecting*, p. 224. The phrase, whether intentionally or not, could be taken as a succinct summary of Wittgenstein's concept of forms of life.
36. See Ricoeur, *The Conflict of Interpretations*, Part 1.
37. Iser, *Prospecting*, pp. 224–5.
38. Ibid., pp. 227, 228.
39. See Gérard Genette, *Figures* (Paris, 1969) and A.J. Greimas, *Sémantique structurale* (Paris, 1966).
40. Jacques Derrida, *L'Ecriture et la différence* (Paris, 1967), p. 29.
41. Lévi-Strauss, *Structural Anthropology*, p. 224.
42. Ibid., p. 229.
43. See Eagleton, *The Ideology of the Aesthetic*, Ch. 1.
44. Lévi-Strauss, *Structural Anthropology*, p. 197.
45. Clarke, *The Foundations of Structuralism*, Ch. 8.
46. The critic Geoffrey Hartman has shown that the poetry of William Wordsworth is paradoxical in just this sense, affirming an unruptured continuity between Nature and humanity, or childhood and adulthood, in a language which itself places it firmly on one side of this ontological divide. This ideological project is also continually undermined by a set of forces associated with death, solitude, infinity, groundlessness, the abyssal imagination and the apocalyptic annihilation of Nature, which unmask the pathos of any such dream of untroubled continuity between

Nature and consciousness. See Eagleton, *Trouble with Strangers: A Study of Ethics* Ch.8.

47. Ricoeur, *The Conflict of Interpretations* p. 44.
48. Claude Lévi-Strauss, *The Savage Mind* (London, 1962), p. 26.
49. See Alain Badiou, *Being and Event* (London, 2005).
50. For an excellent account of some analyses of this process in a range of modern literary theorists, see William Ray, *Literary Meaning* (Oxford, 1984). Ray's study seeks to show how structure and event, system and instance, theory and practice, meaning as fact and meaning as act, are indissociable in the literary work, as well as in the practice of criticism. He claims, however, that most critics call a halt to this dialectic in order to retrieve the truth and authority of their own theory from its mutations and dissolutions at the hands of history and critical practice. This need to bolster their own authority by trying to retrieve their theory from being no more than a set of performative acts forces them into inescapable self-contradiction. In Ray's view, only post-structuralist critics such as Paul de Man can avoid this spurious move, acknowledging the self-deconstructing nature of their own theories. What this powerfully suggestive case overlooks is just how powerful a form of authority is involved in the post-structuralist disavowal of authority – how its strength lies in its confession of everybody's impotence, its fullness in its *kenosis*, its knowledge in a pontifical awareness of its ignorance. This, unavoidably, must apply to Ray's own thesis as well. In the post-structuralist game, loser takes all: the point is to emerge with the emptiest pair of hands, and thus as both anti-authoritarian and invulnerable to critique.
51. Ricoeur, *The Conflict of Interpretations*, pp. 92 and 95.
52. Ibid., pp. 92–3.
53. Jan Mukařovský, *Structure, Sign, and Function* (New Haven and London, 1978), p. 4.
54. Perhaps the best introductory approach to Geneva school phenomenology is Poulet, 'Phenomenology of Reading'. See also J. Hillis Miller, *The Disappearance of God* (Cambridge, Mass., 1963). A useful commentary is Robert Magliola, *Phenomenology and Literature* (Lafayette, Ind., 1977).
55. Poulet, 'Phenomenology of Reading', p. 59.
56. If postmodernism, which is much preoccupied with the body, has by and large neglected this magisterial work, it may be partly because the book ranges far beyond a narrow concern with the libidinal body.
57. The work of Alasdair Macintyre has been the most assiduous in promoting this case. See, for example, his *After Virtue* (London, 1981).
58. I take it for granted here that what counts as art is just as problematic as we have discovered the concept of literature to be.
59. For a superb treatment of this conception of the body, see John MacMurray, *The Self as Agent* (London, 1969).
60. Perhaps the most distinguished modern inheritor of this legacy is the Dominican theologian and philosopher Herbert McCabe. See in particular his *Law, Love and Language* (London, 1968).
61. See Denys Turner, *Faith, Reason and the Existence of God* (Cambridge, 2004), Chs 4–6.
62. See Alasdair Macintyre, *Dependent Rational Animals* (London, 1998).
63. This is not a view I ascribe to Aquinas, who believed that the Archangel Gabriel spoke intelligibly to Mary.

64. I should perhaps point out that in what follows I am giving an account of psychoanalytic theory and practice, not an evaluation of it.

65. Philip Rieff, *Freud: The Mind of the Moralist* (Chicago and London, 1959), p. 102.

66. Paul Ricoeur, *Freud and Philosophy* (New Haven and London, 1970), p. 382.

67. Ricoeur, *The Conflict of Interpretations* p. 66.

68. A certain strain of post-structuralism – Deleuze, the early Lyotard, aspects of Foucault – tends to replace a hermeneutics with an 'energetics'.

69. For a discussion of this question, as well as for an excellent brief introduction to Freud's thought, see Richard Wollheim, *Freud* (London, 1971).

70. See Simon O. Lesser, *Fiction and the Unconscious* (London, 1960), pp. 151–2. See also Norman N. Holland, *The Dynamics of Literary Response* (New York 1968).

71. Peter Brooks, *Reading for the Plot* (Oxford, 1984), p. 37.

72. Ibid., p. 61.

73. Burke, *A Rhetoric of Motives*, p. 37.

74. See Eagleton, *Ideology: An Introduction,* pp. 60–1.

75. Etienne Balibar and Pierre Macherey, 'On Literature as an Ideological Form', in Robert Young (ed.), *Untying the Text* (London, 1981), p. 88.

Index